Instructions on the
Revised Roman Rites

Instructions on the Revised Roman Rites

Initiation
Roman Missal
Eucharist outside Mass
Anointing and Pastoral Care of the Sick
Funerals
Marriage
Holy Order
Ministries
Blessing of Oils
Lectionary

COLLINS

Collins Liturgical Publications
187 Piccadilly, London W1V 9DA

ISBN 0 00 599631 7
First published 1979
© compilation 1979 Wm Collins Sons & Co Ltd

Nihil obstat R. J. Cuming DD, *Censor*
Imprimatur Ralph Brown VG
Westminster 12 March 1979

Made and printed in Great Britain
by William Collins Sons & Co Ltd, Glasgow

CONTENTS

ABBREVIATIONS

Documents of the Second Vatican Council

AA *Apostolicam Actuositatem*, Decree on the Apostolate of the Laity

AG *Ad Gentes*, Decree on the Church's Missionary Activity

CD *Christus Dominus*, Decree on the Bishops' Pastoral Office in the Church

DV *Dei Verbum*, Dogmatic Constitution on Divine Revelation

GS *Gaudium et Spes*, Pastoral Constitution on the Church in the Modern World

LG *Lumen Gentium*, Dogmatic Constitution on the Church

PO *Presbyterorum Ordinis*, Decree on the Ministry and Life of Priests

SC *Sacrosanctum Concilium*, Constitution on the Sacred Liturgy

UR *Unitatis Redintegratio*, Decree on Ecumenism

Other Documents

AP Sacred Congregation of Rites, instruction *Actio Pastoralis*, 15 May 1969: *AAS* 61 (1969) 806-11.

EM Sacred Congregation of Rites, instruction, *Eucharisticum Mysterium*, 25 May 1967: *AAS* 59 (1967) 539-73.

ES Sacred Congregation of Rites, general decree, *Ecclesiae semper*, 7 March 1965: *AAS* 57 (1965) 410-12.

IC Congregation for the Discipline of the Sacraments, instruction, *Immensae Caritatis*, 29 January 1973: *AAS* 65 (1973) 264-71.

IOe Sacred Congregation of Rites, instruction, *Inter Oecumenici*, 26 September 1964: *AAS* 56 (1964) 877-900.

MD Congregation for Divine Worship, instruction, *Memoriale Domini*, 29 May 1969: *AAS* 61 (1969) 541-5.

MS Sacred Congregation of Rites, instruction, *Musicam Sacram*, 5 March 1967: *AAS* 59 (1967) 300-20.

CIC Codex Iuris Canonici

INTRODUCTION

CHRISTOPHER WALSH

The recent liturgical reform in the Roman Catholic Church has perhaps suffered more from half hearted and mechanical implementation than it has from active opposition. A large number of the clergy, and their people after them, have misunderstood it, with more or less good grace, as a revision of texts and rubrics. While they would acknowledge that these 'changes' have brought some undoubted benefits, they have implemented them with varying degrees of loyalty, indifference or resentment because they discerned no theological or pastoral necessity arising out of their understanding of the sacraments which would demand such a wholesale upheaval in their habits of worship. 'Old' theology and 'new' liturgy are out of phase. The active opponents have perhaps been more perceptive. For the reform goes far deeper than changes in texts and rubrics. It marks a development not only in liturgical practice but in the theology of the sacraments and of the Church. And if worship and theology are to be in phase, the renewal of the liturgy must be seen in the context of the Church's developing understanding of herself, her structures, her mission, her relationship to her Lord and to the world. Worship is the lived expression of faith; new insights of faith cannot find expression in a fossilised liturgy, a renewed liturgy cannot come alive with an immobile theology.

The Second Vatican Council's Constitution on the Liturgy asserts that 'in the liturgy the sanctification of man is manifested by signs perceptible to the senses and is effected in a way which is proper to each of these signs' (7). This affirmation restores the balance of emphasis in the classical theological axiom *sacramenta significando causant*: it is through and because of their power to signify that the sacraments achieve their effect. For centuries the emphasis in the rites and in the theology which interpreted and supported them had

8

been on the *causant*, the causality of the sacraments. Commentators identified the conditions in which a sacrament could be 'guaranteed effective' and defined the minimum combination of them required for validity. This is a valuable exercise and important in emergencies, but quite inadequate as a basis for a working theology of sacraments or of liturgy. A flicker of an eye and a whispered absolution do indeed satisfy the minimum requirements for a valid confession, but remain an exception, a limit case. A 'private Mass' with no congregation or communion is a valid eucharist, but cannot be accepted as a norm for practice or as a basis for theology. Yet once the minimum essential for validity was achieved, all else could be regarded, not unnaturally, as inessential, adding nothing, mere ceremonial. So one could be content with non-communicating Mass, communion under one kind, wafer bread, a thimbleful of baptismal water, anointings with a slightly greasy thumb, because only one question was being asked: what are the *minimum* conditions necessary for a valid celebration? But the Church wishes us to ask other questions too: what is being symbolised by this sacrament?, how best can this be given expression?, what are the *optimum* conditions for a worthy celebration? If, as the Council asserts, the sanctification of man is manifested and effected in a way which is proper to each of these signs, then the entire ritual complex of actions, objects, words and persons, with all the human dynamics involved, will be integral to the effectiveness of the sacrament. They are the very way by which this sanctification happens. Since Trent the Church has been concerned to uphold the truth that the sacraments really effect what they signify. Now she is as strenuously concerned to ensure that they really signify what they effect. 'Pastors of souls must therefore realise that when the liturgy is celebrated something more is required than the laws governing valid and lawful celebration. It is their duty also to ensure that the faithful take part fully aware of what they are doing, actively engaged in the rite, and enriched by it' (SC 11). In other words, validity is necessary but not sufficient for an adequate liturgical celebration of a sacrament. Dogmatic theology and canon law may specify the essential matter, form and intention, but these will not suffice of themselves to express the fulness of the sacramental reality nor to secure the conscious, active and enriching involvement of the congregation. And so we find in the documents collected in this volume another language emerging besides that of validity, a language which talks of 'fulness', 'completeness' and 'integrity'. Thus, for instance, 'The homily is an integral part of the liturgy and

9

a necessary source of nourishment' (*Missal* 41); 'The sign of communion is more complete when given under both kinds' (*Missal* 240); 'Even though the laying on of hands does not pertain to the valid giving of the sacrament, it is to be strongly emphasised for the integrity of the rite and the fuller understanding of the sacrament' (*Confirmation* 9); 'The form consists of the words of the (entire) consecratory prayer, of which the following belong to the nature of the rite and are consequently required for validity' (*Ordinations*, Apostolic Constitution).

The expressiveness of the sacraments, their ability to communicate, is a major concern of the Council's constitution: 'The purpose of the sacraments is to sanctify men, to build up the Body of Christ, and finally give worship to God. Because they are signs they also instruct. They not only presuppose faith, but by words and objects they also nourish, strengthen and express it. . . . It is therefore of the greatest importance that the faithful should easily understand the sacramental signs' (SC 59). Because sacraments are to instruct, to arouse faith and give expression to it, they had to be revised so as to express more clearly what they effected (SC 21, 71, 72, 77), and to be directly intelligible to those participating in them (SC 21, 34, 59). This conviction led the bishops at Vatican II to lay down certain general principles to be observed not only in the revision of all liturgical rites but also in the celebration of them throughout the Church. The overriding aim in all cases is to secure the conscious, active and wholehearted involvement of the entire congregation, a participation which is their right and their duty (SC 11, 14, 21). To facilitate this, communal forms of celebration are to be preferred to individual or quasi-private ones (SC 26–7); there should be a proper distribution of roles and functions so that each individual carries out all but only those parts which belong to him (SC 28); succinctness, simplicity and clarity should always be aimed at (SC 34); variations and adaptations should be made to meet the needs and capabilities of different groups, peoples and cultures (SC 38).

The work of revision has now been completed, and new texts for all the sacramental celebrations of the Church have now been issued and come into force. But this does not mean that the liturgy has been renewed, only that the ground has been cleared and the tools provided. Revision has now to be translated into renewal, which will become a reality only in the involvement and transformation of the people who celebrate. And, as the Council recognised, it would be quite futile to entertain any hopes of achieving all this until the clergy, in the first place, are themselves fully penetrated with the spirit and power of the liturgy and capable of communicating it to others (SC 14). 'They are to be helped by every suitable means to a fuller understanding of what they are about when they perform the sacred rites, to live the liturgical life, and to share it with the faithful entrusted to their care' (SC 18). On them rests the responsibility for transforming the approach of the faithful and enabling them to achieve and enjoy that participation which is their right and their duty (SC 19, cf. also *Infants* 7, *Confirmation* 18, *Anointing* 37).

A vast educational project is hereby given to the whole Church, and in particular to the clergy. The principal tool put into our hands is the Introductions and Instructions which accompany each of the rites which are here gathered together in English for the first time: 'In drawing up rituals or particular collections of rites, the instructions prefixed to the individual rites in the Roman Ritual, whether they be pastoral and rubrical or whether they have a particular social import, shall not be omitted' (SC 63). Their purpose and character is indicated in the General Instruction on the Roman Missal which begins: 'When Christ the Lord was about to celebrate the passover meal with his disciples and institute the sacrifice of his body and blood, he directed them to prepare a large furnished room. The Church has always taken this command of Christ as bearing on its own responsibility in giving directions concerning the preparation of the minds of the worshippers and the place, rites and texts for the celebration of the Holy Eucharist' (*Missal* 1). The General Instruction on Christian Initiation asks for itself to be 'adapted and augmented' by local conferences of bishops 'so that ministers may fully understand the meaning of the rites and express this effectively in action' (*Initiation* 30). The Introduction to the Rite of Funerals reinforces this point that the quality of celebration will always depend on theological understanding and pastoral sensitivity: 'The celebration of the funeral liturgy with meaning and dignity, and the priest's ministry to the dead, presuppose an integral understanding of the Christian mystery and the pastoral office' (*Funerals* 22).

These Instructions or Introductions vary in length and scope, but each will be seen to follow a more or less uniform pattern: the meaning, importance and dignity of the rite; its structure, elements and parts; offices and ministries and their respective roles; the different forms of celebration; the time, place and requirements for celebration; adaptations allowed to bishops; adaptations allowed to the minister; choice of texts and the preparation of the celebration.

Their first function is *theological*, directed to achieving *conscious* participation. They each provide an authoritative statement of how the Church understands this rite and its place in the Christian mystery. Theology requires those celebrating a sacrament to intend what the Church intends, do what the Church does. These documents are designed to make clear in each case what is meant by each rite, and within it by each action, text and symbol, so that this intention may be more richly and accurately informed, more consciously conformed to the mind and intention of Christ in his Church. This material is the more precious for never having been provided so systematically and accessibly before. The former rites were published with very authoritative rubrics but little authoritative commentary.

Their second function is more directly *liturgical* and *pastoral*, directed to achieving *active* participation. The proper roles and functions of each participant are clearly defined and promoted so that they may cooperate harmoniously in the worship of the whole Christ, Head and members. That the celebration may be more fully and authentically the worship of a particular congregation, guidelines are given for adaptations of the Roman rite to the culture and traditions of a people (by bishops) and to the needs, resources and spiritual condition of an individual congregation (by the minister, in consultation with the participants). This marks a momentous change in the Roman liturgy, relaxing the uniformity and central control of the last four centuries.

A liturgy so adapted, indigenised and particular, cannot be issued invariable and complete for all circumstances. The desired flexibility and adaptation is made possible, first, by the provision of numerous options and alternatives, so that the book for each rite is, in effect, an anthology from which the minister and participants must choose the most appropriate texts. Interestingly, this reflects the format of the earliest 'sacramentaries' or service-books of the Roman liturgy, before the Gregorian and other reforms edited out the alternatives. If the choice made is not to be merely arbitrary and capricious but constructive, ministers and congregations will need secure principles of selection and a firm grasp of the structure and sequence of the rite, both of which are provided clearly in these instructions.

Also in the interests of flexibility are various formulas presented as models, which may be used as they stand but may also be developed or embroidered upon by the minister in words of his own. This too

12

constitutes a welcome recovery of the liturgical practice of the early Church, when the minister was free to improvise upon set traditional themes, and should prove an invaluable and educative stepping-stone to a responsible and informed liturgical freedom (cf. 'Instruction on Translation of Liturgical Texts', *Notitiae* 5, 1969).

An even more significant contribution to flexibility and adaptation is perhaps the evolution in the character and use of rubrics, which are now much less prescriptive, much more indicative. Neither the Congregation in Rome which issues the rites, nor the International Commission on English in the Liturgy which translates them, nor even the Liturgical Commissions which adapt them to the culture and traditions of each country, can prescribe in advance and in detail the unfolding of a celebration at the local level of parish or group. Such is the pluralism in cultural values, devotional tastes and religious development that the level of participation and the form of communication must vary inevitably from congregation to congregation, from context to context, and from celebration to celebration. As president of the liturgical assembly, the priest should stimulate, articulate and coordinate the involvement of the congregation and of other ministers. The revised rites all require him, in every instance, to adapt the celebration to the capacities, needs and circumstances of his particular congregation, rather as the producer of a play or the conductor of an orchestra has to interpret his script or score to bring out the best his particular team are capable of and to make the experience live for his particular audience (except that congregations, of course, are 'audience' and 'performers' at the same time). Like scripts and scores, the texts and instructions of the new rites mark out the individual contributions and their place in the whole and give general guidelines for their harmonious implementation, but they do not attempt or wish to deal in decibels, in the dimensions of gestures, in angles of inclination, or in the design and disposition of props. The meaning of each item is explained, its place in the whole sequence made clear, but the manner of its doing is left, and must be left, to the pastoral sensitivity of the man on the spot. This places a considerable responsibility upon the presiding minister and calls for sensitivities and skills which the 'old' rites did not demand. Many are unprepared for this and would no doubt prefer to surrender this responsibility in favour of something which, like the 'old' liturgy, more or less celebrated itself; but not only the directives but the Church's whole understanding of sacramental liturgy as contained in these documents will not allow them. New wine needs new wineskins.

A renewed liturgy demands a renewed theological appreciation and a renewed approach to celebration.

But even the most sensitive and accomplished minister will be unable to determine the needs and potential of a congregation singlehanded, and these documents make clear he has not the right. Adaptation is not clerical prerogative to be exercised according to the minister's whim or preference, but a service to the participants to be exercised in consultation with them (cf., for instance, *Missal* 73, 313; *Infants* 7; *Penance* 40; *Anointing* 37, 40; *Funerals* 20, 22). If this is not to remain a pious wish, then every community will need to set up a representative team to plan and prepare the liturgy with the priest, and the liturgical formation necessary for all the faithful must begin with them. Here again these introductions and instructions are the principal resource for such formation, and should be in the hands of all who share in any way in the service of liturgical leadership.

We have returned to the necessity of liturgical formation – of clergy and people – with which the Second Vatican Council began. Commentaries and articles, courses and discussions will all play a vital part, but it is one of the most ancient traditions of the Church that liturgy is 'caught not taught', and that the basis of any worthwhile instruction must be the experience of the sacrament itself (cf. the catechetical homilies of the fathers, and *Infants* 3). All sacramental liturgy is made up first of expressive action, secondly of the salvific Word which declares the meaning, authority and object of the action, and thirdly of the Church's reflection on, and response to the action and Word, formulated in the prayers and addresses of the rite. If we would understand the Church's sacraments, we must first experience them in all their dynamic reality; if we would penetrate and reflect upon their meaning, we must turn first of all to the words and texts of the rite, especially to the solemn prayer of blessing, thanksgiving and consecration found at their heart. And in seeking to achieve both the most authentic and enriching experience and the most authoritative and profound understanding, we have no better or more effective tool than that given us by the Church herself: the documents collected in this volume.

Ushaw College
March 1979

CHRISTIAN INITIATION*
GENERAL INTRODUCTION

Structure

* Originally published with the Rite of Baptism for Children, in 1969.

1.   Through the sacraments of Christian initiation men and women are freed from the power of darkness. With Christ they die, are buried and rise again. They receive the Spirit of adoption which makes them God's sons and daughters and, with the entire people of God, they celebrate the memorial of the Lord's death and resurrection.[1]

2.   Through baptism men and women are incorporated into Christ. They are formed into God's people, and they obtain forgiveness of all their sins. They are raised from their natural human condition to the dignity of adopted children.[2] They become a new creation through water and the Holy Spirit. Hence they are called, and are indeed, the children of God.[3]

Signed with the gift of the Spirit in confirmation, Christians more perfectly become the image of their Lord and are filled with the Holy Spirit. They bear witness to him before all the world and eagerly work for the building up of the body of Christ.[4]

Finally they come to the table of the eucharist, to eat the flesh and drink the blood of the Son of Man so that they may have eternal life[5] and show forth the unity of God's people. By offering themselves with Christ, they share in his universal sacrifice: the entire community of the redeemed is offered to God by their high priest.[6] They pray for a greater outpouring of the Holy Spirit so that the whole human race may be brought into the unity of God's family.[7]

Thus the three sacraments of Christian initiation closely combine to bring the faithful to the full stature of Christ and to enable them to carry out the mission of the entire people of God in the Church and in the world.[8]

I   Dignity of Baptism

3.   Baptism is the door to life and to the kingdom of God. Christ offered this first sacrament of the new law to all men that they might have eternal life.[9] He entrusted this sacrament and the gospel to his

---

[1]   AG 14.
[2]   Romans 8:15; Galatians 4:5; Council of Trent, 6th Session, Decree on Justification, Chapter 4, Denz. 796 (1524).
[3]   I John 3:1.
[4]   AG 36.
[5]   John 6:55.
[6]   Saint Augustine, *The City of God*, X, 6: PL 41, 284; LG 11; PO 2
[7]   LG 28.
[8]   *Ibid.*, 31.
[9]   John 3:5.

Church when he told his apostles: 'Go, make disciples of all nations, and baptise them in the name of the Father, and of the Son, and of the Holy Spirit.'[10] Therefore baptism is, above all, the sacrament of that faith by which men and women, enlightened by the Spirit's grace, respond to the gospel of Christ. That is why the Church believes it is her most basic and necessary duty to inspire all, catechumens, parents of children still to be baptised, and godparents, to that true and living faith by which they adhere to Christ and enter into or confirm their commitment to the new covenant. To accomplish this, the Church prescribes the pastoral instruction of catechumens, the preparation of the children's parents, the celebration of God's word, and the profession of baptismal faith.

4.   Further, baptism is the sacrament by which men and women are incorporated into the Church, built into a house where God lives, in the Spirit,[11] into a holy nation and a royal priesthood.[12] It is a sacramental bond of unity linking all who have been signed by it.[13] Because of that unchangeable effect (signified in the Latin liturgy by the anointing of the baptised person with chrism in the presence of God's people), the rite of baptism is held in highest honour by all Christians. It may never lawfully be repeated once it has been validly celebrated, even if by fellow Christians from whom we are separated.

5.   Baptism, the cleansing with water by the power of the living Word,[14] makes us sharers in God's own life[15] and his adopted children.[16] As proclaimed in the prayers for the blessing of the water, baptism is a cleansing water of rebirth,[17] which makes us God's children. The blessed Trinity is invoked over those who are to be baptised. Signed in this name, they are consecrated to the Trinity and enter into fellowship with the Father, the Son, and the Holy Spirit. They are prepared for this high dignity and led to it by the scriptural readings, the prayer of the community, and the threefold profession of faith.

6.   Far superior to the purifications of the old law, baptism produces all these effects by the power of the mystery of the Lord's passion and resurrection. Those who are baptised are engrafted in the likeness of Christ's death.[18] They are buried with him, they are given

---

[10] Matthew 28:19.   [11] Ephesians 2:22.   [12] 1 Peter 2:9.
[13] UR 22.   [14] Ephesians 5:26.   [15] 2 Peter 1:4.
[16] Romans 8:15; Galatians 4:5.   [17] Titus 3:5.   [18] Romans 6:4-5.

life again with him, and with him they rise again.[19] For baptism recalls and effects the paschal mystery itself, because by means of it men and women pass from the death of sin into life. Its celebration, therefore, should reflect the joy of the resurrection, especially when it takes place during the Easter Vigil or on a Sunday.

II Offices and Ministries of Baptism

7. Christian instruction and the preparation for baptism are a vital concern of God's people, the Church, which hands on and nourishes the faith it has received from the Apostles. Through the ministry of the Church, adults are called by the Holy Spirit to the gospel, and infants are baptised and brought up in this faith. Therefore it is most important that catechists and other lay people should work with priests and deacons in making preparations for baptism. In the actual celebration, the people of God (represented not only by the parents, godparents and relatives, but also, as far as possible, by friends, neighbours, and some members of the local church) should take an active part. Thus they will show their common faith and express their joy as the newly baptised are received into the community of the Church.

8. It is a very ancient custom of the Church that an adult is not admitted to baptism without a godparent, a member of the Christian community who will assist him at least in the final preparation for baptism and after baptism will help him persevere in the faith and in his life as a Christian.

In the baptism of children too, the godparent should be present to be added spiritually to the immediate family of the one to be baptised and to represent Mother Church. As occasion offers, he will be ready to help the parents bring up their child to profess the faith and to show this by living it.

9. At least in the final rites of the catechumenate and in the actual celebration of baptism, the godparent is present to testify to the faith of the adult candidate or, together with the parents, to profess the Church's faith, in which the child is being baptised.

10. Pastors of souls should therefore see to it that the godparents, chosen by the catechumen or by the family, is qualified to carry out

[19] Ephesians 2:6.

his proper liturgical functions as specified in no. 9 above. The god-parents should:

   1) be mature enough to undertake this responsibility;

   2) have received the three sacraments of initiation, baptism, con-firmation, and the eucharist;

   3) be a member of the Catholic Church, canonically free to carry out this office.

A baptised and believing Christian from a separated church or com-munity may act as a godparent or Christian witness along with a Catholic godparent, at the request of the parents and in accordance with the norms for various ecumenical cases.

11.   The ordinary ministers of baptism are bishops, presbyters, and deacons. At every celebration of this sacrament they should remember that they act in the Church in the name of Christ and by the power of the Holy Spirit. They should therefore be diligent in the ministry of the word of God and in the celebration of the sacraments. They must avoid any action which the faithful can rightly condemn as favourit-ism.[20]

12.   Bishops are the principal dispensers of the mysteries of God and leaders of the entire liturgical life in the church committed to them.[21] They thus direct the conferring of baptism, by which a sharing of the kingly priesthood of Christ is granted.[22] Therefore they should personally celebrate baptism, especially at the Easter Vigil. The preparation and baptism of adults is commended to them in a special way.

13.   It is the duty of the parish priest to assist the bishop in the instruction and baptism of the adults entrusted to his care, unless the bishop makes other provisions. It is also their duty, with the assistance of catechists or other qualified lay people, to prepare the parents and godparents of children with appropriate pastoral guidance and to administer baptism to the children.

14.   Other priests and deacons, since they are cooperators in the ministry of bishops and parish priests, also prepare candidates for baptism and, with the invitation or consent of the bishop or parish priest, confer the sacrament.

15.   The celebrant may be assisted by other priests and deacons and also by the laity in those parts which pertain to them, especially if

[20] SC 32; GS 29.   [21] CD15.   [22] LG 26.

there are many persons to be baptised. This provision is made in various parts of the rite.

16. In imminent danger of death and especially at the moment of death, when no priest or deacon is available, any member of the faithful, indeed anyone with the right intention, may and sometimes must administer baptism. If it is a question only of danger of death, then the sacrament should be administered by a member of the faithful if possible, according to the shorter rite (nos. 157-64). Even in this case a small community should be formed to assist at the rite, or at least one or two witnesses should be present if possible.

17. All lay persons, since they belong to the priestly people, and especially parents and, by reason of their work, catechists, obstetricians, women who are employed as family or social workers or as nurses of the sick, as well as physicians and surgeons, should know the proper method of baptising in cases of necessity. They should be taught by parish priests, deacons, and catechists. Bishops should provide appropriate means within their diocese for such instruction.

III Requirements for the Celebration of Baptism

18. The water used in baptism should be true water, for the sake of the authentic sacramental symbolism. It should be clean, for reasons of health.

19. The baptismal font, or the vessel in which on occasion the water is prepared for the celebration of the sacrament in the sanctuary, should be very clean and attractive.

20. If the climate requires, provision should be made for the water to be heated beforehand.

21. Except in the case of necessity, the priest or deacon should use only water that has been blessed for the rite. The water consecrated at the Easter Vigil should, if possible, be kept and used throughout the Easter season to signify more clearly the relationship between the sacrament of baptism and the paschal mystery. Outside the Easter season, it is desirable that the water be blessed for each occasion, in order that the words of blessing may clearly express the mystery of salvation which the Church recalls and proclaims. If the baptistry is supplied with flowing water, the blessing will be given to the water as it flows.

22.   Either the rite of immersion, which is more suitable as a symbol of participation in the death and resurrection of Christ, or the rite of infusion may lawfully be used in the celebration of baptism.

23.   The words for baptism in the Latin Church are: 'I baptise you in the name of the Father, and of the Son, and of the Holy Spirit.'

24.   A suitable place for celebrating the liturgy of the word of God should be provided in the baptistry or in the church.

25.   The baptistry is the area where the baptismal font flows or has been placed. It should be reserved for the sacrament of baptism, and should be a worthy place for Christians to be reborn in water and the Holy Spirit. It may be situated in a chapel either inside or outside the church, or in some other part of the church easily seen by the faithful; it should be large enough to accommodate a good number of people. After the Easter season, the Easter candle should be given a place of honour in the baptistry, so that when it is lighted for the celebration of baptism, the candles of the newly baptised may easily be lighted from it.

26.   In the celebration, the parts of the rite which are to be performed outside the baptistry should be celebrated in different areas of the church which most conveniently suit the size of the congregation and the several stages of the baptismal liturgy. When the baptistry cannot accommodate all the catechumens and the congregation, the parts of the rite which are customarily performed in the baptistry may be transferred to some other suitable area of the church.

27.   As far as possible, all recently born babies should be baptised at a common celebration on the same day. Except for a good reason, baptism should not be celebrated more than once on the same day in the same church.

28.   Further details concerning the time of baptism of adults and children will be found in the respective rites. The celebration of the sacrament should always suggest its paschal character.

29.   Parish priests should carefully and without delay record in the baptismal register the names of those baptised, the minister, parents and godparents, and the place and date of baptism.

IV Adaptations by Conferences of Bishops

30.   According to the Constitution on the Sacred Liturgy (no. 63b), it is within the competence of conferences of bishops to compose for their local rituals a section corresponding to this one in the Roman Ritual, adapted to the needs of their respective regions. When this has been reviewed by the Apostolic See, it should be used in the regions for which it was prepared.

In this connection, it is the responsibility of the conferences of bishops:

1) to determine the adaptations, according to no. 39 of the Constitution on the Sacred Liturgy;

2) carefully and prudently to consider what elements of a country's distinctive culture may suitably be admitted into divine worship. Adaptations considered useful or necessary should then be submitted to the Apostolic See with whose consent they may be introduced;

3) to retain distinctive elements of existing local rituals as long as they conform with the Constitution on the Sacred Liturgy and correspond to contemporary needs; or to modify these elements;

4) to prepare translations of the texts that genuinely reflect the characteristics of various languages and cultures and to add music for the texts when appropriate;

5) to adapt and augment the introduction contained in the Roman Ritual, so that the ministers may fully understand the meaning of the rites and express this effectively in action;

6) to arrange the material in the various editions of the liturgical books prepared under the guidance of the conferences of bishops so that these books may be best suited for pastoral use.

31.   As stated in nos. 37-40 and 65 of the Constitution on the Sacred Liturgy, it is the responsibility of the conferences of bishops in mission countries to judge whether certain initiation ceremonies in use among some peoples can be adapted for the rite of Christian baptism and to decide whether these rites are to be incorporated into it.

32.   When the Roman Ritual for baptism provides a choice of several formulas, local rituals may add other formulas of the same kind.

33.   The celebration of baptism is greatly enhanced by the use of song. It stimulates a sense of unity among those present, it gives

warmth to their common prayer, and it expresses the joy of Easter. Conferences of bishops should encourage and help musical specialists to compose settings for texts suitable for congregational singing at baptism.

V Adaptations by the Minister of Baptism

34. The minister, taking into account existing circumstances and needs, as well as the wishes of the faithful, should freely use the various choices allowed in the rite.

35. In addition to the adaptations which are provided in the Roman Ritual for the dialogue and blessings, the minister may make other adaptations for special circumstances. These adaptations will be indicated more fully in the introduction to the rites of baptism for adults and for children.

RITE OF CHRISTIAN INITIATION OF ADULTS*: INTRODUCTION

Structure

* Promulgated by Decree dated 6 January 1972.

1. The rite of Christian initiation described below is intended for adults. They hear the preaching of the mystery of Christ, the Holy Spirit opens their hearts, and they freely and knowingly seek the living God and enter the path of faith and conversion. By God's help, they will be strengthened spiritually in their preparation and at the proper time they will receive the sacraments fruitfully.

2. This order includes not only the celebration of the sacraments of baptism, confirmation, and the eucharist, but also all the rites of the catechumenate. Approved by the ancient practice of the Church and adapted to contemporary missionary work throughout the world, this catechumenate was so widely requested that the Second Vatican Council decreed its restoration, revision, and accommodation to local traditions.[1]

3. In order to be better suited to the work of the Church and to the circumstances of individuals, parishes, and missions, the rite of initiation first gives the complete or common form, intended for the preparation of a large number of people (see nos. 68-239). By simple changes, pastors may adapt this form for one person. Then, for special cases, there is a simple form, which may be celebrated on a single occasion (see nos. 240-73) or in several parts (see nos. 274-7), as well as a brief form for those in danger of death (see nos. 278-92.)

I Structure of the Initiation of Adults

4. The initiation of catechumens takes place step by step in the midst of the community of the faithful. Together with the catechumens, the faithful reflect upon the value of the paschal mystery, renew their own conversion, and by their example lead the catechumens to obey the Holy Spirit more generously.

5. The rite of initiation is suited to the spiritual journey of adults, which varies according to the many forms of God's grace, the free cooperation of the individuals, the action of the Church, and the circumstances of time and place.

6. On this journey, besides the period for making inquiry and maturing (see no. 7, below), there are stages or steps by which the catechumen moves forward, as it were, through a gateway or up another step.

[1] See SC 64-6; AG 14; CD 14.

a) First stage: at the point of initial conversion, he wishes to become a Christian and is accepted as a catechumen by the Church.

b) Second stage: when his faith has grown and the catechumenate is almost completed, he is admitted to a more profound preparation for the sacraments.

c) Third stage: after the spiritual preparation is completed, he receives the sacraments by which a Christian is initiated.

These three stages, steps, or gateways are to be considered as major, more serious moments of initiation and are marked by liturgical rites: the first by the rite of becoming a catechumen, the second by the election or choice, and the third by the celebration of the sacraments.

7. These stages lead to periods of investigation and maturation, or the latter prepare for the stages.

a) The first period consists of inquiry by the candidate and evangelisation and the precatechumenate on the part of the Church. It ends with entrance into the order of catechumens.

b) The second period, which begins with this entrance into the order of catechumens and may last for several years, includes catechesis and the rites connected with catechesis. It is completed on the day of election.

c) The third period, shorter in length, ordinarily occupies the Lenten preparation for the Easter celebration and the sacraments. It is a time of purification and enlightenment or 'illumination'.

d) The final period goes through the whole Easter season and is called the post-baptismal catechesis or 'mystagogia'. It is a time for deepening the Christian experience, for gaining spiritual fruit, and for entering more closely into the life and unity of the community of the faithful.

Thus there are four continuous periods:

—the precatechumenate, a time for hearing the first preaching of the Gospel;

—the catechumenate, set aside for a complete catechesis;

—the period of purification and enlightenment or illumination (Lent) for a more profound spiritual preparation; and

—the postbaptismal catechesis or mystagogia (Easter season), marked with the new experience of the sacraments and of the Christian community.

8. The whole initiation has a paschal character, since the initiation of Christians is the first sacramental sharing in the death and rising

of Christ and since, moreover, the time of purification and enlightenment or illumination ordinarily takes place during Lent,[2] with the postbaptismal catechesis or mystagogia during the Easter season. In this way Lent achieves its full force as a profound preparation of the elect, and the Easter Vigil is considered the proper time for the sacraments of initiation.[3] Because of pastoral needs, however, the sacraments of initiation may be celebrated outside these seasons.

A. Evangelisation and Precatechumenate

9. Although the rite of initiation begins with admission to the catechumenate, the preceding period or precatechumenate is of great importance and ordinarily should not be omitted. It is a time of evangelisation: in faith and constancy the living God is proclaimed, as is Jesus Christ, whom he sent for the salvation of all men. Thus those who are not yet Christians, their hearts opened by the Holy Spirit, may believe and be freely converted to the Lord. They sincerely adhere to him who is the way, the truth, and the life, and who fulfils all their spiritual expectations, indeed goes far beyond them.[4]

10. From evangelisation, conducted with the help of God, come faith and initial conversion, by which each one feels himself called away from sin and drawn toward the mystery of God's love. The whole period of the precatechumenate is set aside for this evangelisation, so that the true desire of following Christ and seeking baptism may mature.

11. During this time, catechists, deacons, and priests, as well as lay persons, suitably explain the Gospel to the candidates. They receive the help they are looking for, so that they may cooperate with God's grace with a pure and certain intention and may meet with the families and communities of Christians with greater ease.

12. In addition to the evangelisation that is proper to this period, the episcopal conferences may provide, if necessary and according to local circumstances, a method to receive interested inquirers ('sympathisers'), those who, even if they do not fully believe, show an inclination toward the Christian faith.

---

[2] See SC 109.
[3] This derogates from canon 790 of the Code of Canon Law.
[4] AG 13.

INSTRUCTIONS ON THE REVISED ROMAN RITES

1) Such a reception, which is optional and will be carried out without any rite, expresses the inquirers' sound intention rather than faith.

2) The reception will be adapted to local conditions and opportunities. Some candidates need to know and experience the spirit of Christians in a special way. For others, whose catechumenate has been delayed for various reasons, this first external act by them and the community is appropriate.

3) The reception should be carried out at meetings and gatherings of the local community, on a suitable occasion of friendly exchange. The inquirer or sympathiser is presented by a friend, and then he is welcomed and received by the priest or by some other appropriate and worthy member of the community.

13. During the period of the precatechumenate, pastors should help the inquirers with suitable prayers.

B. Catechumenate

14. The rite of becoming a catechumen is of very great importance. Assembling publicly for the first time, the candidates make their intention known to the Church; the Church, carrying out its apostolic mission, admits those who intend to become members. God showers his grace on them, since this celebration manifests their desire publicly and the Church expresses their reception and first consecration.

15. Before this step is taken, the candidates are required to be grounded in the basic fundamentals of the spiritual life and Christian teaching:[5] the faith first conceived at the time of the precatechumentate; the initial conversion and desire to change one's life and to enter into contact with God in Christ; thus the first sense of repentance and the practice of calling on God and praying; and the first experience of the society and spirit of Christians.

16. With the help of the sponsors (see no. 42, below), catechists, and deacons, it is the responsibility of pastors to judge the external indications of these dispositions.[6] It is also their duty, in view of the power of sacraments already validly received (see General Introduction, no. 4), to see that a baptised person is not baptised again for any reason whatever.

[5] See AG 14.　　　　[6] AG 13.

17. After the celebration of the rite, the names are written at once in the register of catechumens, along with the names of the minister and sponsors and the date and place of admission.

18. From this time on the catechumens, who have been welcomed by the Church with a mother's love and concern, are joined to the Church and are part of the household of Christ.[7] They are nourished by the Church on the word of God and helped by liturgical celebrations. They should be eager, then, to take part in the liturgy of the word and to receive blessings and sacramentals. When two catechumens marry or when a catechumen marries an unbaptised person, the appropriate rite is celebrated.[8] One who dies during the catechumenate receives a Christian burial.

19. The catechumenate is an extended period during which the candidates are given pastoral formation and are trained by suitable discipline.[9] In this way, the dispositions manifested at the entrance rite into the catechumenate are brought to maturity. This is achieved in four ways:

1) A fitting formation by priests, deacons, or catechists and other lay persons, given in stages and presented integrally, accommodated to the liturgical year and enriched by celebrations of the word, leads the catechumens to a suitable knowledge of dogmas and precepts and also to an intimate understanding of the mystery of salvation in which they desire to share.

2) Familiar with living the Christian way of life and helped by the example and support of sponsors and godparents and the whole community of the faithful, the catechumens will learn to pray to God more easily, to witness to the faith, to be constant in the expectation of Christ in all things, to follow supernatural inspiration in their deeds, and to exercise charity towards neighbours to the point of self-renunciation. Thus formed, 'new converts set out on a spiritual journey. Already sharing through faith in the mystery of Christ's death and resurrection, they pass from the old man to the new one made perfect in Christ. This transition, which brings with it a progressive change of outlook and morals, should become evident together with its social consequences and should be gradually developed during the time of the catechumenate. Since the Lord in whom he believes is a sign of contradiction, the convert often

---

[7] See LG 14; AG 14.   [8] *Rite of Marriage*, nos. 55-6.   [9] See AG 14.

experiences human divisions and separations, but he also tastes the joy which God gives without measure'.[10]

3) By suitable liturgical rites, Mother Church helps the catechumens on their journey, cleanses them little by little, and strengthens them with God's blessing. Celebrations of the word are encouraged for their benefit, and they may also attend the liturgy of the word with the faithful, thus better preparing themselves for participation in the eucharist in time to come. Ordinarily, however, when they are present in the assembly of the faithful, they should be dismissed in a friendly manner before the eucharistic celebration begins, unless there are difficulties; they must await their baptism which will bring them into the priestly people and allow them to participate in the Christian worship of the new covenant.

4) Since the Church's life is apostolic, catechumens should also learn how to work actively with others to spread the Gospel and build up the Church by the testimony of their lives and the profession of their faith.[11]

20. The period of time suitable for the catechumenate depends on the grace of God and on various circumstances, such as the plan of instruction to be given, the number of catechists, deacons, and priests, the cooperation of the individual catechumens, the means necessary to reach the place of the catechumenate and to live there, and the help of the local community. Nothing can be determined a priori. The bishop has the responsibility of setting the period of time and directing the discipline of the catechumenate. After considering the conditions of their people and region,[12] episcopal conferences should regulate this matter more specifically.

C. Period of Purification and Enlightenment

21. The time of purification and enlightenment or illumination of the catechumens customarily coincides with Lent; both in its liturgy and in its liturgical catechesis, Lent is a memorial or a preparation for baptism and a time of penance.[13] It renews the community of the faithful together with the catechumens and makes them ready to celebrate the paschal mystery which the sacraments of initiation apply to each individual.[14]

[10] See AG 13. [11] See AG 14. [12] See SC 64.
[13] SC 109. [14] AG 14.

22. The second stage of initiation begins the period of purification and enlightenment or illumination, marked by a more intense preparation of heart and spirit. At this stage the Church makes the 'election', that is, the choice and admission of the catechumens who because of their dispositions are worthy to take part in the next celebration of the sacraments of initiation. This stage is called election because the admission made by the Church is founded in the election by God, in whose name the Church acts. It is also called the enrolment or inscription of names because the candidates, as a pledge of fidelity, write their names in the book of the elect.

23. Before the election is celebrated, the candidates are expected to have a conversion of mind and morals, a sufficient knowledge of Christian teaching, and a sense of faith and charity; a consideration of their worthiness is also required. Later, in the actual celebration of the rite, the manifestation of their intention and the decision of the bishop or his delegate should take place in the presence of the community. It is thus clear that the election, which enjoys such great solemnity, is the turning point in the whole catechumenate.

24. From the day of their election and admission, catechumens are called the 'elect'. They are also called *competentes*, mature catechumens who strive together or contend to receive the sacraments of Christ and the gift of the Holy Spirit. They are also called the enlightened or illumined, because baptism itself is called enlightenment or illumination and by baptism the neophytes are illumined in the light of faith. In our day, other terms may be used which are better adapted to common understanding according to the nature of the languages and civil cultures of various regions.

25. During this period, a more intense preparation of the mind, which involves spiritual recollection more than catechesis, is intended to purify minds and hearts by the examination of conscience and by repentance and also to enlighten those minds and hearts by a deeper knowledge of Christ the Saviour. This is accomplished in various rites, especially in the scrutinies and presentations.

1) The scrutinies, which are celebrated solemnly on Sundays, have a twofold purpose: revealing anything that is weak, defective, or sinful in the hearts of the elect, so that it may be healed, and revealing what is upright, strong, and holy, so that it may be strengthened. The scrutinies are intended to free them from sin and the devil and to give them strength in Christ, who is the way, the truth, and the life for his chosen ones.

2) The presentations, by which the Church hands on to the elect its ancient documents of faith and prayer (the profession of faith or the creed and the Lord's Prayer), lead them to enlightenment or illumination. The profession of faith recalls the wonderful work of God for the salvation of man; it deepens the faith and joy of the elect. In the Lord's Prayer, they acknowledge more firmly the new spirit of sonship by which they will call God their Father, especially in the midst of the congregation assembled for the eucharist.

26. In the immediate preparation of the sacraments:

1) The elect should be instructed that on Holy Saturday they should rest from their ordinary work as far as possible, spend the time in prayer and recollection of mind, and fast according to their ability.[15]

2) That same day, if there is a meeting of the elect, some of the immediately preparatory rites may be celebrated, such as the recitation of the profession of faith, the ephphetha or opening of ears and mouth, the choosing of a Christian name, and, if it is to be done, the anointing with the oil of catechumens.

D. *Sacraments af Initiation*

27. The sacraments of baptism, confirmation, and the eucharist are the final stage in which the elect come forward and, with their sins forgiven, are admitted into the people of God, receive the adoption of the sons of God, and are led by the Holy Spirit into the promised fullness of time and, in the eucharistic sacrifice and meal, to the banquet of the Kingdom of God.

a. *Celebration of the Baptism of Adults*

28. The celebration of baptism, which reaches its high point at the washing with water in the name of the Holy Trinity, is prepared for by the blessing of water and the profession of faith, which are closely connected with the rite of washing with water.

29. The blessing of water recalls the dispensation of the paschal mystery and the choice of water for the sacramental operation of the mystery. The Holy Trinity is called upon for the first time, water is given a religious meaning, and the working of the divine mystery is shown before all.

[15] See SC 110.

30. The rites of the renunciation of sin and the profession of faith also recall, in the active faith of those to be baptised, the same paschal mystery which has been recalled in the blessing of water and briefly professed by the celebrant in the words of baptism. Adults are not saved unless they come forward of their own accord and are willing to accept the gift of God by faith. Baptism is the sacrament of faith, not only the faith of the Church, but also the candidates' own faith, and it is expected that it will be an active faith in them. When they are baptised, they should not receive such a sacrament passively, for of their own will they enter into a covenant with Christ, rejecting their errors and adhering to the true God.

31. As soon as they have professed their living faith in the paschal mystery of Christ, they come forward to receive that mystery expressed in the washing with water. After they have professed faith in the Holy Trinity, the Trinity, called on by the celebrant, brings about the numbering of the elect among the adopted children of God and unites them to his people.

32. Since the washing with water is a sign of mystical sharing in the death and rising of Christ, by which believers in his name die to sin and rise to eternal life, it achieves its full importance in the celebration of baptism. The rite of immersion or of infusion or of pouring is chosen according to what is more suitable in individual cases, so that, according to various traditions and circumstances, it may be understood that the washing is not merely a rite of purification but a sacrament of union with Christ.

33. The anointing with chrism after baptism is a sign of the royal priesthood of the baptised and their enrolment in the fellowship of the people of God. The white robe is a symbol of their new dignity, and the lighted candle shows their vocation of living as befits the children of light.

b. Celebration of the Confirmation of Adults

34. According to the ancient practice maintained in the Roman liturgy, an adult is not to be baptised unless he receives confirmation immediately afterward (see no. 44), provided no serious obstacles exist. This connection signifies the unity of the paschal mystery, the close relationship between the mission of the Son and the pouring out of the Holy Spirit, and the joint celebration of the sacraments by which the Son and the Spirit come with the Father upon those who are baptised.

35. Confirmation is celebrated after the complementary rites of baptism; the postbaptismal anointing is omitted (no. 224).

c. First Sharing in the Eucharist by the Newly Baptised

36. Finally the eucharist is celebrated and for the first time the neophytes have the full right to take part. This is the culminating point of their initiation. In the eucharist, the neophytes who have received the dignity of the royal priesthood have an active part in the general intercessions (prayer of the faithful) and, as far as possible, in the rite of bringing the offerings to the altar. With the whole community they take part in the action of the sacrifice and they say the Lord's Prayer, thus showing the spirit of adoption as God's children which they have received in baptism. Then, by receiving the body that was handed over and the blood that was shed, they confirm the gifts they have received and acquire a foretaste of eternal things.

E. Period of Postbaptismal Catechesis or Mystagogia

37. After this last stage has been completed, the community and the neophytes move forward together, meditating on the Gospel, sharing in the eucharist, and performing works of charity. In this way they understand the paschal mystery more fully and bring it into their lives more and more. The period of postbaptismal catechesis or mystagogia is the final period of initiation of the newly baptised.

38. A fuller, more fruitful understanding of the 'mysteries' is acquired by the newness of the account given to the neophytes and especially by their experience of receiving the sacraments. They have been renewed in mind, have tasted more intimately the good word of God, have shared in the Holy Spirit, and have come to discover the goodness of the Lord. From this experience, which is proper to the Christian and is increased by the way he lives, they draw a new sense of the faith, the Church, and the world.

39. This new frequenting of the sacraments enlightens the neophytes' understanding of the holy scriptures and also increases their knowledge of men and develops the experience in the community itself. As a result, the relationship of the neophyte with the rest of the faithful becomes easier and more beneficial. The time of postbaptismal catechesis is of great importance so that the neophytes,

helped by their sponsors, may enter into a closer relationship with the faithful and bring them renewed vision and a new impetus.

40. Since the nature and force proper to this period came from the new, personal experience of the sacraments and of the community, the main place for the postbaptismal catechesis or mystagogia will be the Masses for neophytes, that is, the Sunday Masses of the Easter season. In these celebrations, besides meeting with the community and sharing in the mysteries, the newly baptised will find the readings of the Lectionary appropriate for them, especially the readings of Year A. For this reason, the whole local community should be invited to these Masses along with the neophytes and their sponsors. The texts for the Masses may be used even when the initiation is celebrated outside the usual time.

II Ministries and Offices

41. Besides what is explained in the General Introduction (no. 7), the people of God, represented by the local church, should always understand and show that the initiation of adults is its concern and the business of all the baptised.[16]

Therefore the community must always be ready to fulfil its apostolic vocation by giving help to those who need Christ. In the various circumstances of daily life, as in the apostolate, each disciple of Christ has the obligation of spreading the faith according to his capability.[17] Hence, the community must help the candidates and catechumens throughout their whole period of initiation, during the precatechumenate, the catechumenate, and the period of post-baptismal catechesis or mystagogia. In particular:

1) During the time of evangelisation and the precatechumenate, the faithful should remember that the apostolate of the Church and all its members is directed first to making known to the world the message of Christ through their words and deeds and to communicating his grace.[18] Therefore they will be ready to open up the spirit of the Christian community to the candidates, to invite them into their families, to engage them in private conversation, and to invite them to some community gatherings.

2) The faithful should be present at the celebration of the catechumenate whenever possible and share actively in the responses, prayer, singing, and acclamations.

[16] See AG 14. [17] See LG 17. [18] See AA 6.

3) On the day of election, when the community is to be enlarged, the faithful should be sure to give honest and prudent testimony about the catechumens.

4) During Lent, the time of purification and enlightenment or illumination, the faithful should be present at and attentive to the rites of the scrutinies and presentations and give the catechumens the example of their own renewal in the spirit of penance, faith, and charity. At the Easter Vigil, they should renew their own baptismal promises in their hearts.

5) The faithful should take part in the Masses for the newly baptised during the period immediately after baptism, welcome them with charity, and help them to sense the joy of belonging to the community of the baptised.

42. The candidate should be accompanied by a sponsor when he asks to be admitted as a catechumen. This sponsor is to be a man or woman who knows the candidate, helps him, and witnesses to his morals, faith, and intention. It may happen that this sponsor is not able to fulfil the function of godparent in the period of purification and enlightenment or illumination and in the period of postbaptismal catechesis or mystagogia. In this case, another person takes on this responsibility.

43. The godparent,[19] however, who is close to the candidate because of his example, character, and friendship, is delegated by the local Christian community and approved by the priest. He accompanies the candidate on the day of election, in the celebration of the sacraments, and during the period of postbaptismal catechesis. It is his responsibility to show the catechumen in a friendly way the place of the Gospel in his own life and in society, to help him in doubts and anxieties, to give public testimony for him, and to watch over the progress of his baptismal life. Already a friend before the election, this person exercises his office publicly from the day of election when he gives his testimony about the catechumen before the community. His responsibility remains important when the neophyte has received the sacraments and needs to be helped to remain faithful to his baptismal promises.

44. It is for the bishop,[20] in person or through his delegate, to set up, regulate, and promote the pastoral formation of catechumens

[19] See General Introduction, no. 8.
[20] See SC 64.

and to admit the candidates to their election and to the sacraments. It is to be hoped that, if possible, presiding at the Lenten liturgy, he will himself celebrate the rite of election and, at the Easter Vigil, the sacraments of initiation. Finally, as a part of his pastoral care, the bishop should appoint catechists who are truly worthy and properly prepared to celebrate the minor exorcisms.[21]

45. Besides the usual ministry exercised in any celebration of baptism, confirmation, and the eucharist,[22] presbyters have the responsibility of attending to the pastoral and personal care of the catechumen,[23] especially those who seem hesitant and weak, in order to provide for their catechesis with the help of deacons and catechists. They also are to approve the choice of godparents and gladly listen to them and help them. Finally, presbyters should be diligent in the correct celebration and adaptation of the rites throughout the entire rite of Christian initiation (see no. 67, below).

46. When the bishop is absent, the presbyter who baptises an adult or child of catechetical age should also confer confirmation, unless this sacrament is to be given at another time (see no. 56).[24]

When there are very many to be confirmed, the minister of the sacrament of confirmation may associate other presbyters with himself in its administration.

It is necessary that these presbyters:

a) have a particular function or office in the diocese, namely, that of vicars general, episcopal vicars or delegates, district or regional vicars, or those who by mandate of the ordinary hold equivalent offices;

b) be the parish pastors of the places where confirmation is celebrated or pastors of the places where the candidates belong, or presbyters who did special work in this catechetical preparation.[25]

47. Deacons who are available should be ready to help. If the episcopal conference judges it opportune to have permanent deacons, it should make provision that their number is adequate to permit the stages, periods, and exercise of the catechumenate to take place everywhere when required by pastoral needs.[26]

[21] This abrogates Canon 1153 of the Code of Canon Law.
[22] See General Introduction, nos. 13-15
[23] See PO 6.
[24] See Rite of Confirmation, Introduction, no. 76.
[25] See Rite of Marriage, nos. 55-6.
[26] See LG 26; AG 16.

48. The office of catechists is important for the progress of the catechumens and for the growth of the community. As often as possible, they should have an active part in the rites. When they are teaching, they should see that their instruction is filled with the spirit of the Gospel, adapted to the liturgical signs and the course of the Church year, and enriched by local traditions as far as possible. When so delegated by the bishop, they may perform minor exorcisms (no. 44) and blessings,[27] as mentioned in the Ritual nos. 113-24.

III Time and Place of Initiation

49. Ordinarily pastors should make use of the rite of initiation in such a way that the sacraments will be celebrated at the Easter Vigil and the election will take place on the First Sunday of Lent. The other rites should be arranged as explained above (nos. 6-8, 14-40). For serious pastoral needs, however, the plan of the entire rite of initiation may be differently arranged, as indicated below (nos. 58-62).

A. Lawful or Customary Time

50. The following should be noted about the time of celebrating the rite of becoming catechumens:

1) It should not be too early, but should be delayed until the candidates, according to their own dispositions and situations, have had sufficient time to conceive an elementary faith and to show the first signs of conversion (no. 20, above).

2) When the number of candidates is unusually large, the rite should be postponed until the group is large enough for catechesis and the liturgical rites.

3) Two days or, if necessary, three days or periods of the year should be set aside for the usual celebration of this rite.

51. The rite of election or enrolment of names should usually be celebrated on the First Sunday of Lent. It may be anticipated somewhat or even celebrated during the week.

52. The scrutinies should take place on the Third, Fourth and

[27] See SC 79.

Fifth Sundays of Lent or if necessary, on the other Sundays of Lent or even on more suitable weekdays. Three scrutinies should be celebrated, but for serious reasons the bishop may dispense from one of them or even from two in extraordinary circumstances. When time is lacking and the election is anticipated, the first scrutiny may also be held earlier. But in this case, the time of purification and enlightenment or illumination must not be extended beyond eight weeks.

53. By ancient usage, the presentations, since they take place after the scrutinies, belong to the same period of purification and enlightenment or illumination. They are celebrated during the week. The profession of faith is given during the week after the first scrutiny, and the Lord's Prayer after the third scrutiny. For pastoral reasons, however, to enrich the liturgy of the period of the catechumenate, the presentations may be transferred and celebrated during the catechumenate as rites of transition (see nos. 125-6).

54. On Holy Saturday, when the elect refrain from work (see no. 26) and spend their time in recollection, the various immediately preparatory rites may be performed: the recitation of the creed, the ephphetha or opening of ears and mouth, the choosing of a Christian name, and even the anointing with the oil of catechumens (see nos. 193-207).

55. The sacraments of the initiation of adults should be celebrated at the Easter Vigil (see nos. 8, 49). If there are very many catechumens, the majority receive the sacraments that night, and the rest may be postponed to the days within the octave of Easter, when they receive the sacraments either in the principal churches or in secondary stations. In this case, either the Mass of the day or the ritual Mass for Christian initiation should be used, with readings from the Easter Vigil.

56. In certain cases, confirmation may be postponed until near the end of the period of postbaptismal catechesis or mystagogia, for example, Pentecost Sunday (see no. 237).

57. The Masses for neophytes are celebrated on all the Sundays after the First Sunday of Easter. The community, the newly baptised and their godparents are urgently invited to participate (see no. 40).

B. *Outside the Customary Times*

58.   The rite of initiation is normally arranged so that the sacraments will be celebrated during the Easter Vigil. Because of unusual circumstances and pastoral needs, however, the rite of election and the period of purification and enlightenment or illumination may be held outside Lent and the sacraments may be celebrated outside the Vigil or Easter Sunday. Even in ordinary circumstances, but only for serious pastoral needs (for example, if there is a very large number of persons to be baptised), apart from the plan of initiation carried on as usual during Lent, another time for celebrating the sacraments of initiation may be chosen, particularly in the Easter season. In these cases, although the times of the liturgical year are changed, the arrangement of the whole rite with its appropriate intervals remains the same. Adaptations should be made as follows.

59.   As far as possible, the sacraments of initiation are celebrated on Sunday, using the Sunday Mass or the proper ritual Mass (see no. 55).

60.   The rite of becoming catechumens takes place at a suitable time, as explained in no. 50.

61.   The election is celebrated almost six weeks before the sacraments of initiation so that there is sufficient time for the scrutinies and the presentations. Care should be taken that the celebration of the election does not fall on a solemnity of the liturgical year. The readings given in the ritual should be used, and the Mass of the day or the ritual Mass will be celebrated.

62.   The scrutinies should not be celebrated on solemnities, but on Sundays or even on weekdays, observing the usual intervals and using the readings given in the ritual. The Mass of the day or the ritual Mass will be celebrated (see no. 374a).

C. *Places for the Rite of Initiation*

63.   The rites should take place in suitable locations, as indicated in the ritual. Consideration should be given to special needs which arise in secondary stations of missionary regions.

IV Adaptations by Episcopal Conferences which use the Roman Ritual

64. Besides the adaptations mentioned in the General Introduction (nos. 30-3), episcopal conferences may make other changes in the rite of initiation of adults.

65. Episcopal conferences may freely choose:

1) To provide, where it seems suitable, some method of receiving interested inquirers (or sympathisers) prior to the catechumenate (see no. 12).

2) Wherever false worship flourishes, to insert the first exorcism and the first renunciation in the rite of becoming catechumens (nos. 79-80).

3) To decree that the gesture of signing the forehead be done in front of the forehead in places where the act of touching may not seem proper (no. 83).

4) Where it is the practice of non-Christian religions to give a new name to the initiated at once, to decree that the new name be given in the rite for becoming catechumens (no. 88).

5) According to local custom, to add auxiliary rites to show that the catechumens have been received into the community (no. 89).

6) Besides the usual rites during the period of the catechumenate (nos. 106-24), to restore the rites of transition by anticipating the presentations (nos. 125-6), the ephphetha or opening of ears and mouth, the recitation of the profession of faith, or even the anointing with the oil of catechumens (nos. 127-9).

7) To decide to omit the anointing with the oil of catechumens (no. 218), to transfer it to the immediately preparatory rites (nos. 206-7), or to use it during the period of catechumenate as a rite of transition (nos. 127-32).

8) To make the formulas of renunciation more detailed and richer (see nos. 80, 217).

V Competence of the Bishop

66. For his diocese, the bishop has the responsibility:

1) To set up the formation of the catechumenate and give suitable norms as needed (see no. 44).

2) As circumstances suggest, to decree whether and when the rite of initiation may be celebrated outside the ordinary times (see no. 58).

3) Because of serious obstacles, to dispense from one scrutiny or even from two scrutinies in extraordinary circumstances (see no. 240).

4) To permit the simple rite to be used in whole or in part (see no. 240).

5) To assign catechists who are truly worthy and properly prepared to give the exorcisms and blessings (see nos. 44, 47).

6) To preside at the rite of election and to ratify personally, or through a delegate, the admission of the elect (see no. 44).

VI Adaptations by the Minister

67. It is for the celebrant to use fully and intelligently the freedom which is given to him either in the General Introduction (no. 34) or in the rubrics of the rite. In many places the manner of acting or praying is intentionally left undetermined or two possibilities are offered, so that the celebrant may accommodate the rite, according to his prudent pastoral judgment, to the circumstances of the candidates and others who are present. The greatest freedom is left in the introductions and intercessions, which may always be shortened, changed, or even increased with new intentions in order to correspond with the circumstances or special situation of the candidates (for example, a sad or joyful event occurring in a family) or of the others present (for example, joy or sorrow common to the parish or town).

The celebrant will also adapt the text by changing the gender and number as needed.

RITE OF BAPTISM OF CHILDREN*:
INTRODUCTION

Structure

* Promulgated by Decree dated 5 May 1969.

43

I Importance of Baptising Children

1. Children or infants are those who have not yet reached the age of discernment and therefore cannot have or profess personal faith.

2. From the earliest times, the Church, to which the mission of preaching the gospel and of baptising was entrusted, has baptised children as well as adults. Our Lord said: 'Unless a man is reborn in water and the Holy Spirit, he cannot enter the kingdom of God.'[1] The Church has always understood these words to mean that children should not be deprived of baptism, because they are baptised in the faith of the Church. This faith is proclaimed for them by their parents and godparents, who represent both the local Church and the whole society of saints and believers: 'The Church is at once the mother of all and the mother of each.'[2]

3. To fulfil the true meaning of the sacrament, children must later be formed in the faith in which they have been baptised. The foundation of this formation will be the sacrament itself, which they have already received. Christian formation, which is their due, seeks to lead them gradually to learn God's plan in Christ, so that they may ultimately accept for themselves the faith in which they have been baptised.

II Ministries and Roles in the Celebration of Baptism

4. The people of God, that is the Church, made present in the local community, has an important part to play in the baptism of both children and adults.

Before and after the celebration of the sacrament, the child has a right to the love and help of the community. During the rite, in addition to the ways of congregational participation mentioned in no. 7 of the General Introduction, the community exercises its duty when it expresses its assent together with the celebrant after the profession of faith by the parents and godparents. In this way it is clear that the faith in which the children are baptised is not the private possession of the individual family, but is the common treasure of the whole Church of Christ.

5. Because of the natural relationships, parents have a more

[1] John 3:5.
[2] Saint Augustine, Epistle 98, 5: PL 33, 362.

important ministry and role in the baptism of infants than the god-parents.

1) Before the celebration of the sacrament, it is of great importance that parents, moved by their own faith or with the help of friends or other members of the community, should prepare to take part in the rite with understanding. They should be provided with suitable means such as books, instructions, and catechisms written for families. The parish priest should make it his duty to visit them, or see that they are visited, as a family or as a group of families, and prepare them for the coming celebration by pastoral counsel and common prayer.

2) It is very important that the parents should be present in the celebration in which their child is reborn in water and the Holy Spirit.

3) In the celebration of baptism, the father and mother have special parts to play. They listen to the words addressed to them by the celebrant, they join in prayer along with the congregation, and they exercise a special function when:

a) they publicly ask that the child be baptised;
b) they sign their child with the sign of the cross after the celebrant;
c) they renounce Satan and make their profession of faith;
d) they (and especially the mother) carry the child to the font;
e) they hold the lighted candle;
f) they are blessed with the special prayers for the mothers and fathers.

4) If one of the parents cannot make the profession of faith (if, for example, he is not a Catholic), he may keep silent. All that is asked of him, when he requests baptism for the child, is that he should make arrangements, or at least give permission, for the child to be instructed in the faith of its baptism.

5) After baptism it is the responsibility of the parents, in their gratitude to God and in fidelity to the duty they have undertaken, to enable the child to know God, whose adopted child it has become, to receive confirmation, and to participate in the holy eucharist. In this duty they are again to be helped by the parish priest by suitable means.

6. Each child may have a godfather and a godmother; the word 'godparents' is used in the rite to describe both.

7. In addition to what is said about the ordinary minister of

baptism in the General Introduction (nos. 11-15), the following should be noted:

1) It is the duty of the priest to prepare families for the baptism of their children and to help them in the task of Christian formation which they have undertaken. It is the duty of the bishop to co-ordinate such pastoral efforts in the diocese, with the help also of deacons and lay people.

2) It is also the duty of the priest to arrange that baptism is always celebrated with proper dignity and, as far as possible, adapted to the circumstances and wishes of the families concerned. Everyone who performs the rite of baptism should do so with care and devotion; he must also try to be understanding and friendly to all.

III Time and Place for the Baptism of Children

8.   As for the time of baptism, the first consideration is the welfare of the child, that it may not be deprived of the benefit of the sacrament; then the health of the mother must be considered, so that, as far as possible she too may be present. Then, as long as they do not interfere with the greater good of the child, there are pastoral considerations such as allowing sufficient time to prepare the parents and for planning the actual celebration to bring out its paschal character:

1) If the child is in danger of death, it is to be baptised without delay, as is laid down in no. 21.

2) In other cases, as soon as possible and even before the child is born, the parents should be in touch with the parish priest concerning the baptism, so that proper preparation may be made for the celebration.

3) An infant should be baptised within the first weeks after birth. The conference of bishops may, for sufficiently serious pastoral reasons, determine a longer interval of time between birth and baptism.

4) When the parents are not yet prepared to profess the faith or to undertake the duty of bringing up their children as Christians, it is for the parish priest, keeping in mind whatever regulations may have been laid down by the conference of bishops, to determine the time for the baptism of infants.

9.   To bring out the paschal character of baptism, it is recommended

that the sacrament be celebrated during the Easter Vigil or on Sunday, when the Church commemorates the Lord's resurrection. On Sunday, baptism may be celebrated even during Mass, so that the entire community may be present and the necessary relationship between baptism and eucharist may be clearly seen, but this should not be done too often. Regulations for the celebration of baptism during the Easter Vigil or at Mass on Sunday are set out below.

10. So that baptism may clearly appear as the sacrament of the Church's faith and of admittance into the people of God, it should normally be celebrated in the parish church, which must have a baptismal font.

11. The bishop, after consulting the local parish priest, may permit or direct that a baptismal font be placed in another church or public oratory within the parish boundaries. In these places, too, it is the normal right of the parish priest to celebrate baptism.

12. Except in case of danger of death, baptism should not be celebrated in private houses.

13. Unless the bishop decides otherwise (see no. 11), baptism should not be celebrated in hospitals, except in cases of emergency or for some other pastoral reason of a pressing kind. Care should always be taken that the parish priest is notified and that the parents are suitably prepared beforehand.

14. While the liturgy of the word is being celebrated, it is desirable that the children should be taken to some other place. Provision should be made for the mothers or godmothers to attend the liturgy of the word; the children should therefore be entrusted to the care of other women.

IV Structure of the Rite of Baptising Children

a. Order of Baptism Celebrated by the Ordinary Minister
15. Baptism, whether for one child, or for several, or even for a larger number, should be celebrated by the ordinary minister and with the full rite when there is no immediate danger of death.

16. The rite begins with the reception of the children. This is to indicate the desire of the parents and godparents, as well as the

intention of the Church, concerning the celebration of the sacrament of baptism. These purposes are expressed in action when the parents and the celebrant trace the sign of the cross on the foreheads of the children.

17. Then the liturgy of the word is directed toward stirring up the faith of the parents, godparents, and congregation, and praying in common for the fruits of baptism before the sacrament itself. This part of the celebration consists of the reading of one or more passages from holy scripture; a homily, followed by a period of silence; the prayer of the faithful; and finally a prayer, drawn up in the style of an exorcism, to introduce either the anointing with the oil of catechumens or the laying on of hands.

18. 1) The celebration of the sacrament is immediately preceded by:
   a) the solemn prayer of the celebrant, who, by invoking God and recalling his plan of salvation, blesses the water of baptism or commemorates its previous blessing;
   b) the renunciation of Satan on the part of parents and god-parents, and their profession of faith, to which is added the assent of the celebrant and the community; and the final interrogation of the parents and godparents.
   2) The celebration of the sacrament is performed by washing in water, by way of immersion or infusion, according to local custom, and by the invocation of the blessed Trinity.
   3) The celebration of the sacrament is completed, first by the anointing with chrism, which signifies the royal priesthood of the baptised and enrolment in the fellowship of God's people; then by the ceremonies of the white garment, lighted candle, and *Ephphetha* (the last of which is optional).

19. After the celebrant speaks of the future reception of the eucharist by the baptised children, the Lord's Prayer, in which God's children pray to their Father in heaven, is recited before the altar. Finally, a prayer of blessing is said over the mothers, fathers, and all present, to ask God's grace in abundance for all.

b. Shorter Rite of Baptism

20. In the shorter rite of baptism designed for the use of catechists,[3] the reception of the children, the celebration of the word of God, or the instruction by the minister, and the prayer of the faithful are

[3] SC 68.

retained. Before the font, the minister offers a prayer invoking God and recalling the history of salvation as it relates to baptism. After the baptismal washing, an adapted formula is recited in place of the anointing with chrism, and the whole rite concludes in the customary way. The omissions, therefore, are the exorcism, the anointing with oil of catechumens and with chrism, and the *Ephphetha*.

21. The shorter rite for baptising a child in danger of death and in the absence of the ordinary minister has a twofold structure:

1) At the moment of death or when there is urgency because of imminent danger of death, the minister,[4] omitting all other ceremonies, pours water (not necessary blessed but real and natural water), on the head of the child, and pronounces the customary formula.[5]

2) If it is prudently judged that there is sufficient time, several of the faithful may be gathered together, and, if one of them is able to lead the others in a short prayer, the following rite may be used: an explanation by the minister of the sacrament, a short common prayer, the profession of faith by the parents or one godparent, and the pouring of the water with the customary words. But if those present are uneducated, the minister of the sacrament should recite the profession of faith aloud and baptise according to the rite for use at the moment of death.

22. In danger of death, the priest or deacon may also use this shorter form if necessary. If there is time and he has the sacred chrism, the parish priest or other priest enjoying the same faculty should not fail to confer confirmation after baptism. In this case he omits the postbaptismal anointing with chrism.

V Adaptations by Conferences of Bishops or by Bishops

23. In addition to the adaptations provided for in the General Introduction (nos. 30-3), the baptismal rite for infants admits other variations, to be determined by the conferences of bishops.

24. As is indicated in the Roman Ritual, the following matters are left to the discretion of the conferences:

1) As local customs may dictate, the questioning about the name of the child may be arranged in different ways: the name may have

---

[4] General Introduction, 16.   [5] *Ibid.*, 23.

been given already or may be given during the rite of baptism.

2) The anointing with oil of catechumens may be omitted (nos. 50, 87).

3) The formula of renunciation may be shortened or extended (nos. 57, 94, 121).

4) If the number to be baptised is very great, the anointing with chrism may be omitted (no. 125).

5) The rite of *Ephphetha* may be retained (nos. 65, 101).

25. In many countries parents are sometimes not ready for the celebration of baptism or they ask for their children to be baptised, although the latter will not afterwards receive a Christian education and will even lose the faith. Since it is not enough to instruct the parents and to inquire about their faith in the course of the rite itself, conferences of bishops may issue pastoral directives, for the guidance of parish priests, to determine a longer interval between birth and baptism.

26. It is for the bishop to judge whether in his diocese catechists may give an improvised homily or speak only from a written text.

VI Adaptations by the Minister

27. During meetings to prepare the parents for the baptism of their children, it is important that the instruction should be supported by prayer and religious rites. The various elements provided in the rite of baptism for the celebration of the word of God will prove helpful.

28. When the baptism of children is celebrated as part of the Easter Vigil, the ritual should be arranged as follows:

1) At a convenient time and place before the Easter Vigil, the rite of receiving the children is celebrated. The liturgy of the word may be omitted at the end, according to circumstances, and the prayer of exorcism is said, followed by the anointing with oil of catechumens.

2) The celebration of the sacrament (nos. 56-8, 60-3) takes place after the blessing of the water, as is indicated in the Rite of the Easter Vigil.

3) The assent of the celebrant and community (no. 59) is omitted, as are the presentation of the lighted candle (no. 64) and the rite of *Ephphetha* (no. 65).

4) The conclusion of the rite (nos. 67-71) is omitted.

29. If baptism takes place during Sunday Mass, the Mass for that Sunday is used, and the celebration takes place as follows:

1) The rite of receiving the children (nos. 33-43) takes place at the beginning of Mass, and the greeting and penitential rite are omitted.

2) In the liturgy of the word:

a) The readings are taken from the Mass of the Sunday or, for special reasons, from those provided in the baptismal rite.

b) The homily is based on the sacred texts, but should take account of the baptism which is to take place.

c) The creed is not said, since the profession of faith by the entire community before baptism takes its place.

d) The general intercessions are taken from those used in the rite of baptism (nos. 47-8, 217-20). At the end, however, before the invocation of the saints, petitions are added for the universal Church and the needs of the world.

3) The celebration of baptism continues with the prayer of exorcism, anointing, and other ceremonies in the rite (nos. 49-66).

4) After the celebration of baptism, the Mass continues in the usual way with the offertory.

5) For the blessing at the end of Mass, the priest may use one of the formulas provided in the rite of baptism (nos. 70, 247-9).

30. If baptism is celebrated during Mass on weekdays, it is arranged in the same way as on Sundays; the readings for the liturgy of the word may be taken from those that are provided in the rite of baptism (nos. 44, 186-94, 204-15).

31. In accordance with no. 34 of the General Introduction, the minister may make some adaptations in the rite, as circumstances require, such as:

1) If the child's mother died in childbirth, this should be taken into account in the opening instruction (no. 36), general intercessions (nos. 47, 217-20), and final blessing (nos. 70, 247-8).

2) In the dialogue with the parents (nos. 37-8, 76-7), their answer should be taken into account: if they have not answered 'baptism,' but 'faith', or 'the grace of Christ,' or 'entrance into the Church,' or 'everlasting life,' then the minister does not begin by saying 'baptism,' but uses 'faith,' or 'the grace of Christ,' and so forth.

3) The rite of bringing a baptised child to the church (nos. 165-85), which has been drawn up for use only when the child has been baptised in danger of death, should be adapted to cover other

contingencies, for example, when children have been baptised during a time of religious persecution or temporary disagreement between the parents.

In England and Wales, the Hierarchy direct that the anointing with the oil of catechumens is not to be omitted; the Ephphetha need not be performed unless specially requested by the parents, and then only after explanation to the people; baptism is to be conferred on children as soon as possible after the mother has recovered from childbirth, and should not be delayed for more than one month after the birth of the child, except for serious reasons. (See paras. 24 and 25.)
In Ireland, the Hierarchy direct that the anointing with the oil of catechumens and the Ephphetha are to be retained (see para. 24). The alternative text of the Our Father is permitted.
In Scotland, the Hierarchy direct that the anointing with the oil of catechumens and the Ephphetha are to be retained (see para. 24).

RITE OF CONFIRMATION
APOSTOLIC CONSTITUTION

PAUL, BISHOP
Servant of the Servants of God For an Everlasting Memorial

The sharing of the divine nature which is granted to men through the grace of Christ has a certain likeness to the origin, development, and nourishing of natural life. The faithful are born anew by baptism, strengthened by the sacrament of confirmation, and finally are sustained by the food of eternal life in the eucharist. By means of these sacraments of Christian initiation, they thus receive in increasing measure the treasures of divine life and advance toward the perfection of charity. It has rightly been written: 'The body is washed, that the soul may be cleansed; the body is anointed, that the soul may be consecrated; the body is signed, that the soul too may be fortified; the body is overshadowed by the laying on of hands, that the soul too may be enlightened by the Spirit; the body is fed on the body and blood of Christ, that the soul too should be nourished by God.'[1]

Conscious of its pastoral purpose, the Second Vatican Ecumenical Council devoted special attention of these sacraments of initiation. It prescribed that the rites should be suitably revised in order to make them more suited to the understanding of the faithful. Since the *Rite for the Baptism of Children*, revised at the mandate of that General Council and published at our command, is already in use, it is now fitting to publish the rite of confirmation, in order to show the unity of Christian initiation in its true light.

In fact, careful attention and application have been devoted in these last years to the task of revising the manner of celebrating this sacrament. The aim of this work has been that 'the intimate connection which this sacrament has with the whole of Christian initiation should be more lucidly set forth'.[2] The link between confirmation and the other sacraments of initiation is shown forth more clearly

[1] Tertullian, *De resurrectione mortuorum*, VIII, 3: *CCL*, 2, 931.
[2] SC 71.

not only by closer association of these sacraments but also by the rite and words by which confirmation is conferred. This is done so that the rite and words of this sacrament may 'express more clearly the holy things which they signify. The Christian people, so far as possible, should be able to understand them with ease and take full and active part in the celebration as a community.'[3]

For that purpose, it has been our wish also to include in this revision what concerns the very essence of the rite of confirmation, through which the faithful receive the Holy Spirit as a Gift.

The New Testament shows how the Holy Spirit assisted Christ in fulfilling his messianic mission. On receiving the baptism of John, Jesus saw the Spirit descending on him (see Mark 1:10) and remaining with him (see John 1:32). He was impelled by the Spirit to undertake his public ministry as the Messiah, relying on the Spirit's presence and assistance. Teaching the people of Nazareth, he shows by what he said that the words of Isaiah, 'The Spirit of the Lord is upon me,' referred to himself (see Luke 4:17-21).

He later promised his disciples that the Holy Spirit would help them also to bear fearless witness to their faith even before persecutors (see Luke 12:12). The day before he suffered, he assured his apostles that he would send the Spirit of truth from his Father (see John 15:26) to stay with them 'for ever' (John 14:16) and help them to be his witnesses (see John 15:26). Finally, after his resurrection, Christ promised the coming descent of the Holy Spirit: 'You will receive power when the Holy Spirit comes down on you; then you are to be my witnesses' (Acts 1:8; see Luke 24:49).

And in fact, on the day of the feast of Pentecost, the Holy Spirit came down in an extraordinary way on the Apostles as they were gathered together with Mary the mother of Jesus and the group of disciples. They were so 'filled with' the Holy Spirit (Acts 2:4) that by divine inspiration they began to proclaim 'the mighty works of God'. Peter regarded the Spirit who had thus come down upon the Apostles as the gift of the messianic age (see Acts 2:17-18). Those who believed the Apostles' preaching were then baptised and they too received 'the gift of the Holy Spirit' (Acts 2:38). From that time on the apostles, in fulfilment of Christ's wish, imparted the gift of the Spirit to the newly baptised by the laying on of hands to complete the grace of baptism. Hence it is that the Letter to the Hebrews lists among the first elements of Christian instruction the teaching about

[3]   *Ibid.*, 21.

baptisms and the laying on of hands (Hebrews 6:2). This laying on of hands is rightly recognised by Catholic tradition as the beginning of the sacrament of confirmation, which in a certain way perpetuates the grace of Pentecost in the Church.

This makes clear the specific importance of confirmation for sacramental initiation by which the faithful 'as members of the living Christ are incorporated into him and made like him through baptism and through confirmation and the eucharist'.[4] In baptism, the newly baptised receive forgiveness of sins, adoption as sons of God, and the character of Christ, by which they are made members of the Church and for the first time become sharers in the priesthood of their Saviour (see 1 Peter 2:5, 9). Through the sacrament of confirmation, those who have been born anew in baptism receive the inexpressible Gift, the Holy Spirit himself, by which 'they are endowed . . . with special strength'.[5] Moreover, having received the character of this sacrament, they are 'bound more intimately to the Church'[6] and 'they are more strictly obliged to spread and defend the faith both by word and by deed as true witnesses of Christ'.[7] Finally, confirmation is so closely linked with the holy eucharist[8] that the faithful, after being signed by holy baptism and confirmation, are incorporated fully into the body of Christ by participation in the eucharist.[9]

From ancient times the conferring of the gift of the Holy Spirit has been carried out in the Church with various rites. These rites underwent many changes in the East and the West, while always keeping the significance of a conferring of the Holy Spirit.[10]

In many Eastern rites, it seems that from early times a rite of anointing, not then clearly distinguished from baptism, prevailed for the conferring of the Holy Spirit. That rite continues in use today in the greater part of the churches of the East.

In the West there are very ancient witnesses concerning the part of Christian initiation which was later distinctly recognised as the sacrament of confirmation. After the baptismal washing and before the eucharistic meal, the performance of many rites is indicated, such

---

[4] See AG 36. [5] See LG 11. [6] *Ibid.*
[7] *Ibid.*, see AG 11. [8] See PO 5. [9] See *ibid.*
[10] See Origen, *De Principiis*, I, 3, 2: *GCS*, 22, 49 sq.; *Comm. in Ep. ad Rom.*, V, 8; *PG*, 14, 1038; Cyril of Jerusalem, *Catech.* XVI, 26; XXI, 1-7: *PG*, 33, 956; 1088-1093.

as anointing, the laying on of the hand and consignation.[11] These are contained both in liturgical documents[12] and in many testimonies of the Fathers. In the course of the centuries, problems and doubts arose as to what belonged with certainty to the essence of the rite of confirmation. It is fitting to mention at least some of the elements which, from the thirteenth century onwards, in the ecumenical councils and in the documents of the popes, cast light on the importance of anointing while at the same time not allowing the laying on of hands to be obscured.

Our predecessor Innocent III wrote: 'By the anointing of the forehead the laying on of the hand is designated, which is otherwise called confirmation, since through it the Holy Spirit is given for growth and strength.'[13] Another of our predecessors, Innocent IV, recalls that the Apostles conferred the Holy Spirit 'through the laying on of the hand, which confirmation or the anointing of the forehead represents'.[14] In the profession of faith of Emperor Michael Palaeologus, which was read at the Second Council of Lyons, mention is made of the sacrament of confirmation, which 'bishops confer by the laying on of the hands, anointing with chrism those who have been baptised'.[15] The Decree for the Armenians, issued by the Council of Florence, declares that the 'matter' of the sacra-

---

[11] See Tertullian, *De Baptismo*, VII-VIII: *CCL*, 1, 282 sq.; B. Botte, *La tradition apostolique de Saint Hippolyte*: *Liturgiewissenschaftliche Quellen und Forschungen*, 39 (Münster in W., 1963) 52-4; Ambrose, *De Sacramentis*, II, 24; III, 2, 8; VI, 2, 9: *CSEL*, 73, pp. 36, 42, 74-5; *De Mysteriis*, VII, 42: *ibid.* p. 106.

[12] *Liber Sacramentorum Romanae Ecclesiae Ordinis Anni circuli*, ed. L. C. Mohlberg: *Rerum Ecclesiasticarum Documenta, Fontes*, IV (Rome, 1960) 75; *Das Sacramentarium Gregorianum nach dem Aachener Urexemplar*, ed. H. Lietzman: *Liturgiegeschichtliche Quellen*, 3 (Münster in W., 1921) 53 sq.; *Liber Ordinum*, ed. M. Ferotin: *Monumenta Ecclesiae Liturgica*, V (Paris, 1904) 33 sq.; *Missale Gallicanum Vetus*, ed. L. C. Mohlberg: *Rerum Ecclesiasticarum Documenta, Fontes*, III (Rome, 1958) 42: *Missale Gothicum*, ed. L. C. Mohlberg: *Rerum Ecclesiasticarum Documenta*, V (Rome 1961) 67; C. Vogel - R. Elze, *Le Pontifical Romano-Germanique de XIIe siècle*, *Le Texte*, *II*; *Studi e Testi*, 227 (Vatican City, 1963) 109; M. Andrieu, *Le Pontifical Romain au Moyen-Age*, t. 1, *Le Pontifical Romain du XIIe siècle: Studi e Testi*, 86 (Vatican City, 1938) 247 sq., 289; t. 2, *Le Pontifical de la Curie Romaine au XIIIe siècle: Studi e Testi*, 87 (Vatican City, 1940) 452 sq.

[13] Ep. *Cum venisset: PL*, 215, 285. The profession of faith which the same pope prescribed for the Waldensians includes the following:
Confirmationem ab episcopo factam, id est impositionem manuum, sanctam et venerande accipiendam esse censemus: PL, 215, 1511.

[14] Ep. *Sub Catholicae professione*: Mansi, *Conc. Coll.*, t. 23, 579.

[15] Mansi, *Conc. Coll.*, t. 24, 71.

ment of confirmation is 'chrism made of olive oil . . . and balsam',[16] and, quoting the words of the Acts of the Apostles concerning Peter and John, who gave the Holy Spirit through the laying on of hands (see Acts 8:17), it adds: 'in place of that laying on of the hand, in the Church confirmation is given'.[17] The Council of Trent, though it had no intention of defining the essential rite of confirmation, only designated it with the name of the holy chrism of confirmation.[18] Benedict XIV made this declaration: 'Therefore let this be said, which is beyond dispute: in the Latin Church the sacrament of confirmation is conferred by using sacred chrism or olive oil, mixed with balsam and blessed by the bishop, and by tracing the sign of the cross by the minister of the sacrament on the forehead of the recipient, while the same minister pronounces the words of the form'.[19]

Many theologians, taking account of these declarations and traditions, maintained that for valid administration of confirmation there was required only anointing with chrism, done by placing the hand on the forehead. In spite of this, however, in the rites of the Latin Church a laying of hands upon those to be confirmed was always prescribed before the anointing.

With regard to the words of the rite by which the Holy Spirit is given, it should be noted that, already in the primitive Church, Peter and John, in order to complete the initiation of those baptised in Samaria, prayed for them to receive the Holy Spirit and then laid hands on them (see Acts 8:15-17). In the East, in the fourth and fifth centuries there appear in the rite of anointing the first indications of the words 'signaculum doni Spiritus Sancti'.[20] These words were quickly accepted by the Church of Constantinople and are still used by the Churches of the Byzantine rite.

In the West, however, the words of this rite, which completed baptism, were not defined until the twelfth and thirteenth centuries.

---

[16] *Epistolae Pontificiae ad Concilium Florentinum spectantes*, ed. G. Hofmann: *Concilium Florentinum*, vol. I, ser. A. part II (Rome, 1944) 128.

[17] *Ibid.*, 129.

[18] *Concilii Tridentini Actorum pars altera*, ed. S. Ehses: *Concilium Tridentinum*, V, Act. 11 (Fribourg Br., 1911) 996.

[19] Ep. *Ex quo primum tempore*, 52: *Benedicti XIV . . . Bullarium*, t. III (Prato, 1847) 320.

[20] See Cyril of Jerusalem, *Catech.* XVIII, 33, 1056; Asterius, Bishop of Amasea, *In parabolam de filio prodigo*, in 'Photii Bibliotheca', Cod. 271: *PG*, 104, 213. See also *Epistola cuiusdam Patriarchae Constantinopolitani ad Martyrium Episcopum Antiochenum*: *PG*, 119, 900.

But in the twelfth century Roman Pontifical the formula which later became the common one first occurs: 'I sign you with the sign of the cross and confirm you with the chrism of salvation. In the name of the Father and of the Son and of the Holy Spirit'.[21]

From what we have recalled, it is clear that in the administration of confirmation in the East and the West, though in different ways, the most important place was occupied by the anointing, which in a certain way represents the apostolic laying on of hands. Since this anointing with chrism well represents the spiritual anointing of the Holy Spirit, who is given to the faithful, we intend to confirm its existence and importance.

As regards the words which are pronounced in confirmation, we have examined with due consideration the dignity of the venerable formula used in the Latin Church, but we judge preferable the very ancient formula belonging to the Byzantine rite, by which the Gift of the Holy Spirit himself is expressed and the outpouring of the Spirit which took place on the day of Pentecost is recalled (see Acts 2:1-4, 38). We therefore adopt this formula, rendering it almost word for word.

Therefore, in order that the revision of the rite of confirmation may fittingly embrace also the essence of the sacramental rite, by our supreme apostolic authority we decree and lay down that in the Latin Church the following should be observed for the future:

The Sacrament of Confirmation is conferred through the anointing with chrism on the forehead, which is done by the laying on of the hand, and through the words: 'Accipe Signaculum Doni Spiritus Sancti.'

Although the laying of hands on the candidates, which is done with the prescribed prayer before the anointing, does not belong to the essence of the sacramental rite, it is nevertheless to be held in high esteem, in that it contributes to the integral perfection of that rite and to a clearer understanding of the sacrament. It is evident that this preceding laying on of hands differs from the laying on of the hand by which the anointing is done on the forehead.

Having established and declared all these elements concerning the essential rite of the sacrament of confirmation, we also approve by our apostolic authority the order for the same sacrament, which has

---

[21] M. Andrieu, *Le Pontifical Romain au Moyen-Age*, t. 1. *Le Pontifical Romain du XIIe siècle: Studi e Testi*, 86 (Vatican City, 1938) 247.

been revised by the Congregation for Divine Worship, after consultation with the Congregations for the Doctrine of the Faith, for the Discipline of the Sacraments, and for the Evangelisation of Peoples as regards the matters which are within their competence. The Latin edition of the order containing the new form will come into force as soon as it is published; the editions of the vernacular languages, prepared by the episcopal conferences and confirmed by the Apostolic See, will come into force on the dates to be laid down by the individual conferences. The old order may be used until the end of the year 1972. From 1 January 1973, however, only the new order is to be used by those concerned.

We intend that everything that we have laid down and prescribed should be firm and effective in the Latin Church, notwithstanding, where relevant, the apostolic constitutions and ordinances issued by our predecessors, and other prescriptions, even if worthy of special mention.

Given in Rome, at Saint Peter's, on the fifteenth day of August, the Solemnity of the Assumption of the Blessed Virgin Mary, in the year 1971, the ninth of our pontificate.

PAUL PP. VI

RITE OF CONFIRMATION*:
INTRODUCTION

Structure

I Dignity of Confirmation 1-2

II Offices and Ministries in the Celebration of Confirmation 3-8

III Celebration of the Sacrament 9-15

IV Adaptations in the Rite of Confirmation 16-18

V Preparations 19

* Promulgated by Decree dated 22 August 1971.

I Dignity of Confirmation

1. Those who have been baptised continue on the path of Christian initiation through the sacrament of confirmation. In this sacrament they receive the Holy Spirit, who was sent upon the apostles by the Lord on Pentecost.

2. This giving of the Holy Spirit conforms believers more perfectly to Christ and strengthens them so that they may bear witness to Christ for the building up of his body in faith and love. They are so marked with the character or seal of the Lord that the sacrament of confirmation cannot be repeated.

II Offices and Ministries in the Celebration of Confirmation

3. It is the responsibility of the people of God to prepare the baptised for confirmation. It is the responsibility of the pastors to see that all the baptised come to the fullness of Christian initiation and are carefully prepared for confirmation.

Adult catechumens, who are to be confirmed immediately after baptism, have the help of the Christian community and, in particular, the formation which is given to them during the catechumenate, catechesis, and common liturgical celebrations. Catechists, sponsors, and members of the local church should participate in the catechumenate. The steps of the catechumenate will be appropriately adapted to those who, baptised in infancy, are confirmed only as adults.

The initiation of children into the sacramental life is for the most part the responsibility and concern of Christian parents. They are to form and gradually increase a spirit of faith in the children and, with the help of catechetical institutions, prepare them for the fruitful reception of the sacraments of confirmation and the eucharist. The role of the parents is also expressed by their active participation in the celebration of the sacraments.

4. Attention should be paid to the festive and solemn character of the liturgical service, especially its significance for the local church, especially if all the candidates are assembled for a common celebration. The whole people of God, represented by the families and friends of the candidates and by members of the local community, will be invited to take part in the celebration and will express its faith in the fruits of the Holy Spirit.

5. Ordinarily there should be a sponsor for each of those to be confirmed. The sponsor brings the candidate to receive the sacrament, presents him to the minister for the anointing, and will later help him to fulfil his baptismal promises faithfully under the influence of the Holy Spirit.

In view of contemporary pastoral circumstances, it is desirable that the godparent at baptism, if present, also be the sponsor at confirmation; canon 796, no. 1 is abrogated. This change expresses more clearly the relationship between baptism and confirmation and also makes the function and responsibility of the sponsor more effective.

Nonetheless the choice of a special sponsor for confirmation is not excluded. Even the parents themselves may present their children for confirmation. It is for the local Ordinary to determine diocesan practice in the light of local circumstances.

6. Pastors will see that the sponsor, chosen by the candidate or his family, is spiritually qualified for the office and satisfies these requirements:

a) that he be sufficiently mature for this role;

b) that he belong to the Catholic Church and have been initiated in the three sacraments of baptism, confirmation, and the eucharist;

c) that he be not prohibited by law from exercising the role of sponsor.

7. The ordinary minister of confirmation is the bishop. Ordinarily the sacrament is administered by the bishop so that there will be a more evident relationship to the first pouring forth of the Holy Spirit on Pentecost. After the apostles were filled with the Holy Spirit, they themselves gave the Spirit to the faithful through the laying on of their hands. Thus the reception of the Spirit through the ministry of the bishop shows the close bond which joins the confirmed to the Church and the mandate to be witnesses of Christ among men.

In addition to the bishop, the law gives the faculty to confirm to the following:

a) apostolic administrators who are not bishops, prelates or abbots *nullius*, vicars and prefects apostolic, vicars capitular, within the limits of their territory and while they hold office;

b) priests who, in virtue of an office which they lawfully hold, baptise an adult or a child old enough for catechesis or receive a validly baptised adult into full communion with the Church;

c) in danger of death, provided a bishop is not easily available or is lawfully impeded: pastors and parochial vicars; in their absence, parochial associates; priests who are in charge of special parishes lawfully established; administrators; substitutes; and assistants;[1] in the absence of all of the preceding, any priest who is not subject to censure or canonical penalty.

8. In case of true necessity and special reason, for example, the large number of persons to be confirmed, the minister of confirmation mentioned in no. 7 or the extraordinary minister designated by special indult of the Apostolic See or by law may associate other priests with himself in the administration of this sacrament.

It is required that these priests:

a) have a particular function or office in the diocese, namely, vicars general, episcopal vicars or delegates, district or regional vicars,[2] or those who by mandate of the Ordinary hold equivalent offices; or

b) be the pastors of the places where confirmation is conferred, pastors of the places where the candidates belong, or priests who have had a special part in the catechetical preparation of the candidates.

III Celebration of the Sacrament

9. The sacrament of confirmation is conferred through the anointing with chrism on the forehead, which is done by the laying on of the hand, and through the words: **Be sealed with the Gift of the Holy Spirit.**

Even though the laying of hands on the candidates with the prayer **All-powerful God** does not pertain to the valid giving of the sacrament, it is to be strongly emphasised for the integrity of the rite and the fuller understanding of the sacrament.

Priests who are sometimes associated with the principal minister in conferring the sacrament join him in laying their hands on all the candidates together, but they do not say the prayer.

The whole rite has a twofold meaning. The laying of hands on the candidates by the bishop and the concelebrating priests is the biblical gesture by which the gift of the Holy Spirit is invoked. This is well

[1] See canons 451, 471, 476, 216, §4, 472, 474, 475.
[2] See canon 217, §1.

63

adapted to the understanding of the Christian people. The anointing with chrism and the accompanying words express clearly the effects of the giving of the Holy Spirit. Signed with the perfumed oil, the baptised person receives the indelible character, the seal of the Lord, together with the gift of the Spirit, which conforms him more closely to Christ and gives him the grace of spreading the Lord's presence among men.

10. The chrism is consecrated by the bishop in the Mass which is ordinarily celebrated on Holy Thursday for this purpose.

11. Adult catechumens and children who are baptised at an age when they are old enough for catechesis should ordinarily be admitted to confirmation and the eucharist at the same time they receive baptism. If this is impossible, they should receive confirmation in a common celebration (see no. 4). Similarly, adults who were baptised in infancy should, after suitable preparation, receive confirmation and the eucharist in a common celebration.

With regard to children, in the Latin Church the administration of confirmation is generally postponed until about the seventh year. For pastoral reasons, however, especially to strengthen the faithful in complete obedience to Christ the Lord and in loyal testimony to him, episcopal conferences may choose an age which seems more appropriate, so that the sacrament is given at a more mature age after appropriate formation.

In this case the necessary precautions should be taken so that children will be confirmed at the proper time, even before the use of reason, where there is danger of death or other serious difficulty. They should not be deprived of the benefit of this sacrament.

12. One must be baptised to receive the sacrament of confirmation. In addition, if the baptised person has the use of reason, it is required that he be in a state of grace, properly instructed, and able to renew his baptismal promises.

It is the responsibility of the episcopal conferences to determine more precisely the pastoral methods for the preparation of children for confirmation.

With regard to adults, the same principles should be followed, with suitable adaptations, which are in effect in individual dioceses for the admission of catechumens to baptism and the eucharist. In particular, suitable catechesis should precede confirmation, and there should be sufficient effective relationship of the candidates with the Christian community and with individual members of the faithful to assist in their formation. This formation should be directed toward their giving the witness of a Christian life and exercising the Christian apostolate, while developing a genuine desire to participate in the eucharist (see *Christian Initiation of Adults, Introduction*, 19).

Sometimes the preparation of a baptised adult for confirmation is part of his preparation for marriage. In such cases, if it is foreseen that the conditions for a fruitful reception of confirmation cannot be satisfied, the local Ordinary will judge whether it is better to defer confirmation until after the marriage.

If one who has the use of reason is confirmed in danger of death, he should be prepared spiritually, so far as possible, depending upon the circumstances of the individual case.

13. Ordinarily confirmation takes place within Mass in order to express more clearly the fundamental connection of this sacrament with the entirety of Christian initiation. The latter reaches its culmination in the communion of the body and blood of Christ. The newly confirmed should therefore participate in the eucharist which completes their Christian initiation.

If the candidates for confirmation are children who have not received the eucharist and are not admitted to their first communion at this liturgical celebration or if there are other special circumstances, confirmation should be celebrated outside Mass. When this occurs, there should first be a celebration of the word of God.

It is fitting that the minister of confirmation celebrate the Mass or, better, concelebrate the Mass, especially with the priests who may join him in the administration of the sacrament.

If the Mass is celebrated by someone else, it is proper that the bishop preside over the liturgy of the word and that he give the blessing at the end of Mass.

Emphasis should be given to the celebration of the word of God which begins the rite of confirmation. It is from the hearing of the word of God that the many-sided power of the Holy Spirit flows upon the Church and upon each one of the baptised and confirmed, and it is by this word that God's will is manifest in the life of Christians.

The saying of the Lord's Prayer by the newly confirmed with the rest of the people is also of very great importance, whether during Mass before communion or outside Mass before the blessing. because it is the Spirit who prays in us, and in the Spirit the Christian says '*Abba*, Father'.

INSTRUCTIONS ON THE REVISED ROMAN RITES

14. The pastor should record the names of the minister, those con-firmed, parents and sponsors, and the date and place of confirmation in a special book. The notation in the baptismal register should also be made according to law.

15. If the pastor of the newly-confirmed person is not present, the minister should promptly inform him of the confirmation, either personally or through a representative.

IV Adaptations in the Rite of Confirmation

16. In virtue of the Constitution on the Sacred Liturgy (art. 63b), episcopal conferences have the right to prepare a title in particular rituals corresponding to this title of the Roman Pontifical on confirmation. This is to be adapted to the needs of individual regions so that, after confirmation of their action by the Apostolic See, the ritual may be used in the territory.[3]

17. The episcopal conference will consider whether, in view of local circumstances and the culture and traditions of the people, it is opportune:

a) to make suitable adaptations of the formulas for the renewal of baptismal promises and professions, either following the text in the rite of baptism or accommodating these formulas to the circumstances of the candidates for confirmation;

b) to introduce a different manner for the minister to give the sign of peace after the anointing, either to each individual or to all the newly confirmed together.

18. The minister of confirmation may introduce some explanations into the rite in individual cases in view of the capacity of candidates for confirmation. He may also make appropriate accommodations in the existing texts, for example, by expressing these in a kind of dialogue, especially with children.

When confirmation is given by a minister who is not a bishop, whether by concession of the general law or by special indult of the Apostolic See, it is fitting for him to mention in the homily that the bishop is the original minister of the sacrament and the reason why priests receive the faculty to confirm from the law or by an indult of the Apostolic See.

[3] See Christian Initiation, General Instruction, nos. 30-3, above.

V Preparations

19. The following should be prepared for confirmation:

a) vestments for the celebration of Mass, for the bishop and for the priests who concelebrate with him; if the bishop does not concelebrate the Mass, he and the priests who may administer confirmation with him should participate in the Mass wearing the vestments for confirmation: alb, stole, and for the minister of confirmation, cope; these vestments are also worn for confirmation outside Mass;

b) chairs for the bishop and the priests;

c) vessel or vessels of chrism;

d) Roman Pontifical or Ritual;

e) preparations for Mass and, for communion under both kinds, if it is given in this way;

f) preparations for the washing of the ministers' hands after the anointing.

THE ROMAN MISSAL
APOSTOLIC CONSTITUTION

Promulgation of the Roman Missal
revised by Decree of
the Second Vatican Ecumenical Council

PAUL, BISHOP
Servant of the Servants of God For an Everlasting Memorial

The Roman Missal, promulgated in 1570 by our predecessor, Saint
Pius V, by decree of the Council of Trent,[1] has been accepted by all
as one of the many admirable results which that council had throughout the entire Church of Christ. For four centuries it furnished the
priests of the Latin Rite with norms for the celebration of the eucharistic sacrifice, and heralds of the Gospel carried it to almost all the
world. Innumerable holy men nourished their piety towards God
with its readings from scripture and its prayers, the arrangement and
major part of which go back to Saint Gregory the Great.

Since that period a liturgical renewal has developed and spread
among the Christian people. According to Pius XII, this seemed to
be a sign of God's providence in the present time, a saving action
of the Holy Spirit in his Church.[2] The renewal also showed clearly
that the formulas of the Roman Missal had to be revised and enriched. This was begun by Pope Pius XII in the restoration of the
Easter Vigil and the Holy Week services,[3] which formed the first
stage in accommodating the Roman Missal to contemporary
mentality.

The Second Vatican Ecumenical Council, in the constitution
Sacrosanctum Concilium, laid down the basis for the general revision
of the Roman Missal: 'both texts and rites should be drawn up so

---

[1]   See apostolic const. *Quo primum*, 14 July 1570.
[2]   See Pius XII, Discourse to the participants in the First International Congress
       of Pastoral Liturgy at Assisi, 22 May 1956: *AAS* 48 (1956) 712.
[3]   See Sacred Congregation of Rites, general decree *Dominicae Resurrectionis*,
       9 February 1951: *AAS* 43 (1951) 128ff.; general decree *Maxima Redemptionis
       nostrae mysteria*, 16 November 1955: *AAS* 47 (1955) 838ff.

that they express more clearly the holy things they signify,'[4] 'the rite of the Mass is to be revised in such a way that the intrinsic nature and purpose of its several parts, and also the connection between them, may be more clearly manifested and that devout and active participation by the faithful may be more easily accomplished,'[5] 'the treasures of the Bible are to be opened up more lavishly, so that richer fare may be provided for the faithful at the table of God's word,'[6] 'a new rite for concelebration is to be drawn up and incorporated into the Roman Pontifical and Missal'.[7]

No one should think, however, that this revision of the Roman Missal has been accomplished suddenly. The progress of liturgical science in the last four centuries has certainly prepared the way. After the Council of Trent, the study 'of ancient manuscripts in the Vatican library and elsewhere', as Saint Pius V indicated in the apostolic constitution *Quo primum*, helped greatly in the correction of the Roman Missal. Since then, however, other ancient sources have been discovered and published, and liturgical formulas of the Eastern Church have been studied. Many wish that these doctrinal and spiritual riches not be hidden in libraries, but be brought to light to illuminate and nourish the minds and spirit of Christians.

Now we wish to indicate, in broad terms, the new plan of the Roman Missal. First, a *General Instruction* or preface for the book gives the new regulations for the celebration of the eucharistic sacrifice, the rites, the functions of each of the participants, furnishings, and sacred places.

The chief innovation affects the eucharistic prayer. Although the Roman rite, in the first part of this prayer (the preface), preserved a variety of texts over the centuries, the second part, or *Canon Actionis*, became unchangeable during the period of the fourth and fifth centuries. The Eastern liturgies, on the other hand, allowed variety in the anaphoras. Now the eucharistic prayer is enriched with a great number of prefaces, derived from the older tradition of the Roman Church or recently composed. In this way the different aspects of the mystery of salvation will be emphasised, and there will be richer themes of thanksgiving. Besides this, we have decided to add three new canons to the eucharistic prayer. For pastoral reasons, however, and to facilitate concelebration, we have directed that the words of the Lord be identical in each form of the canon.

[4] SC 21.
[5] See SC 50.
[6] See SC 51.
[7] See SC 58.

Thus, in each eucharistic prayer, we wish that the words be as follows: over the bread: *Accipite et manducate ex hoc omnes: Hoc est enim Corpus meum, quod pro vobis tradetur;* over the chalice: *Accipite et bibite ex eo omnes: Hic est enim calix Sanguinis mei novi et aeterni testamenti, qui pro vobis et pro multis effundetur in remissionem peccatorum. Hoc facite in meam commemorationem.* The words *Mysterium fidei,* now taken out of the context of the words of Christ, are said by the priest as an introduction to the acclamation of the faithful.

In the Order of Mass, the rites have been 'simplified, with due care to preserve their substance'.[8] 'Elements which, with the passage of time, came to be duplicated or were added with but little advantage'[9] have been eliminated, especially in the offering of bread and wine, the breaking of the bread, and communion.

Also, 'other elements which suffered injury through accidents of history' are restored 'to the earlier norm of the holy Fathers',[10] for example, the homily,[11] the general intercessions or prayer of the faithful,[12] and the penitential rite or act of reconciliation with God and the brethren at the beginning of Mass, where its proper significance is restored.

According to the decree of the Second Vatican Council, that 'a more representative portion of the holy scriptures be read to the people over a set period of years',[13] the Sunday readings are arranged in a cycle of three years. In addition, on Sundays and feasts the epistle and gospel are preceded by an Old Testament reading or, at Easter, the Acts of the Apostles. This is to accentuate the dynamism of the mystery of salvation, shown in the words of divine revelation. These broadly selected biblical readings, which give the faithful on feastdays the most important part of sacred scripture, are complemented by the other parts of the Bible read on other days.

All this has been planned to develop among the faithful a greater hunger for the word of God.[14] Under the guidance of the Holy Spirit, this word leads the people of the New Covenant to the perfect unity of the Church. We are fully confident that both priests and faithful will prepare their minds and hearts more devoutly for the Lord's Supper, meditating on the scriptures, nourished day by day with the words of the Lord. According to the hopes of the Second Vatican

[8] See SC 50.
[9] See *ibid.*
[10] See *ibid.*
[11] See SC 52.
[12] See SC 53.
[13] See SC 51
[14] See Amos 8:11.

Council, sacred scripture will then be a perpetual source of spiritual life, the chief instrument for handing down Christian doctrine, and the centre of all theological study.

This revision of the Roman Missal, in addition to the three changes already mentioned (the eucharistic prayer, the Order of Mass, and the readings), has also corrected and considerably modified other parts: the proper of seasons, the proper of saints, the common of saints, ritual Masses and votive Masses. In all of these changes, particular care has been taken with the prayers. Their number has been increased, so that the new forms might better correspond to new needs, and the text of older prayers has been restored on the basis of the ancient sources. Each weekday of the principal liturgical seasons, Advent, Christmas, Lent, and Easter, now has its own prayer.

Even though the music of the Roman Gradual has not been changed, the responsorial psalm, which Saint Augustine and Saint Leo the Great often mention, has been restored for easier comprehension, and the entrance and communion antiphons have been adapted for recited Masses.

In conclusion, we wish to give force and effect to what we have set forth concerning the new Roman Missal. In promulgating the first edition of the Roman Missal, Saint Pius V presented it to the people of Christ as an instrument of liturgical unity and as a witness to purity of worship in the Church. Even if there is room in the new Missal, according to the decree of the Second Vatican Council, 'for legitimate variations and adaptations',[15] we hope similarly that it will be received by the faithful as a help and witness to the common unity of all. Thus, in the great diversity of languages, one single prayer will rise as an acceptable offering to our Father in heaven, through our High Priest Jesus Christ, in the Holy Spirit.

What we have prescribed in this constitution shall begin to be in force from the First Sunday of Advent of this year, 30 November. We decree that these laws and prescriptions be firm and effective now and in the future, notwithstanding, to the extent necessary, the apostolic constitutions and ordinances issued by our predecessors and other prescriptions, even those deserving particular mention and derogation.

Given at Rome, at Saint Peter's, on Holy Thursday, 3 April 1969, the sixth year of our pontificate.

PAUL PP. VI

[15] SC 38.

GENERAL INSTRUCTION ON THE ROMAN MISSAL*

Structure

---

* Promulgated by Decree dated 26 March 1970. The text of the General Instruction given here, taken from the English edition of the Roman Missal published on 6 January 1975, has been amended to include further variations
announced in *Notitiae*, 111-12, November-December 1975. Footnotes inter-
polated from *Notitiae* are indicated by ª, e.g. 18ª etc.

Introduction

1. When Christ the Lord was about to celebrate the passover meal
with his disciples and institute the sacrifice of his body and blood, he
directed them to prepare a large, furnished room (Luke 22:12). The
Church has always taken this command of Christ as bearing on its
own responsibility in giving directions concerning the preparation of
the minds of the worshippers and the place, rites, and texts for the
celebration of the holy eucharist. Today, in response to the decision
of the Second Vatican Council, there are new norms and this new
missal, to be used from now on for the Mass of the Roman rite.
These bear witness to the unity and coherence of the Church's
tradition. Although they introduce some new elements into the
celebration, they show the Church's continued concern for the
eucharist, its faith, and its unchanging love of this great mystery.

A Witness to Unchanging Faith

2. The sacrificial nature of the Mass was solemnly proclaimed by
the Council of Trent in agreement with the tradition of the universal
Church.[1] The Second Vatican Council reaffirmed this teaching in
these significant words: 'At the Last Supper our Saviour instituted
the eucharistic sacrifice of his body and blood to perpetuate the
sacrifice of the cross throughout the centuries until he comes again.
He entrusted it to his bride, the Church, as a memorial of his death
and resurrection.'[2]

This teaching of the Council is expressed constantly in the prayers
of the Mass. The Leonine Sacramentary states the doctrine concisely:
'The work of our redemption is carried out whenever we celebrate
the memory of this sacrifice',[3] and it is properly and carefully
presented in the eucharistic prayers. At the anamnesis or memorial,
the priest speaks to God in the name of all the people and offers in
thanksgiving the holy and living sacrifice, which is the Church's
offering, the Victim pleasing to God himself[4]; he prays that the body
and blood of Christ may be a sacrifice acceptable to the Father,
bringing salvation to the whole world.[5]

In this new missal, then, the Church's rule of prayer corresponds

[1] See Session XXII, 17 September 1562.
[2] SC 47; see LG 3, 28; PO 2, 4, 5.
[3] *Sacramentarium Veronense*, ed. Mohlberg, no. 93.
[4] See Eucharistic Prayer III.
[5] See Eucharistic Prayer IV.

to the Church's enduring rule of faith. It teaches us that the sacrifice of the cross and its sacramental renewal in the Mass are one and the same, differing only in the manner of offering. At the Last Supper Christ the Lord instituted this sacramental renewal and commanded his apostles to do it in memory of him. It is at once a sacrifice of praise and of thanksgiving, a sacrifice that reconciles us to the Father and makes amends to him for the sins of the world.

3. The Church believes that the Lord Jesus is really present among us in a wonderful way under the eucharistic species. The Second Vatican Council[6] and other pronouncements of the Church's magisterium[7] have reaffirmed the same doctrine and the same meaning proposed by the Council of Trent for our belief.[8] At Mass this presence of Christ is proclaimed not only by the words of consecration, by which Christ is made present through transubstantiation, but also by the sense of deep reverence and adoration which are evident in the liturgy of the eucharist. His presence is further recognised by Christians when they honour the eucharist in a special way on Holy Thursday and on Corpus Christi.

4. The distinctive nature of the ministerial priesthood is clear from the prominent place the presbyter occupies and the functions he takes in the rite itself: he offers sacrifice in the person of Christ and presides over the assembly of God's holy people. His priestly role is explained precisely and in greater detail in the preface of the eucharistic prayer at the chrism Mass on Holy Thursday, when the institution of the priesthood is celebrated. That preface describes the responsibilities of the priestly office, explains how the power of the priesthood is conferred by the laying on of hands, and declares it to be the continuation of the power of Christ, the High Priest of the New Testament.

5. The ministerial priesthood throws light on another and important priesthood, namely, the royal priesthood of believers. Their spiritual sacrifice to God is accomplished through the ministry of presbyters, in union with the sacrifice of Christ, our one and only Mediator.[9]

[6] See SC 7, 47; PO 5, 18.
[7] See Pius XII, encyclical letter *Humani generis*: *AAS* 42 (1950) 570-1; Paul VI, encyclical letter *Mysterium Fidei*: AAS 57 (1965) 762-9; Solemn Profession of Faith, 30 June 1968: *AAS* 60 (1968) 442-3; Congregation of Rites (= SRC), instruction *Eucharisticum mysterium* (= EM), 25 May, 1967, nos. 3f, 9: *AAS* 59 (1967) 543, 547.
[8] See Session XIII, 11 October, 1551.
[9] See PO 2.

The celebration of the eucharist is the action of the whole Church, in which each individual should take his own full part and only his part, as determined by his particular position in the people of God. In this way greater attention is given to some aspects of the eucharistic celebration which have sometimes been overlooked in the course of time. The worshipping community is the people of God, won by Christ with his blood, called together by the Lord, and nourished by his word. It is a people called to offer God the prayers of the entire human family, a people which gives thanks in Christ for the mystery of salvation by offering his sacrifice. It is a people brought together and strengthened in unity by sharing in the body and blood of Christ. This people is holy in origin, but by conscious, active, and fruitful participation in the mystery of the eucharist it constantly grows in holiness.[10]

A Witness to Unbroken Tradition

6. The Second Vatican Council, in setting forth its decrees for the revision of the Order of Mass, directed, among other things, that some rites be restored 'to the ancient usage of the holy Fathers',[11] quoting the apostolic letter *Quo primum* of 1570, in which Saint Pius V promulgated the Tridentine missal. The fact that the same words are used in reference to both Roman missals indicates that, although separated by four centuries, both embrace one and the same tradition. And when the more profound elements of this tradition are considered, it becomes clear how remarkably this new missal complements the older one.

7. The old missal was promulgated in difficult times. There were attacks upon Catholic faith about the sacrificial nature of the Mass, the ministerial priesthood, and the real and permanent presence of Christ under the eucharistic species. Saint Pius V was especially concerned to preserve the recent tradition of the Church then unjustly under attack, and only very slight changes were introduced into the sacred rites. In fact, the missal of 1570 differs very little from the first printed edition of 1474, which in turn faithfully follows the missal used at the time of Pope Innocent III (1198-1216). Manuscripts in the Vatican Library provided some verbal emendations, but did not permit research into the 'ancient and approved authors' beyond some liturgical commentators of the Middle Ages.

[10] See SC 11.
[11] SC 50.

8. Today, on the other hand, countless writings of scholars have clarified the 'usage of the holy Fathers' followed by the revisers of the missal under Saint Pius V. After the Gregorian sacramentary was first published in 1571, many critical studies of other ancient Roman and Ambrosian sacramentaries appeared. Ancient Spanish and Gallican liturgical books also became available, bringing to light many prayers of profound spirituality that had been previously unknown.

Traditions dating back to the first centuries, before the development of the Eastern and Western rites, are also better known today because so many liturgical documents have been discovered.

Progress has been made, moreover, in studying the actual works of the holy Fathers. The teachings of such outstanding saints as Irenaeus, Ambrose, Cyril of Jerusalem, and John Chrysostom have shed light on the theology of the eucharistic mystery in Christian antiquity.

9. The 'usage of the holy Fathers' does not require only the preservation of what our immediate ancestors passed on to us. The entire past of the Church and all its customs must be studied profoundly and understood: the Christian communities which flourished among the Semitic, Greek, and Latin peoples differed from one another in the forms of human and social culture by which they professed one common faith. This broader prospect shows us how the Holy Spirit keeps the people of God faithful in preserving the deposit of faith unchanged, while prayers and rites differ greatly.

Adaptation to Modern Conditions

10. This new missal bears witness to the Roman Church's rule of prayer. It guards the deposit of faith handed down by recent councils. At the same time, it marks a major step forward in liturgical tradition.

The Fathers of the Second Vatican Council reaffirmed the dogmatic statements of the Council of Trent, but they spoke to a far different age in the world's history. They were able, therefore, to bring forward proposals and plans of a pastoral nature which could not have been foreseen four centuries ago.

11. The Council of Trent recognised the great catechetical value of the celebration of Mass, but was unable to make full use of this value in the actual life of the Church. Many people were demanding that the vernacular be permitted in the eucharistic sacrifice. But the

council, judging the conditions of that age, felt bound to answer such demands with a reaffirmation of the Church's traditional teaching. This teaching is that the eucharistic sacrifice is, first and foremost, the action of Christ himself; the unique efficacy of Christ's action is not affected by the manner in which the faithful participate. The council, therefore, stated firmly, but with restraint: 'Although the Mass contains much instruction for the faithful, it did not seem expedient to the Fathers that it be celebrated everywhere in the vernacular.'[12] The council accordingly condemned the proposition 'that the rite of the Roman Church, in which part of the canon and the words of consecration are spoken in a low voice, should be rejected or that the Mass must be celebrated in the vernacular.'[13] Although the Council of Trent thus prohibited the use of the vernacular in the Mass, it did direct pastors of souls to substitute appropriate catechesis: 'So that the sheep of Christ may not go hungry . . . this holy Synod commands pastors and all who have the care of souls to explain to their people some of the things read at Mass. They are to do this often, personally or through others, during the celebration, especially on Sundays and feast days. They are to explain, among other things, some mystery of this holy sacrifice.'[14]

12.   The Second Vatican Council was assembled to adapt the Church to the contemporary requirements of its apostolic task. The council therefore examined thoroughly, as had Trent, the educational and pastoral character of the sacred liturgy.[15] Since no Catholic would now deny the lawfulness and efficacy of a sacred rite celebrated in Latin, the council was able to declare that 'the use of the mother tongue frequently may be of great advantage to the people' and gave permission for its use.[16] This decision was received everywhere with so much enthusiasm that, under the leadership of the bishops and the Apostolic See, all liturgical celebrations in which the people participate may now be carried out in the vernacular so that the mystery may be more fully understood.

13.   The use of the vernacular in the liturgy may certainly be considered most helpful in presenting more clearly the catechesis of the mystery which is celebrated. Nevertheless, the Second Vatican

---

[12] Session XXII, Teaching on the Holy Sacrifice of the Mass, chapter 8.
[13] *Ibid.*, chapter 9.   [14] *Ibid.*, chapter 8.
[15] See SC 33.   [16] SC 36.

Council also ordered the observance of certain directives, prescribed by the Council of Trent but not obeyed everywhere. These include, for example, the preaching of a homily on Sundays and feast days[17] and permission to interject some explanations into the sacred rites themselves.[18]

Most importantly, the Second Vatican Council strongly urged 'that more complete form of participation in the Mass when, after the priest's communion, the faithful receive the Lord's body from the same sacrifice'.[19] Thus the council sought to give effect to the recommendation of the Fathers of Trent that for fuller participation in the holy eucharist 'the faithful present at each Mass should communicate not only by spiritual desire but also by sacramental communion'.[20]

14. Moved by the same spirit of pastoral concern, the Second Vatican Council was able to reconsider the norm laid down by Trent about communion under both kinds. The Church teaches that the full effect of communion is received under the one species of bread; since that doctrine is rarely if ever challenged today, the Council gave permission for communion to be received sometimes under both kinds. This clearer form of the sacramental signs offers the faithful 'a special opportunity for deepening their appreciation of the mystery in which they share'.[21]

15. The Church faithfully fulfils its responsibility as the teacher of truth to guard the 'old', that is, the deposit of tradition. At the same time, it fulfils another responsibility, that of examining and prudently introducing the 'new' (see Matthew 13:52).

Part of this new missal arranges the prayers of the Church with a clearer relation to the needs of our time. The best examples are in the ritual Masses and the Masses for special intentions. These combine tradition with new ideas. Some prayers remain unchanged from the most ancient tradition of the Church, which successive editions of the Roman missal reflect. Other prayers have been adapted to contemporary needs and conditions. Still others are new compositions, such as the prayers for the Church, for the laity, for blessing of man's labour, the whole community of nations, and for certain contemporary needs. They voice the thoughts and sometimes the words of the recent conciliar documents.

[17] See SC 52.   [19] See SC 55.
[20] Session XXII, Teaching on the Holy Sacrifice of the Mass, chapter 6.
[21] See SC 55.

The same awareness of the new state of the world also influenced the changes made in texts from very ancient tradition. It seemed that this cherished treasury of prayers would not be harmed if some phrases were adapted to the language of modern theology and to the current discipline of the Church. Thus some expressions were changed which referred to the value and use of the good things of the earth or which encouraged a particular form of external penance more suited to another age in the history of the Church.

In short, the liturgical norms of the Council of Trent have been completed and perfected in many ways by those of the Second Vatican Council. The council has brought to fulfilment the efforts of the last four hundred years to move the faithful closer to the sacred liturgy, especially the effort of recent times and above all the liturgical movement promoted by Saint Pius X and his successors.

CHAPTER I

IMPORTANCE AND DIGNITY OF THE EUCHARISTIC CELEBRATION

1.   The celebration of Mass is the action of Christ and the people of God hierarchically assembled. For both the universal and the local Church, and for each person, it is the centre of the whole Christian life.[1] The Mass reaches the high point of the action by which God in Christ sanctifies the world and the high point of men's worship of the Father, as they adore him through Christ, his Son.[2] During the course of the year the mysteries of redemption are recalled at Mass so that they are in some way made present.[3] All other actions and works of the Christian iife are related to the eucharistic celebration, leading up to it and flowing from it.[4]

2.   It is of the greatest importance that the celebration of the Mass, the Lord's Supper, be so arranged that the ministers and the faithful may take their own proper part in it and thus gain its fruits more fully.[5] For this Christ the Lord instituted the eucharistic sacrifice of

---

[1]   See SC 41; LG 11; PO 2, 5, 6; CD 30; UR 15; EM 3e, 6.
[2]   See SC 10.   [3]   See SC 102.
[4]   See PO 5; SC 10.   [5]   See SC 14, 19, 26, 28, 30.

his body and blood and entrusted it to his bride, the Church, as a memorial of his passion and resurrection.[6]

3. The purpose will be accomplished if the celebration takes into account the nature and circumstances of each assembly and is planned to bring about conscious, active, and full participation of the people, motivated by faith, hope, and charity. Such participation of mind and body is desired by the Church, is demanded by the nature of the celebration, and is the right and duty of Christians by reason of their baptism.[7]

4. The presence and active participation of the people show plainly the ecclesial nature of the celebration.[8] Although at times this participation may be lacking, the eucharistic celebration, in which the priest always acts for the salvation of the people, retains its efficacy and dignity as the action of Christ and the Church.[9]

5. The celebration of the eucharist, and the entire liturgy, is carried out by the use of outward signs. By these signs faith is nourished, strengthened, and expressed.[10] It is thus very important to select and arrange the forms and elements proposed by the Church, which, taking into account individual and local circumstances, will best foster active and full participation and promote the spiritual welfare of the faithful.

6. This instruction is intended to give general guidelines for celebrating the eucharist and also norms for each form of celebration.[10a] In accord with the Constitution on the Liturgy, each conference of bishops may establish additional norms for its territory to suit the traditions and character of the people, regions, and various communities.[11]

---

[6] See SC 47.
[7] See SC 14.
[8] See SC 41.
[9] See PO 13.
[10] See SC 59.
[10a] For Masses in particular gatherings see AP; for Masses with Children, see *Directory on Masses with Children*, 1 November 1973: AAS 66 (1974) 30-46; for how to combine the Liturgy of the Hours with the Mass, see *General Instruction on the Liturgy of the Hours*, 93-8.
[11] See SC 37-40.

CHAPTER II
STRUCTURE, ELEMENTS, AND PARTS OF THE MASS

I General Structure of the Mass

7. The Lord's Supper or Mass gathers together the people of God, with a priest presiding in the person of Christ, to celebrate the memorial of the Lord or eucharistic sacrifice.[12] For this reason the promise of Christ is particularly true of such a local congregation of the Church: 'Where two or three are gathered in my name, there am I in their midst' (Matthew 18:20). In the celebration of Mass, which perpetuates the sacrifice of the cross,[13] Christ is really present in the assembly itself, which is gathered in his name, in the person of the minister, in his word, and indeed substantially and unceasingly under the eucharistic species.[14]

8. Although the Mass is made up of the liturgy of the word and the liturgy of the eucharist, the two parts are so closely connected as to form one act of worship.[15] The table of God's word and of Christ's body is prepared and from it the faithful are instructed and nourished.[16] In addition, the Mass has introductory and concluding rites.

II Different Elements of the Mass

Reading and Explaining the Word of God
9. When the scriptures are read in the Church, God himself speaks to his people, and it is Christ, present in his word, who proclaims the Gospel.

The readings should be listened to with respect; they are a principal element of the liturgy. In the biblical readings God's word is addressed to all men of every era and is understandable in itself, but a homily, as a living explanation of the word, increases its effectiveness and is an integral part of the service.[17]

---

[12] See PO 5; SC 33.
[13] Council of Trent, Session XXII, chapter I; see Paul VI, Solemn Profession of Faith, 30 June 1968, no. 24: AAS 60 (1968) 442.
[14] See SC 7; Paul VI, encyclical letter *Mysterium Fidei*, 3 September 1965; EM 9.
[15] See SC 56; EM 10.
[16] See SC 48, 51; DV 21; PO 4.
[17] See SC 7, 33, 52.

Prayers and Other Parts Assigned to the Priest

10.   Among the parts assigned to the priest, the eucharistic prayer has precedence; it is the high point of the whole celebration. Next are the prayers: the opening prayer or collect, the prayer over the gifts, and the prayer after communion. The priest, presiding in the person of Christ, addresses the prayers to God in the name of the entire assembly of God's people and of all present,[18] and thus they are called presidential prayers.

11.   As president of the congregation, the priest gives instructions and words of introduction and conclusion that are indicated within the rite. The nature of the instructions does not require him to adhere to every single word of the form provided in the Missal; rather, he may carry them out in each case by adapting them to whatever the real needs of the community happen to be.[18a] He proclaims the Word of God and gives the final blessing. He may also very briefly introduce the Mass of the day (before the celebration begins), the liturgy of the word (before the readings), and the eucharistic prayer (before the preface); he may make concluding comments before the dismissal.

12.   The nature of the presidential prayers demands that they be spoken in a loud and clear voice so that everyone present may hear and pay attention.[19] While the priest is speaking, there should be no other prayer or song, and the organ and other musical instruments should be silent.

13.   As president the priest prays in the name of the whole community. Besides this, he prays at times in his own name so that he may exercise his ministry with attention and devotion. These prayers are said quietly.

Other Texts in the Celebration

14.   Since the celebration of Mass is a communal action,[20] the dialogue between the celebrant and the congregation and the acclamations are of special value.[21] These are not only the external signs of the communal celebration but are also the means of greater communication between priest and people.

---

[18] See SC 33.
[18a] See SRC *Circular Letter on the Eucharistic Prayers*, 27 April 1973, no. 14: AAS 65 (1973) 346.
[19] See MS 14.   [20] See SC 26, 27; EM 3d.   [21] See SC 30.

15. In every form of Mass the acclamations and the responses to the greetings of the priest and the prayers should be made by the faithful. This extent of participation is needed to express clearly and to develop the action of the entire community.[22]

16. Other parts, important in manifesting and stimulating the people's active participation, are also assigned to the whole congregation, especially the penitential rite, the profession of faith, the general intercessions, and the Lord's Prayer.

17. Finally, there are other texts:
a) those which constitute an independent rite, such as the *Gloria*, the responsorial psalm, *Alleluia* and verse before the Gospel, the *Sanctus*, the memorial acclamation, and the song after communion;
b) those which accompany a rite, such as the songs at the entrance, offertory, breaking of the bread (*Agnus Dei*), and communion.

Texts Said Aloud or Sung

18. In texts which are to be said in a clear, loud voice, whether by the priest or by the ministers or by everyone, the tone of voice should correspond to the nature of the text, which may be a reading, a prayer, an instruction, an acclamation, or a song; the tone also depends on the form of celebration and the solemnity of the assembly. The characteristics of different languages and peoples should be considered.

In the rubrics and in the norms of this instruction, the words 'say' or 'proclaim' are used for both singing and speaking and should be understood in the light of these principles.

Importance of Singing

19. The faithful who gather to await the Lord's coming are urged by the Apostle Paul to sing psalms, hymns, and inspired songs (see Colossians 3:16). Song is the sign of the heart's joy (see Acts 2:46), and Saint Augustine said: 'To sing belongs to lovers.'[23] Even in antiquity it was proverbial to say, 'He prays twice who sings well.'

Singing should be widely used at Mass, depending on the type of people and the capability of each congregation, but it is not always necessary to sing all the texts which were composed for singing.

Preference should be given to the more significant parts, especially those to be sung by the priest or ministers with the people responding

[22] See MS 16a.
[23] Sermon 336, 1: PL 38, 1472.

or those to be sung by the priest and people together.[24]

Since people frequently come together from different countries, it is desirable that they know how to sing at least some parts of the Ordinary of Mass in Latin, especially the profession of faith and the Lord's Prayer, set to simple melodies.[25]

Actions and Postures

20. A common posture, observed by all, is a sign of the unity of the assembly and its sense of community. It both expresses and fosters the inner spirit and purpose of those who take part in it.[26]

21. For the sake of uniformity in actions and postures, the people should follow the directions given by the deacon, priest, or other minister during the celebration. Unless other provision is made, at every Mass they should stand from the beginning of the entrance song or when the priest enters until the opening prayer or collect inclusive; for the singing of the alleluia before the gospel; while the gospel is proclaimed; during the profession of faith and the general intercessions; from the prayer over the gifts to the end of the Mass, with the exceptions below. They should sit during the readings before the gospel and during the responsorial psalm; for the homily and the preparation of the gifts at the offertory; and after communion if there is a period of silence. They should kneel at the consecration unless prevented by lack of space, large numbers, or other reasonable cause.

The conference of bishops may adapt the actions and postures described in the Order of the Roman Mass to the usage of the people,[27] but these adaptations must correspond to the character and meaning of each part of the celebration.

22. The actions include the procession at the entrance of the priest, the bringing forward of the gifts, and the communion. These actions should be carried out with dignity, and the accompanying songs should follow the respective norms.

---

[24] See MS 7, 16; see Praenotanda to *Missale Romanum, Ordo cantus Missae,* ed. typ. (1972).
[25] See SC 54; IOe 59; MS 47.
[26] See SC 30.
[27] See SC 39.

Silence

23. Silence should be observed at designated times as part of the celebration.[28] Its character will depend on the time it occurs in the particular celebration. At the penitential rite and again after the invitation to pray, each one should become recollected; at the conclusion of a reading or the homily, each one meditates briefly on what he has heard; after communion, he praises God in his heart and prays.

III Individual Parts of the Mass

A. *Introductory Rites*

24. The parts preceding the liturgy of the word, namely, the entrance song, greeting, penitential rite, *Kyrie*, *Gloria*, and opening prayer or collect, have the character of beginning, introduction, and preparation.

The purpose of these rites is to make the assembled people a unified community and to prepare them properly to listen to God's word and celebrate the eucharist.

Entrance Song

25. After the people have assembled, the entrance song begins, and the priest and ministers come in. The purpose of this song is to open the celebration, deepen the unity of the people, introduce them to the mystery of the season or feast, and accompany the procession.

26. The entrance song is sung alternatively by the choir and people or by the cantor and the people; or it is sung entirely by the people or the choir alone. The antiphon and psalm of the Roman Gradual or the Simple Gradual may be used, or another song appropriate for this part of the Mass, the day, or the season. The text of such a song is to be approved by the conference of bishops.

If there is no singing at the entrance, the antiphon in the missal is recited either by the people, by some of them, or by a reader. Otherwise it is said by the priest after the greeting.

---

[28] See SC 30; MS 17.

Veneration of the Altar and Greeting of the People

27. When the priest and the ministers come to the presbyterium, they greet the altar. As a sign of veneration, the priest and deacon kiss the altar; the priest may also incense it.

28. After the entrance song, the priest and congregation make the sign of the cross. Then through a greeting the priest expresses the presence of the Lord to the assembled community. This greeting and the people's response manifest the mystery of the Church that is gathered together.

Penitential Rite

29. After greeting the people, the priest or other suitable minister may very briefly introduce the Mass of the day. Then the priest invites the congregation to take part in the penitential rite, which is a general confession made by the entire assembly and is concluded by the priest's absolution.

Lord, Have Mercy

30. After the penitential rite, the *Kyrie* is begun, unless it has already been included as a part of the penitential rite. This acclamation, which praises the Lord and implores his mercy, is ordinarily made by all, that is, with parts for the people and for the choir or cantor.

Each acclamation is normally made twice, but, because of the nature of the language, the music, or other circumstances, the number may be greater or a short verse (trope) may be inserted. If the *Kyrie* is not sung, it is to be recited.

Gloria

31. The *Gloria* is an ancient hymn in which the Church, assembled in the Spirit, praises and prays to the Father and the Lamb. It is sung by the congregation, by the people alternately with the choir, or by the choir alone. If not sung, it is to be recited by all together or in alternation.

The *Gloria* is sung or said on Sundays outside Advent and Lent, on solemnities and feasts, and at solemn local celebrations.

Opening Prayer or Collect

32. Next the priest invites the people to pray, and together they spend some moments in silence so they may realise that they are in God's presence and may make their petitions. The priest then says

the prayer which is called the opening prayer or collect. This expresses the theme of the celebration and by the words of the priest a petition is addressed to God the Father through the mediation of Christ in the Holy Spirit.

The people make the prayer their own and give their assent by the acclamation, *Amen.*

At Mass only one opening prayer is said; this rule applies also to the prayer over the gifts and the prayer after communion.

The opening prayer ends with the longer conclusion:
—if the prayer is directed to the Father:
>We ask this (We make our prayer) (Grant this)
>through our Lord Jesus Christ, your Son,
>who lives and reigns with you and the Holy Spirit,
>one God, for ever and ever;

—if it is directed to the Father, but the Son is mentioned at the end:
>Who lives and reigns with you and the Holy Spirit,
>one God, for ever and ever;

—if it is directed to the Son:
>You live and reign with the Father and the Holy Spirit,
>one God, for ever and ever.

The prayer over the gifts and the prayer after communion end with the shorter conclusion:

—if the prayer is directed to the Father:
>We ask this (Grant this) through Christ our Lord, *or*
>We ask this (Grant this) in the name of Jesus the Lord;

—if it is directed to the Father, but the Son is mentioned at the end:
>Who lives and reigns with you for ever and ever, *or*
>You are Lord for ever and ever.

—if it is directed to the Son:
>You live and reign for ever and ever.

B. Liturgy of the Word

33. Readings from scripture and the chants between the readings form the main part of the liturgy of the word. The homily, profession of faith, and general intercessions or prayers of the faithful develop and complete it. In the readings, explained by the homily, God

speaks to his people[29] of redemption and salvation and nourishes their spirit; Christ is present among the faithful through his word.[30] Through the chants the people make God's word their own and express their adherence to it through the profession of faith. Finally, moved by this word, they pray in the general intercessions for the needs of the Church and for the world's salvation.

Scripture Readings

34. In the readings the treasures of the Bible are opened to the people; this is the table of God's word.[31] Reading the scriptures is traditionally considered a ministerial, not a presidential, function. It is desirable that the gospel be read by a deacon or, in his absence, by a priest other than the one presiding; the other readings are proclaimed by a reader. In the absence of a deacon or another priest, the celebrant reads the gospel.[32]

35. The liturgy teaches that the reading of the gospel should be done with great reverence; it is distinguished from the other readings by special marks of honour. A special minister is appointed to proclaim it, preparing himself by a blessing or prayer. By standing to hear the reading and by their acclamations, the people recognise and acknowledge that Christ is present and speaking to them. Marks of reverence are also given to the book of gospels itself.

Chants between the Readings

36. The responsorial psalm or gradual comes after the first reading. The psalm is an integral part of the liturgy of the word and is ordinarily taken from the lectionary, since these texts are directly related to and depend upon the respective readings. To make the people's response easier, however, some texts of psalms and responses have also been selected for the several seasons of the year or for the different groups of saints. These may be used, whenever the psalm is sung, instead of the text corresponding to the reading.

The cantor of the psalm sings the verse at the lectern or other suitable place, while the people remain seated and listen. Ordinarily the congregation takes part by singing the response, unless the psalm is sung straight through without response.

If sung, the following texts may be chosen: the psalm in the lectionary, the gradual in the Roman Gradual, or the responsorial or alleluia psalm in the Simple Gradual, as these books indicate.

[29] See SC 33.   [30] See SC 7.   [31] See SC 51.   [32] See IOe 50.

37.   According to the season, the second reading is followed by the alleluia or other chant.

a) The alleluia is sung outside Lent. It is begun by all present or by the choir or cantor; it may then be repeated. The verses are taken from the lectionary or the Gradual.

b) The other chant consists of the verse before the gospel or another psalm or tract, as found in the lectionary or the Gradual.

38.   When there is only one reading before the gospel:

a) during the time when the alleluia is sung, either the alleluia psalm, or the psalm and alleluia with its verse, or only the psalm or alleluia may be used;

b) during the time when the alleluia is not sung, either the psalm or the verse before the gospel may be used.

39.   If the psalm after the reading is not sung, it is to be recited. The alleluia or the verse before the gospel may be omitted if not sung.

40.   Except on Easter Sunday and Pentecost the sequences are optional.

Homily

41.   The homily is strongly recommended as an integral part of the liturgy[33] and as a necessary source of nourishment of the Christian life. It should develop some point of the readings or of another text from the Ordinary or the Mass of the day. The homilist should keep in mind the mystery that is being celebrated and the needs of the particular community.[34]

42.   The homily is to be given on Sundays and holydays of obligation at all Masses which are celebrated with a congregation. It is recommended on other days, especially on the weekdays of Advent, Lent, and the Easter season, as well as on other feasts and occasions when the people come to church in large numbers.[35]

The homily should ordinarily be given by the celebrating priest.

Profession of Faith

43.   In the profession of faith or creed the people have the opportunity to respond and give assent to the word of God which they have heard in the readings and the homily. It is also a time for the people to recall the teachings of the faith before they begin to celebrate the eucharist.

[33] See SC 52.   [34] See IOe 54.   [35] See IOe 53.

44.   On Sundays and solemnities the profession of faith is to be said by the priest and the people. It may also be said at solemn local celebrations.

If it is sung, this is ordinarily done by the people together or in alternation.

General Intercessions

45.   In the general intercessions or prayers of the faithful, the people exercise their priestly function by interceding for all mankind. It is appropriate that this prayer be included in all Masses celebrated with a congregation, so that intercessions may be made for the Church, for civil authorities, for those oppressed by various needs, for all mankind, and for the salvation of the world.[36]

46.   As a rule the sequence of intentions is:
   a) for the needs of the Church,
   b) for public authorities and the salvation of the world,
   c) for those oppressed by any need,
   d) for the local community.

In particular celebrations, such as confirmations, marriages, funerals, etc., the list of intentions may be more closely concerned with the special occasion.

47.   The priest directs the prayer: with a brief introduction he invites the people to pray; after the intentions he says the concluding prayer. It is desirable that the intentions be announced by the deacon, cantor, or other person.[37] The congregation makes its petition either by a common response after each intention or by silent prayer.

C. Liturgy of the Eucharist

48.   At the Last Supper Christ instituted the paschal sacrifice and meal. In this meal the sacrifice of the cross is continually made present in the Church when the priest, representing Christ, carries out what the Lord did and handed over to his disciples to do in his memory.[38]

Christ took bread and the cup, gave thanks, broke, and gave to his disciples, saying: 'Take and eat, this is my body. Take and drink, this is the cup of my blood. Do this in memory of me.' The Church has arranged the celebration of the eucharistic liturgy to correspond to these words and actions of Christ:

---

[36] See SC 53.   [37] See IOe 56.   [38] See SC 47; EM 3a, 30.

1) In the preparation of the gifts, bread, wine, and water are brought to the altar, the same elements which Christ used.

2) The eucharistic prayer is the hymn of thanksgiving to God for the whole work of salvation; the offerings become the body and blood of Christ.

3) The breaking of the one bread is a sign of the unity of the faithful, and in communion they receive the body and blood of Christ as the Apostles did from his hands.

Preparation of the Gifts

49.   At the beginning of the liturgy of the eucharist, the gifts which will become the Lord's body and blood are brought to the altar.

First the altar, the Lord's table, is prepared as the centre of the eucharistic liturgy.[39] The corporal, purificator, missal and chalice are placed on it.

The offerings are then brought forward: it is desirable for the faithful to present the bread and wine which are accepted by the priest or deacon at a suitable place. These are placed on the altar with the accompanying prayers. The rite of carrying up the gifts continues the spiritual value and meaning of the ancient custom when the people brought bread and wine for the liturgy from their homes.

This is also the time to bring forward or to collect money or gifts for the poor and the Church. These are to be laid in a suitable place but not on the altar.

50. The procession with the gifts is accompanied by the offertory song, which continues at least until the gifts are placed on the altar. The rules for the offertory song are the same as those for the entrance song (no. 26). If the antiphon is not sung, it is omitted.

51.   The gifts on the altar and the altar itself may be incensed. This is a symbol of the Church's offering and prayer going up to God. Afterwards the deacon or other minister may incense the priest and the people.

52.   The priest washes his hands as an expression of his desire for inward purification.

53.   The preparation of the gifts concludes with the invitation to pray with the priest and the prayer over the gifts, followed by the eucharistic prayer.

[39] See IOe 91; EM 24.

Eucharistic Prayer

54. The eucharistic prayer, a prayer of thanksgiving and sanctification, is the centre and high point of the entire celebration. In an introductory dialogue the priest invites the people to lift their hearts to God in prayer and thanks; he unites them with himself in the prayer he addresses in their name to the Father through Jesus Christ. The meaning of the prayer is that the whole congregation joins Christ in acknowledging the works of God and in offering the sacrifice.

55. The chief elements of the eucharistic prayer are these:

a) *Thanksgiving* (expressed especially in the preface): in the name of the entire people of God, the priest praises the Father and gives him thanks for the work of salvation or for some special aspect of it in keeping with the day, feast, or season.

b) *Acclamation*: united with the angels, the congregation sings or recites the *Sanctus*. This acclamation forms part of the eucharistic prayer, and all the people join with the priest in singing or reciting it.

c) *Epiclesis*: in special invocations the Church calls on God's power and asks that the gifts offered by men may be consecrated, that is, become the body and blood of Christ and that the victim may become a source of salvation for those who are to share in communion.

d) *Narrative of the institution and consecration*: in the words and actions of Christ, the sacrifice he instituted at the Last Supper is celebrated, when under the appearances of bread and wine he offered his body and blood, gave them to his Apostles to eat and drink, and commanded them to carry on this mystery.

e) *Anamnesis*: in fulfilment of the command received from Christ through the Apostles, the Church keeps his memorial by recalling especially his passion, resurrection, and ascension.

f) *Offering*: in this memorial, the Church—and in particular the Church here and now assembled—offers the victim to the Father in the Holy Spirit. The Church's intention is that the faithful not only offer the spotless victim but also learn to offer themselves and daily to be drawn into ever more perfect union, through Christ the Mediator, with the Father and with each other, so that at last God may be all in all.[40]

g) *Intercessions*: the intercessions make it clear that the eucharist is celebrated in communion with the whole Church of heaven and

[40] See SC 48; EM 12.

earth, and that the offering is made for the Church and all its members, living and dead, who are called to share in the salvation and redemption acquired by the body and blood of Christ.

h) *Final doxology*: the praise of God is expressed in the doxology which is confirmed and concluded by the acclamation of the people.

All should listen to the eucharistic prayer in silent reverence and share in it by making the acclamations.

Communion Rite

56. Since the eucharistic celebration is the paschal meal, in accord with his command, the body and blood of the Lord should be received as spiritual food by the faithful who are properly disposed.[41] This is the purpose of the breaking of the bread and the other preparatory rites which lead directly to the communion of the people:

a) *Lord's Prayer*: this is a petition both for daily food, which for Christians means also the eucharistic bread, and for forgiveness from sin, so that what is holy may be given to those who are holy. The priest invites all the faithful to sing or say the Lord's Prayer with him. He alone adds the embolism, *Deliver us*; and the people conclude this with the doxology. The addition to the Lord's Prayer develops the last petition and begs in the name of the community deliverance from the power of evil. The invitation, the prayer itself, the embolism, and the people's doxology are sung or spoken aloud.

b) *Rite of peace*: before they share in the same bread, the people express their love for one another and beg for peace and unity in the Church and with all mankind.

The form of this rite is left to the conference of bishops to decide in accord with the customs and mentality of the people.

c) *Breaking of bread*: this gesture of Christ at the Last Supper gave the entire eucharistic action its name in apostolic times. In addition to its practical aspect, it signifies that in communion we who are many are made one body in the one bread of life which is Christ (see 1 Corinthians 10:17).

d) *Commingling*: the celebrant drops a part of the host into the chalice.

e) *Agnus Dei*: during the breaking of the bread and the commingling the *Agnus Dei* is ordinarily sung by the choir or cantor with the people responding; or it may be said aloud. This invocation may be repeated as often as necessary to accompany the breaking of the

---

[41] See EM 12, 33a.

bread, and is brought to a close by the words, *grant us peace.*

f) *Private preparation of the priest*: the priest prepares himself to receive the body and blood of Christ by praying quietly. The faithful also do this by praying in silence.

g) The priest then shows the eucharistic bread to the faithful. He invites them to participate in the meal and leads them in an act of humility, using words from the gospel.

h) It is most desirable that the faithful should receive the body of the Lord in hosts consecrated at the same Mass and should share the cup when it is permitted. Communion is thus a clearer sign of sharing in the sacrifice that is actually being celebrated.[42]

i) The song during the communion of the priest and people expresses the spiritual union of the communicants who join their voices in a single song, shows the joy of all, and makes the communion procession an act of brotherhood. This song begins when the priest receives communion and continues as long as convenient. The communion song should be concluded in time if there is to be an additional hymn after communion.

An antiphon from the Roman Gradual, with or without the psalm, an antiphon with a psalm from the Simple Gradual, or another suitable song approved by the conference of bishops may be used. It is sung by the choir alone or by the choir or cantor with the people.

If there is no singing, the antiphon in the Missal is recited either by the people, by some of them, or by a reader. Otherwise the priest himself says it after he receives communion and before he gives communion to the congregation.

j) After communion, the priest and people may spend some time in silent prayer. If desired, a hymn, psalm, or other song of praise may be sung by the entire congregation.

k) In the prayer after communion the priest petitions for the effects of the mystery just celebrated, and by their acclamation, *Amen*, the people make the prayer their own.

D. Concluding Rite

57. The concluding rite consists of:

a) the priest's greeting and blessing which is on certain days and occasions expanded by the prayer over the people or other solemn form;

[42] EM 31, 32. Regarding the faculty for communicating twice on the same day, see IC 2.

b) the dismissal which sends each member of the congregation to do good works, praising the Lord.

CHAPTER III

OFFICES AND MINISTRIES IN THE MASS

58. Everyone in the eucharistic assembly has the right and duty to take his own part according to the diversity of orders and functions.[43] In exercising his function, everyone, whether minister or layman, should do that and only that which belongs to him,[44] so that in the liturgy the Church may be seen in its variety of orders and ministries.

I Offices and Ministries of Holy Orders

59. Every authentic celebration of the eucharist is directed by the bishop, either in person or through the presbyters, who are his helpers.[45]

Whenever he is present at a Mass with a congregation the bishop should preside over the assembly and associate the presbyters with himself in the celebration. If possible, they should concelebrate.

This is done not to add external solemnity but to express in a clearer light the mystery of the Church, which is the sacrament of unity.[46]

If he does not celebrate the eucharist, but assigns another to celebrate, the bishop may properly preside during the liturgy of the word and may give a blessing at the end of Mass.

60. Within the community of the faithful a presbyter also possesses the power of orders to offer sacrifice in the person of Christ.[47] He presides over the assembly and leads its prayer, proclaims the message of salvation, leads the people in offering sacrifice through Christ in the Spirit to the Father, gives them the bread of eternal life, and shares it with them. At the eucharist he should serve God and the people with dignity and humility. By his actions and by his proclama-

---

[43] See SC 14, 26. [44] See SC 28.
[45] See LG 26, 28; SC 42.
[46] See SC 26. [47] See PO 2; LG 28.

tions of the word he should impress upon the faithful the living presence of Christ.

61. The deacon, whose order was held in high honour in the early Church, has first place among the ministers. At Mass he has his own functions: he proclaims the gospel, sometimes preaches God's word, leads the general intercessions of the faithful, assists the priest, gives communion to the faithful (in particular, ministering the chalice), and sometimes gives directions to the congregation.

II Office and Function of the People of God

62. In the celebration of Mass the faithful form a holy people, a chosen race, a royal priesthood: they give thanks to the Father and offer the victim not only through the hands of the priest but also with him, and they learn to offer themselves.[48] They should make this clear by their deep sense of religion and their charity to everyone who shares in the celebration.

Any appearance of individualism or division among the faithful should be avoided, since they all are brothers in the sight of the one Father.

They should become one body, hearing the word of God, joining in prayers and song, and offering sacrifice and sharing the Lord's table together. This unity is especially evident in the common postures and actions observed by the faithful.

The people should serve willingly when asked to perform some particular ministry in the celebration.

63. The schola or choir exercises a liturgical function within the assembly. It sings the different parts proper to it and encourages active participation of the people in singing.[49] What is said about the schola of singers applies in a similar way to other musicians, especially the organist.

64. There should be a cantor or a choirmaster to direct and encourage the people in singing. If there is no choir, the cantor leads the various songs, and the people take their own part.[50]

[48] See SC 48; EM 12.
[49] See MS 19.
[50] MS 21.

III Special Ministries

65. The acolyte is instituted to serve at the altar and to assist the priest and deacon. In particular he prepares the altar and the vessels and, as an auxiliary minister of the eucharist, he gives communion to the faithful.

66. The reader is instituted to proclaim the scripture readings, with the exception of the gospel. He may also announce the intentions of the general intercessions and, in the absence of a cantor of the psalm, sing or read the psalm between the readings.

The reader, although a layman, has his own proper function in the eucharistic celebration and should exercise this even though ministers of a higher rank are present.

It is necessary that those who exercise the ministry of reading, even if they have not received institution, be qualified and carefully prepared so that the reading should develop in the faithful a profound appreciation of scripture.[51]

67. The cantor of the psalm is to sing the psalm or other biblical song between the readings. He should be trained in the area of singing psalms and be able to speak clearly and distinctly.

68. Some ministers perform their function in the presbyterium, including those who carry the missal, cross, candles, bread, wine, water, and censer.

Others serve outside the presbyterium:

a) The commentator gives explanations and directives to the people; he introduces the celebration and helps the people to understand it better. His comments should be carefully prepared, clear, and succinct.

He stands in a suitable place in the sight of the people, but it is not very appropriate for him to stand at the lectern where the scriptures are read.

b) In some places ushers meet the people at the door, lead them to their places, and direct processions.

c) Those who take up collections in church.

69. Especially in larger churches and communities, a person should be designated to arrange the services and to see that they are carried out by the ministers in a devout and orderly manner.

[51] See SC 24.

70. Laymen, even if they have not received institution as ministers, may perform all the functions below those reserved to deacons. Services performed outside the presbyterium may also be given to women at the discretion of the rector of the church. The conference of bishops may permit women to proclaim the readings prior to the Gospel and to announce the intentions of the general intercessions; furthermore, they may determine the appropriate place in a liturgical gathering from which the word of God is to be proclaimed by a woman.[51a]

71. If there are several persons present who can exercise the same ministry, different parts of it may be assigned to them. For example, one deacon may take the sung parts, another serve at the altar. If there are several readings, it is better to distribute them among a number of readers, and likewise with other functions.

72. If there is only one minister at a Mass with a congregation, he may carry out several different functions.

73. All concerned should work together in preparing the ceremonies, pastoral arrangements, and music for each celebration. They should work under the direction of the rector and should consult the people about the parts which belong to them.

CHAPTER IV
DIFFERENT FORMS OF CELEBRATION

74. Among the various ways of celebrating the eucharist in the local Church, first place should be given to Mass at which the bishop presides with the college of presbyters and the ministers,[52] and with the people taking full and active part. This is the principal sign of the Church.

75. Mass celebrated by any community, but especially by the parish community, has special meaning in representing the universal Church gathered at a given time and place. This is particularly true of the common celebration on the Lord's day.[53]

[51a] See Sacred Congregation of Rites, Instruction *Liturgicae instaurationes*, 5 September 1970, 7: AAS 62 (1970) 700-1.
[52] See SC 41.
[53] See SC 42; EM 26; LG 28; PO 5.

76. The conventual Mass, which is a part of the daily office, and the 'community' Mass have a special position in some communities. Although such Masses do not have their own form of celebration, it is most suitable that they be celebrated with singing, with the full participation of all the members of the community, religious or canons. In these Masses individuals should exercise their own unction according to the ordination or ministry they have received. For that reason all the priests who are not bound to celebrate individually for the pastoral care of the faithful should concelebrate at the conventual or community Mass if possible. All priests belonging to the community who are bound to celebrate individually for the pastoral care of the faithful may also concelebrate at the conventual or community Mass on the same day.[54]

I Mass with a Congregation

77. By Mass with a congregation is meant one in which the people take part. As far as possible and especially on Sundays and holydays of obligation, this Mass should be celebrated with song and with a suitable number of ministers.[55] It may, however, be celebrated without music and with only one minister.

78. It is desirable that an acolyte, a reader and a cantor assist the celebrant. The form described below is called the common or typical rite, but it also allows for a greater number of ministers.
  A deacon may exercise his office in any form of celebration.

Preparations

79. The altar is to be covered with at least one cloth. On or near it are placed a cross and at least two lighted candles. Four or six candles may be used or, if the diocesan bishop celebrates, seven. The cross and candles may be carried in the entrance procession. The gospel book, if distinct from the book of other readings, may be placed on the altar, unless it is carried in the entrance procession.

80. The following should also be prepared:
  a) near the priest's chair: the missal and a book with the chants, as occasion demands;
  b) at the lectern: the lectionary;

[54] See EM 47; Sacred Congregation of Rites, *Declaration on Concelebration*, 7 August 1972: AAS 64 (1972) 561-3.
[55] EM 26; MS 16, 27.

c) on the side table: the chalice, corporal, purificator, and if needed, a pall; a paten and ciboria, if needed, with the bread for the communion of the priest, the ministers, and the people, together with cruets with wine and water, unless all of these are presented by the faithful at the offertory; communion plate; and the requisites for the washing of hands. The chalice should be covered with a veil, which may always be white.

81.   In the sacristy the vestments for the priest and ministers should be prepared according to the form of celebration:

a) for the priest: alb, stole, and chasuble;

b) for the deacon: alb, stole, and dalmatic; the latter may be omitted if necessary or if less solemnity is desired;

c) for the other ministers: albs or other vestments lawfully approved.

Anyone who wears an alb should use a cincture and an amice unless other provision is made.

A. Common Form

Introductory Rites

82.   The priest and the ministers put on their vestments and, when the people have assembled, go to the altar in this order:

a) a minister with a lighted censer, if incense is used;

b) ministers with lighted candles, according to circumstances; between them, if the occasion demands, a minister with the cross;

c) the acolytes and other ministers;

d) the priest.

If incense is used, the priest puts some in the censer before the procession begins.

83.   The entrance song is sung during the procession to the altar (see nos. 25-6).

84.   At the altar the priest and ministers make a low bow. If there is a tabernacle containing the blessed sacrament, they genuflect.

If the cross has been carried in the procession, it is placed near the altar or wherever is suitable; the candles carried by the ministers are placed near the altar or on the side table; and the gospel book is placed on the altar.

85.   The priest goes up to the altar and kisses it. If incense is used, he walks around the altar while incensing it.

86.   The priest then goes to the chair. After the entrance song, while all are standing, the priest and the faithful make the sign of the cross. The priest says: *In the name of the Father, and of the Son, and of the Holy Spirit*; the people answer: *Amen.*

Then the priest, facing the people, extends his hands and greets all present, using one of the forms indicated. He or some other suitable minister may very briefly introduce the Mass of the day.

87.   After the penitential act, the *Kyrie* and *Gloria* are said according to the rubrics (nos. 30-1). Either the priest or the cantors or everyone together may begin the *Gloria.*

88.   With his hands joined, the priest invites the people to pray: *Let us pray.* All pray silently with the priest for a while. Then the priest extends his hands and says the opening prayer, at the end of which the people respond: *Amen.*

Liturgy of the Word

89.   After the opening prayer, the reader goes to the lectern for the first reading. All sit and listen and make the acclamation at the end.

90.   After the reading, the cantor of the psalm, or the reader, sings or recites the psalm, and the people make the response (see no. 36).

91.   If there is a second reading before the gospel, it is read at the lectern, as before. All sit and listen and make the acclamation at the end.

92.   The alleluia, or other chant according to the season, follows (see nos. 37-9).

93.   During the singing of the alleluia or other chant, if incense is being used, the priest puts some in the censer. Then he bows before the altar, with his hands joined, and says quietly: *Almighty God, cleanse my heart.*

94.   If the gospel book is on the altar, he takes it and goes to the lectern. The ministers, who may carry the censer and candles, walk ahead of him.

95.   At the lectern the priest opens the book and says: *The Lord be with you.* Then he says: *A reading from . . .* , and makes the sign of the cross with his thumb on the book and on his forehead, mouth, and breast. If incense is used, he incenses the book. After the acclamation of the people, he proclaims the gospel. At the end he

kisses the book, saying quietly: *May the words of the gospel wipe away our sins.* After the reading the people make the customary acclamation.

96. If no reader is present, the priest proclaims all the readings at the lectern and, if necessary, also the chants between the readings. If incense is used, he puts some in the censer and then, bowing, says: *Almighty God, cleanse my heart.*

97. The homily is given at the chair or at the lectern.

98. The profession of faith is said by the priest and people (see no. 44). At the words: *by the power of the Holy Spirit*, etc. all bow. On the feasts of the Annunciation and Christmas all genuflect.

99. The general intercessions (prayer of the faithful), in which the people take part, follow the profession of faith. The priest directs the intercessions from his chair or at the lectern (see nos. 45-7).

Liturgy of the Eucharist

100. After the general intercessions, the offertory song begins (see no. 50). The ministers place the corporal, purificator, chalice, and missal on the altar.

101. It is fitting that the participation of the faithful be expressed by their offering the bread and wine for the celebration of the eucharist, together with other gifts for the needs of the Church and of the poor.

The offerings of the people are received by the priest, assisted by the ministers. The bread and wine for the eucharist are taken to the altar, and the other gifts are put in a suitable place.

102. At the altar the priest receives the paten with the bread from the minister. He holds it slightly raised above the altar and says the accompanying prayer. Then he places the paten with the bread on the corporal.

103. The priest stands at the side of the altar and pours wine and a little water into the chalice, saying the accompanying prayer quietly. The minister presents the cruets. Returning to the middle of the altar he raises the chalice a little with both hands and says the appointed prayer. Then he places the chalice on the corporal and may cover it with a pall.

104. The priest bows and says quietly: *Lord God, we ask you to receive.*

105. If incense is used, he incenses the gifts and altar. The minister incenses the priest and people.

106. After the prayer, *Lord God, we ask you to receive,* or after the incensation, the priest washes his hands at the side of the altar, saying the prescribed prayer quietly. The minister pours the water.

107. Standing at the middle of the altar and facing the people, the priest extends and joins his hands while he invites the people to pray: *Pray, brethren.* After the people's answer, the priest says the prayer over the gifts with hands extended. At the end the people respond: *Amen.*

108. The priest then begins the eucharistic prayer. With hands extended, he says: *The Lord be with you.* As he says: *Lift up your hearts,* he raises his hands; with hands extended, he adds: *Let us give thanks to the Lord our God.* When the people have answered: *It is right to give him thanks and praise,* the priest continues the preface. At its conclusion, he joins his hands and sings or says aloud with the ministers and people: *Holy, holy, holy Lord* (see no. 55b).

109. The priest continues the eucharistic prayer according to the rubrics of each prayer.

If the celebrating priest is a bishop, after the words: *with your servant Pope N.* he adds *and me, your unworthy servant.*

A local Ordinary should be named with this formula: *with your servant Pope N. and N., our bishop* (or: *vicar, prelate, prefect, abbot*). Coadjutor and auxiliary bishops should be named in the eucharistic prayer. Where several are to be mentioned, this is done with the following formula: *our bishop N. and his assistant bishops.*[55a] Depending on which eucharistic prayer is being used, these formulae are to be adapted according to normal rules of grammar.

A little before the consecration, the minister may ring a bell as a signal to the people. According to local custom, he also rings the bell at each showing of the bread and wine to the people.

110. After the doxology the priest joins his hands and says the introduction to the Lord's Prayer. With extended hands, he then sings or says the prayer with the people.

111. After the Lord's Prayer, with hands extended, the priest alone says the embolism, *Deliver us.* At the end the people make the

[55a] See Sacred Congregation of Rites, Decree, 9 October 1972: AAS 64 (1972) 692-4.

acclamation: *For the kingdom.*

112.   Then the priest says aloud the prayer, *Lord Jesus Christ.* After this prayer, extending and joining his hands he gives the greeting of peace: *The peace of the Lord be with you always.* The people answer: *And also with you.* Then the priest may add: *Let us offer each other the sign of peace.* All exchange the sign of peace and love, according to local custom. The priest may give the sign of peace to the ministers.

113.   The priest takes the host and breaks it over the paten. He places a small piece in the chalice, saying quietly: *May this mingling.* Meanwhile the *Agnus Dei* is sung or recited by the choir and congregation (see no. 56e).

114.   Then the priest says quietly the prayer: *Lord Jesus Christ, Son of the living God,* or *Lord Jesus Christ, with faith in your love and mercy.*

115.   After the prayer, the priest genuflects and takes the host. Facing the people, he raises the host slightly over the paten and says: *This is the Lamb of God.* With the people he adds once only: *Lord, I am not worthy to receive you.*

116.   Facing the altar, the priest says quietly: *May the body of Christ bring me to everlasting life,* and reverently consumes the body of Christ. Next he takes the chalice and continues: *May the blood of Christ bring me to everlasting life,* and reverently drinks the blood of Christ.

117.   After this he takes the paten or other vessel and goes to the communicants. If communion is to be given in the form of bread only, before each one he raises the host slightly and shows it to him, saying: *The body of Christ.* The communicant replies: *Amen,* and, holding the communion plate under his chin, receives the sacrament.

118.   For communion under both kinds, the rite described in nos. 240-52 is followed.

119.   The communion song is begun while the priest is receiving the sacrament (see no. 56i).

120.   After communion, the priest returns to the altar and collects any remaining fragments. Standing at the side of the altar or at the side table, he purifies the paten or other vessel over the chalice, then washes the chalice, saying quietly: *Lord, may I receive,* and dries it

with the purificator. If this is done at the altar, the vessels are taken to the side table by the minister. It is also permitted to wash the vessels after Mass when the people have left, especially if there are several vessels. In this case, after communion they may be covered and placed on a corporal either on the altar or on the side table.

121. Afterwards the priest may return to the chair. A period of silence may now follow, or a hymn of praise or psalm may be sung (see no. 56j).

122. Standing at the altar or the chair and facing the people, the priest says: *Let us pray.* There may be a brief period of silence, unless this has been already observed immediately after communion. At the end of the prayer the people respond: *Amen.*

Concluding Rite

123. If there are any brief announcements, they may be made at this time.

124. Then the priest extends his hands and greets the people: *The Lord be with you.* They answer: *And also with you.* The priest adds: *May almighty God bless you,* and, as he makes the sign of the cross over them, continues: *the Father, and the Son, and the Holy Spirit.* The people answer: *Amen.* On certain days and occasions another more solemn form or the prayer over the people may precede this form of blessing as the rubrics direct.

   With his hands joined, the priest adds: *Go in the peace of Christ,* or *Go in peace to love and serve the Lord,* or *The Mass is ended, go in peace,* and the people answer: *Thanks be to God.*

125. Ordinarily the priest kisses the altar, then makes the customary reverence with the ministers, and leaves.

126. If a liturgical service follows the Mass, the concluding rite (greeting, blessing, and dismissal) is omitted.

B. Functions of the Deacon

127. When there is a deacon to exercise his ministry, the above norms apply with the following exceptions.

   In general the deacon:
   a) assists the priest and walks at his side;

b) at the altar, assists with the chalice or the book;

c) if there is no other minister present, fulfils the duties of others when necessary.

Introductory Rites

128. The deacon vests and then, carrying the gospel book, precedes the priest on the way to the altar; otherwise he walks at the priest's side.

129. He and the priest make the reverence and go up to the altar. After placing the gospel book on it, the deacon and the priest kiss the altar together. If incense is used, he assists the priest.

130. After the incensation, he goes to the chair with the priest, takes his place beside him, and assists him when needed.

Liturgy of the Word

131. If incense is used, the deacon assists the priest when he puts incense in the censer during the singing of the alleluia or other chant. Then he bows before the priest and asks for the blessing, saying in a low voice: *Father, give me your blessing.* The priest blesses him: *The Lord be in your heart.* The deacon answers: *Amen.* If the gospel book is on the altar, he takes it and goes to the lectern, preceded by the ministers, if present, who may carry the candles and censer. There he greets the people, incenses the book, and proclaims the gospel. After the reading, he kisses the book, saying quietly: *May the words of the gospel wipe away our sins*, and returns to the priest. If there is no homily or profession of faith, he may remain at the lectern for the general intercessions, but the ministers leave.

132. After the priest introduces the general intercessions, the deacon announces the intentions at the lectern or other suitable place.

Liturgy of the Eucharist

133. At the offertory, while the priest remains at the chair, the deacon, assisted by other ministers, prepares the altar. The deacon himself takes care of the vessels and also assists the priest in receiving the people's gifts. He then hands the priest the paten with the bread, prepares the chalice with wine and a little water either at the altar or at the side table, and hands it to the priest. As he pours the water into the chalice the deacon says quietly: *By the mystery of this water and wine.* If incense is used, the deacon assists the priest as he incenses the

offerings and altar, and afterwards he, or another minister, incenses the priest and people.

134. During the eucharistic prayer, the deacon stands near the priest, but a little behind. When necessary he assists the priest with the chalice or the missal.

135. At the doxology, the deacon stands beside the priest and raises the chalice while the priest raises the paten with the host, until the people have responded *Amen*.

136. After the priest has said the prayer for peace and the greeting, *The peace of the Lord be with you always*, and the people have answered, *And also with you*, the deacon invites all to exchange the sign of peace, according to circumstances, saying: *Let us offer each other the sign of peace.* He himself receives the sign of peace from the priest and may give it to the other ministers near him.

137. After the priest's communion, the deacon receives under both kinds and then assists the priest in giving communion to the people. If communion is given under both kinds, the deacon ministers the chalice to the communicants and is the last to drink from it.

138. After communion, the deacon returns to the altar with the priest and collects any remaining fragments. He then takes the chalice and other vessels to the side table, where he washes them and arranges them in the usual way; the priest returns to the chair. The deacon may cover the vessels and leave them on a corporal on the side table to be washed after Mass when the people have left.

Concluding Rite

139. After the prayer after communion, if there are any brief announcements, the deacon may make them unless the priest prefers to do so himself.

140. After the blessing, the deacon dismisses the people, saying: *Go in the peace of Christ*, or *Go in peace to love and serve the Lord*, or *The Mass is ended, go in peace*.

141. Ordinarily the deacon kisses the altar with the priest. Then he makes the customary reverence and leaves in the same order as at the beginning of the Mass.

C. Functions of the Acolyte

142. The acolyte may have functions of various kinds, and some of these may occur at the same time. It is therefore desirable that the functions be suitably distributed among several acolytes. If there is only a single acolyte present, however, he should perform the more important functions, and the rest are distributed among the other ministers.

Introductory Rites

143. In the procession to the altar the acolyte may carry the cross; he walks between two ministers with lighted candles. When he comes to the altar, he places the cross near it and takes his own place in the sanctuary.

144. Throughout the celebration the acolyte goes to the priest or the deacon, whenever necessary, to hold the book for them and to assist them in other ways. Thus it is appropriate, if possible, for him to have a place from which he can conveniently exercise his ministry, either at the chair or at the altar.

Liturgy of the Eucharist

145. After the general intercessions, the priest remains at the chair and the acolyte places the corporal, purificator, chalice, and missal on the altar. Then, if needed, he assists the priest in receiving the gifts of the people and he may bring the bread and wine to the altar and present them to the priest. If incense is used, the acolyte gives the censer to the priest and assists him as he incenses the offerings and the altar.

146. The acolyte may assist the priest as a special minister in giving communion to the people.[56] If communion is given under both kinds, the deacon ministers the chalice to the communicants or he holds the chalice if communion is given by intinction.

147. After communion, the acolyte helps the priest and deacon to wash the vessels and arrange them. If there is no deacon, the acolyte takes the vessels to the side table, where he washes them and arranges them.

[56] Paul VI, *Motu Proprio Ministeria quaedam*, 15 August 1972, no. VI: AAS 54 (1972) 532.

D. Functions of the Reader

Introductory Rites

148. In the procession to the altar, if there is no deacon, the reader may carry the gospel book and precede the priest; otherwise he walks with the other ministers.

149. When the reader comes to the altar, he makes the reverence with the priest, goes up to the altar, and places the gospel book on it. Then he takes his place in the sanctuary with the other ministers.

Liturgy of the Word

150. The readings which precede the gospel are read at the lectern. If there is no cantor of the psalm, the reader may also sing or recite the responsorial psalm after the first reading.

151. After the priest gives the introduction to the general intercessions, the reader may announce intentions.

152. If there is no entrance song or communion song and the antiphons in the missal are not said by the people, the reader reads them at the proper time.

II Concelebrated Mass

Introduction

153. In a special way concelebration shows the unity of priesthood and of the sacrifice, and the unity of the people of God. Prescribed by the rite at times, it is also permitted at:

1 a) the chrism Mass and the evening Mass on Holy Thursday;
    b) councils, meetings of bishops, and synods;
    c) the blessing of an abbot.

2 In addition, with the permission of the ordinary, who may decide whether concelebration is suitable:

a) at the conventual Mass and at the principal Mass in churches and oratories when the needs of the faithful do not require that all the priests present celebrate individually;

b) at any kind of meeting of priests, either secular or religious.[57]

154. Where there is a large number of priests, the competent superior may permit concelebration several times on the same day, but at different times or in distinct sacred places.[58]

[57] SC 57.   [58] EM 47.

155. It is for the bishop to regulate the discipline for concelebration in the diocese, in accord with the law, even in churches and semi-public oratories of exempt religious communities. Every ordinary, including the major superior of non-exempt clerical religious institutes and of societies of clerics living in community without vows,[59] has the right to judge the suitability of, and to give permission for, concelebration in his churches and oratories.

156. No one is ever to be admitted to concelebrate in a Mass which has already begun.[60]

157. Concelebration is particularly significant when the priests of a diocese concelebrate with their own bishop, especially at the chrism Mass on Holy Thursday and on the occasion of a synod or pastoral visitation. For the same reason concelebration is recommended whenever priests meet with their bishop during a retreat or any other gathering. At these times the sign of the unity of the priesthood, and of the Church itself, is even more clearly manifested.[61]

158. Because of the occasion or the particular significance of the rite it is permissible to celebrate or concelebrate more than once on the same day in the following cases:

a) One who has celebrated or concelebrated the chrism Mass on Holy Thursday may also celebrate or concelebrate the evening Mass.

b) One who has celebrated or concelebrated the Easter Vigil Mass may celebrate or concelebrate the second Mass of Easter.

c) All priests may celebrate or concelebrate the three Masses of Christmas, provided these are celebrated at the proper times.

d) One who concelebrates with the bishop or his delegates at a synod, at a pastoral visitation, or at meetings of priests may celebrate another Mass for the benefit of the faithful if the bishop so decides.[62] This holds also for meetings of religious with their own ordinary or his delegate.

159. A concelebrated Mass follows the norms for various forms of individual celebration, with the exceptions indicated below.

160. If neither a deacon nor other ministers assist in a concelebrated Mass, their functions are carried out by the concelebrants.

---

[59] See *Ritus servandus in concelebratione Missae*, no. 3.
[60] *Ibid.*, 8.
[61] See ES; EM 47.
[62] See *Ritus servandus in concelebratione Missae*, no. 9.

Introductory Rites

161. In the sacristy or other suitable place the concelebrants put on the usual vestments for Mass. For a good reason, as when there are more concelebrants than vestments, the concelebrants may omit the chasuble but wear the stole over the alb. The celebrant always wears the chasuble.

162. When everything is ready, the procession goes through the church to the altar. The concelebrating priests go ahead of the celebrant.

163. At the altar the concelebrants and the celebrants make the usual reverence, kiss the altar, and go to their chairs. The celebrant may incense the altar and then go to the chair.

Liturgy of the Word

164. During the liturgy of the word the concelebrants remain at their places, sitting or standing as the celebrant does.

165. Ordinarily the celebrant or one of the concelebrants gives the homily.

Liturgy of the Eucharist

166. The offertory rites are carried out by the celebrant; the concelebrants remain at their places.

167. At the end of the offertory, the concelebrants come to the altar and stand around it in such a way that the people are able to see the rite clearly. The concelebrants should remain out of the way of the deacon when he ministers at the altar.

Eucharistic Prayer

168. The preface is said by the celebrant alone. The *Sanctus* is sung or recited by all the concelebrants with the people and the choir.

169. After the *Sanctus*, the concelebrants continue the eucharistic prayer as described below. Only the celebrant makes the gestures, unless otherwise indicated.

170. The parts said by the concelebrants together are to be recited in a low voice and in such a way that the voice of the celebrant is clearly heard by all the people, who should be able to understand the texts easily.

a. Eucharistic Prayer I, the Roman Canon

171.   *We come to you, Father* is said by the celebrant alone, with hands extended.

172.   The intercessions, *Remember, Lord, your people*, and *In union with the whole Church*, may be assigned to one or other of the concelebrants; he alone says the prayers aloud, with hands extended.

In the eucharistic prayer the bishop must be named in this way: *for N. our bishop* (or: *vicar, prelate, prefect, abbot*).

When several are to be named, a general form is used: *for N. our bishop and his assistant bishops.*

173.   *Father, accept this offering* is said by the celebrant alone, with hands extended.

174.   From *Bless and approve our offering* to *Almighty God, we pray* inclusive, all the concelebrants say the prayer together in this manner:

a) They say *Bless and approve our offering* with hands outstretched towards the offerings.

b) They say *The day before he suffered* and *When supper was ended* with hands joined.

c) While saying the words of the Lord, each extends his right hand towards the bread and towards the chalice, if this seems opportune; at the elevation they look at the host and chalice and afterwards bow low.

d) They say *Father, we celebrate the memory of Christ* and *Look with favour* with hands extended.

e) From *Almighty God, we pray* to *the sacred body and blood of your Son* inclusive, they bow with hands joined; then they stand upright and make the sign of the cross at the words, *let us be filled.*

175.   The intercessions, *Remember, Lord, those who have died*, and *For ourselves, too*, may be assigned to one or other of the concelebrants; he alone says the prayers aloud, with hands extended.

176.   At the words, *Though we are sinners*, all the concelebrants strike their breasts.

177.   The prayer, *Through Christ our Lord you give us all these gifts*, is said by the celebrant alone.

178.   In this eucharistic prayer the parts from *Bless and approve our offering* to *Almighty God, we pray* inclusive and the doxology may be sung.

b. Eucharistic Prayer II

179. *Lord, you are holy indeed* is said by the celebrant alone, with hands extended.

180. From *Let your Spirit come* to *May all of us who share* inclusive, all the concelebrants say the prayer together in this manner:

a) They say *Let your Spirit come* with hands outstretched towards the offerings.

b) They say *Before he was given up to death* and *When supper was ended* with hands joined.

c) While saying the words of the Lord, each extends his right hand towards the bread and towards the chalice, if this seems opportune; at the elevation they look at the host and chalice and afterwards bow low.

d) They say *In memory of his death* and *May all of us who share* with hands extended.

181. The intercessions for the living, *Lord, remember your Church*, and for the dead, *Remember our brothers and sisters*, may be assigned to one or other of the concelebrants; he alone says the intercessions with hands extended.

182. In this eucharistic prayer the parts from *Before he was given up to death* to *In memory of his death* inclusive and the doxology may be sung.

c. Eucharistic Prayer III

183. *Father, you are holy indeed* is said by the celebrant alone, with hands extended.

184. From *And so, Father, we bring you these gifts* to *Look with favour* inclusive, all the concelebrants say the prayer together in this manner:

a) They say *And so, Father, we bring you these gifts* with hands outstretched towards the offerings.

b) They say *On the night he was betrayed* and *When supper was ended* with joined hands.

c) While saying the words of the Lord, each extends his right hand towards the bread and towards the chalice, if this seems opportune; at the elevation they look at the host and chalice and afterwards bow low.

d) They say *Father, calling to mind* and *Look with favour* with hands extended.

185. The intercessions, *May he make us an everlasting gift*, and *Lord, may this sacrifice*, may be assigned to one or other of the concelebrants; the concelebrant alone says the intercessions with hands extended.

186. In this eucharistic prayer the parts from *On the night he was betrayed* to *Father, calling to mind* inclusive and the doxology may be sung.

d. Eucharistic Prayer IV

187. *Father, we acknowledge* is said by the celebrant alone, with hands extended.

188. From *Father, may this Holy Spirit* to *Lord, look upon this sacrifice* inclusive, all the concelebrants say the prayer together in this manner:

a) They say *Father, may this Holy Spirit* with hands outstretched towards the offerings.

b) They say *He always loved those* and *In the same way* with hands joined.

c) While saying the words of the Lord, each extends his right hand towards the bread and towards the chalice, if this seems opportune; at the elevation they look at the host and chalice and afterwards bow low.

d) They say *Father, we now celebrate* and *Lord, look upon this sacrifice* with hands extended.

189. The intercessions, *Lord, remember those*, may be assigned to one of the concelebrants, who says them alone, with hands extended.

190. In this eucharistic prayer the parts from *He always loved those* to *Father, we now celebrate* inclusive and the doxology may be sung.

191. The doxology of the eucharistic prayer may be sung or said by the celebrant alone or by all the concelebrants with him.

Communion Rite

192. With hands joined, the celebrant introduces the Lord's Prayer. Then, extending his hands, he sings or says the prayer with the concelebrants and the people.

193. The embolism, *Deliver us*, is said by the celebrant alone, with hands extended. All the concelebrants make the final acclamation with the people: *For the kingdom*.

194. After the deacon (or one of the concelebrants) says: *Let us offer each other the sign of peace*, all exchange the sign of peace. The celebrant gives the sign of peace to those near him and then to the deacon.

195. During the singing of the *Agnus Dei* some of the concelebrants may help the celebrant break the hosts for communion, both for the concelebrants and for the people.

196. After the commingling the celebrant says quietly the prayer, *Lord Jesus Christ, Son of the living God*, or *Lord Jesus Christ, with faith in your love and mercy*.

197. After this prayer the celebrant genuflects and steps back a little. One by one the concelebrants come to the middle of the altar, genuflect, and take the body of Christ. They hold the host in the right hand, with the left hand under it, and return to their places. The concelebrants may, however, remain in their places and take the body of Christ from a paten which is passed from one to another or held by the celebrant or one or more of the concelebrants.

198. Then the celebrant takes the host and, facing the people and holding it slightly raised above the paten, says: *This is the Lamb of God*. With the concelebrants and the people he continues: *Lord, I am not worthy*.

199. Then the celebrant, facing the altar, says quietly: *May the body of Christ bring me to everlasting life*, and reverently consumes the body of Christ. The concelebrants do likewise. After them the deacon receives the body of Christ from the celebrant.

200. The blood of the Lord may be taken by drinking from the chalice, through a tube, with a spoon, or even by intinction.

201. If communion is received directly from the chalice:

a) The celebrant takes the chalice and says quietly: *May the blood of Christ bring me to everlasting life*. He drinks a little and hands the chalice to the deacon or a concelebrant. Then he gives communion to the faithful or returns to the chair. The concelebrants approach the altar one by one or in pairs if two chalices are used. They drink the blood of Christ and return to their seats. The deacon or the concelebrant wipes the chalice with a purificator after each one communicates.

b) Alternatively, the celebrant stands at the middle of the altar and drinks the blood of Christ as usual, but the concelebrants remain at their places.

In this case they drink from the chalice either offered them by the deacon or one of the concelebrants or handed from one to the other. The chalice should always be wiped, either by the one who drinks from it or by the one who is presenting it. After communicating, the concelebrants return to their seats.

202. If communion is received through a tube, the celebrant takes the tube and says quietly: *May the blood of Christ bring me to everlasting life.* He drinks a little and immediately cleans the tube with some water from a container on the altar. Then he places the tube on a paten. The deacon or one of the concelebrants places the chalice in the middle of the altar or at the right side on another corporal. A container of water for washing the tubes is placed near the chalice, with a paten to hold them afterwards.

The concelebrants come forward one by one, take a tube and drink a little. Then they clean the tube with water and place it on the paten.

The concelebrants come forward one by one, take a tube and drink a little. They then clean the tube with water and place it on the paten.

203. If the communion is received from a spoon, this is done in the same way as with a tube. After communion the spoon is placed in a container of water. The acolyte carries this to the side table where he washes and dries the spoons.

204. The deacon receives communion last. Then the deacon drinks what remains in the chalice and takes it to the side table. There he or the acolyte washes and dries the chalice and covers it in the usual way.

205. Concelebrants may also receive from the chalice at the altar immediately after they receive the body of Christ.

In this case, the celebrant communicates under both kinds as he would when celebrating Mass alone, but he follows the same rite as the concelebrant for communion from the chalice.

After the celebrant's communion, the chalice is placed on another corporal at the right side of the altar. The concelebrants come forward one by one, genuflect, and receive the body of the Lord. Then they go to the side of the altar and drink the blood of the Lord following the same rite as the celebrant.

The communion of the deacon and the washing of the chalice take place as already described.

206. If the communion is received by intinction, the celebrant receives the body and blood of the Lord in the usual way, making sure that enough remains in the chalice for the other concelebrants. The deacon or one of the concelebrants arranges the paten with the hosts and the chalice in the centre of the altar or at the right side on another corporal. Each concelebrant approaches the altar, genuflects, and takes a particle; he dips it into the chalice and, holding a paten under his chin, communicates. Afterwards he returns to his chair.

The deacon receives communion in the same way, but from one of the concelebrants. He says: *The body and blood of Christ*, to which the deacon replies: *Amen*. At the altar the deacon drinks all that remains in the chalice, then takes it to the side table. There he or the acolyte washes and dries the chalice and covers it in the usual way.

Concluding Rite

207. The concelebrants remain at their seats, and the celebrant concludes Mass in the usual way.

208. Before leaving, the concelebrants make the usual reverence to the altar. Ordinarily the celebrant kisses the altar.

III Mass Without a Congregation

Introduction

209. This section gives the norms for Mass celebrated by a priest with only one minister to assist him to make the responses.

210. In general this form of Mass follows the rite of Mass with a congregation. The minister takes the people's part when suitable.

211. Mass should not be celebrated without a minister except in serious necessity. In this case the greetings and the blessing at the end of Mass are omitted.

212. The chalice is prepared before Mass, either on a table near the altar or on the altar itself. The missal is placed on the left side of the altar.

Introductory Rites

213. After he reverences the altar, the priest makes the sign of the cross: *In the name of the Father*. He turns to the minister and gives

one of the forms of greeting. They remain standing at the foot of the altar for the penitential rite.

214. The priest goes up to the altar and kisses it. Then he goes to the missal at the left side of the altar and remains there until the end of the general intercessions.

215. He reads the entrance antiphon and says the *Kyrie* and *Gloria*, as the rubrics indicate.

216. Then, with his hands joined, the priest says: *Let us pray.* After a suitable pause, he extends his hands and says the opening prayer, at the end of which the minister responds: *Amen.*

Liturgy of the Word

217. After the opening prayer, the minister or the priest himself reads the first reading and psalm and, when it is to be said, the second reading and the alleluia verse or other chant.

218. The priest remains in the same place, bows, and says: *Almighty God, cleanse my heart.* He then reads the gospel, kissing the book at the end and saying quietly: *May the words of the gospel wipe away our sins.* The minister says the acclamation.

219. If the profession of faith is to be added, the priest says it with the minister.

220. The general intercessions may be said in this form of Mass. The priest gives the intentions, and the minister answers.

Liturgy of the Eucharist

221. The offertory antiphon is omitted, and the minister places the corporal, purificator, and chalice on the altar, unless they were there at the beginning of Mass.

222. The bread and wine are prepared as at Mass with a congregation, with the prayers given in the Order of Mass. After the bread and wine have been placed on the altar, the minister pours the water, and the priest washes his hands at the side of the altar.

223. The prayer over the gifts and the eucharistic prayer are said as described for Mass with a congregation.

224. The Lord's Prayer and the embolism, *Deliver us*, are said as at Mass with a congregation.

225. After the acclamation, *For the kingdom*, the priest says the prayer, *Lord Jesus Christ, you said*. He then adds *The peace of the Lord be with you always*, and the minister answers: *And also with you*. The priest may give the sign of peace to the minister.

226. While he says the *Agnus Dei* with the minister, the priest breaks the host over the paten. After the *Agnus Dei*, he places a particle in the chalice saying quietly: *May this mingling*.

227. After the commingling, the priest says the prayer, *Lord Jesus Christ, Son of the living God*, or *Lord Jesus Christ, with faith in your love and mercy*. Then he genuflects and takes a particle. If the minister is to communicate, the priest turns to him and, holding the host a little above the paten, says: *This is the Lamb of God*, adding once with the minister: *Lord, I am not worthy*. Facing the altar, the priest receives the body of Christ. If the minister is not going to communicate, the priest genuflects, takes the host and, facing the altar, says once: *Lord, I am not worthy*, and eats the body of Christ. The blood of Christ is received as described in the Order of Mass with a congregation.

228. Before giving communion to the minister, the priest says the communion antiphon.

229. The chalice is washed at the side of the altar and then may be carried by the minister to the side table or left on the altar.

230. After this the priest may observe a period of silence. Then he says the prayer after communion.

Concluding Rite
231. The concluding rite is carried out as at Mass with a congregation, but the dismissal is omitted.

IV General Rules for all Forms of Mass

Veneration of the Altar and Gospel Book
232. According to liturgical tradition, the altar and the gospel book are venerated with a kiss. But if this sign of reverence is not in harmony with the traditions or the culture of the region, the conference of bishops may substitute some other sign, after informing the Apostolic See.

Genuflections and Bows

233. Three genuflections are made during Mass: after the elevation of the host, after the elevation of the chalice, and before communion

If there is a tabernacle with the blessed sacrament in the sanctuary, a genuflection is made before and after Mass and whenever passing in front of the sacrament.

234. There are two kinds of bows, a bow of the head and a bow of the body:

a) A bow of the head is made when the three Divine Persons are named together and at the name of Jesus, Mary, and the saint in whose honour Mass is celebrated.

b) A bow of the body is made before the altar, if the blessed sacrament is not present; at the prayers, *Almighty God, cleanse*, and *Lord God, we ask you to receive*; in the profession of faith at the words, *by the power of the Holy Spirit*, in the Roman canon at the words, *Almighty God, we pray*. The same kind of bow is made by the deacon when he asks the blessing before the gospel. The priest, moreover, bows slightly when he says the words of the Lord at the consecration.

Incensation

235. The use of incense is optional in any form of Mass:

a) during the entrance procession;
b) at the beginning of Mass, to incense the altar;
c) at the procession and proclamation of the gospel;
d) at the offertory, to incense the offerings, altar, priest, and people;
e) at the elevation of the host and chalice after the consecration.

236. The priest puts some incense into the censer and blesses it silently, with the sign of the cross.

The altar is incensed in this manner:

a) If the altar is freestanding, the priest incenses it as he walks around it.

b) If the altar is attached to the wall, he incenses it while walking first to the right side, then to the left side.

If there is a cross on the altar or near it, the priest incenses it before he incenses the altar. If the cross is behind the altar, the priest incenses it when he passes in front of it.

Purifications

237. If a fragment of the host adheres to his fingers, especially after the breaking of the bread or the communion of the people, the priest cleanses his fingers over the paten and, if necessary, washes them. He also gathers any fragments which may fall outside the paten.

238. The vessels are washed by the priest or deacon or acolyte after the communion or after Mass, if possible at the side table. The chalice is washed with wine and water, or with water only, which is then drunk by the person who has done the washing. The paten is ordinarily wiped with the purificator.

239. If a host or any particle should fall, it is to be picked up reverently. If any of the precious blood spills, the area should be washed and the water poured into the sacrarium.

Communion under Both Kinds

240. The sign of communion is more complete when given under both kinds, since in that form the sign of the eucharistic meal appears more clearly. The intention of Christ that the new and eternal covenant be ratified in his blood is better expressed, as is the relation of the eucharistic banquet to the heavenly banquet.[63]

241. Priests should use the occasion to teach the faithful the Catholic doctrine on the form of communion, as affirmed by the Council of Trent. They should first be reminded that, according to Catholic faith, they receive the whole Christ and the genuine sacrament when they participate in the sacrament even under one kind and that they are not thus deprived of any grace necessary for salvation.[64]

They should also be taught that the Church may change the manner of celebrating and receiving the sacraments, provided their substance is safeguarded. In doing so, the Church judges when such changes will better meet the devotion or needs of different times and places.[65] At the same time the faithful should be urged to take part in the rite which brings out the sign of the eucharistic meal more fully.

---

[63] See EM 32.
[64] See Council of Trent, Session XXI, Decree on Eucharistic Communion, c. 1-3: Denzinger 929-32 (1725-9).
[65] Ibid., c. 2: Denzinger 931 (1728).

242. At the discretion of the Ordinary and after the necessary explanation, communion from the chalice is permitted for the following:[66]

1) adults at the Mass which follows their baptism; adults at the Mass in which they are confirmed; baptised persons who are being received into communion with the Church;

2) the bride and bridegroom at their wedding Mass;

3) deacons at their ordination Mass;

4) an abbess at the Mass in which she is blessed; virgins at the Mass of their consecration; professed religious, their parents and relatives, and members of their community at the Mass during which they make their first or perpetual vows or renew their vows;

5) those who are instituted into any ministry at the Mass of their institution; lay missionaries at the Mass in which they publicly receive their mission; others at the Mass in which they receive an ecclesiastical mission;

6) the sick person and all present when viaticum is administered at a Mass lawfully celebrated in the home;

7) the deacon and ministers who exercise their office at Mass;

8) when there is a concelebrated Mass:

a) all who exercise a genuine liturgical function in the concelebration and also all seminarians who are present;

b) in their churches or oratories, all members of institutes which profess the evangelical counsels and other societies whose members dedicate themselves to God by religious vows, offering, or promise, as well as all those who live in the houses of such institutes and societies;

9) priests who are present at large celebrations and are not able to celebrate or concelebrate;

10) all who make a retreat or spiritual exercises, at a Mass specially celebrated for the participating group; all who take part in a meeting of the pastoral body, at a Mass celebrated in common;

11) those listed in nos. 2 and 4, at Masses celebrating their jubilees;

12) godparents, parents, wife or husband, and lay catechists of a newly baptised adult at the Mass of initiation;

13) parents, relatives, and special benefactors who participate in the Mass of a newly ordained priest;

14) members of communities at the conventual or community Mass, in accord with no. 76.

[66] See EM 32.

243. Preparations for giving communion under both kinds:

a) If communion is received from the chalice with a tube, silver tubes are needed for the celebrant and each communicant. There should also be a container of water to wash the tubes and a paten on which to place them.

b) If communion is given with a spoon, only one spoon is necessary.

c) If communion is given by intinction, the host should not be too thin or too small, but a little thicker than usual so that it may be partly dipped in the precious blood and easily given to the communicant.

1   Communion under both kinds from the chalice

244. If there is a deacon or another priest or an acolyte:

a) The celebrant receives communion as usual, making sure enough remains in the chalice for the other communicants. He wipes the outside of the chalice with a purificator.

b) The priest gives the chalice and purificator to the minister and takes the paten or other vessel with the hosts. Then the priest and the minister of the chalice both go to a convenient place for the communion of the faithful.

c) The communicants approach, make a suitable reverence, and stand in front of the priest. He shows the host to the communicant and says: *The body of Christ.* The communicant answers: *Amen,* and receives the host from the priest.

d) The communicant then goes and stands in front of the minister, who says: *The blood of Christ.* The communicant answers: *Amen* and the minister holds out the chalice and purificator. The communicant may raise the chalice to his mouth with his own hands. He holds the purificator under his mouth with his left hand and drinks a little from the chalice, taking care not to spill it. Then he returns to his place. The minister wipes the outside of the chalice with the purificator.

e) The minister places the chalice on the altar after all who are receiving under both kinds have drunk from it. If there are others who do not receive communion under both kinds, the priest returns to the altar when he finishes giving communion to them. The priest or minister drinks whatever remains in the chalice, and it is washed in the usual way.

245. If there is no deacon, other priest, or acolyte:

a) The priest receives communion as usual, making sure enough remains in the chalice for the other communicants. He wipes the outside of the chalice with the purificator.

b) The priest then goes to a convenient place and distributes the body of Christ as usual to all who are receiving under both kinds. The communicants approach, make a suitable reverence, and stand in front of the priest. After receiving the body of Christ, they step back a little.

c) After all have received, the priest places the vessel on the altar and takes the chalice and purificator. The communicants again come forward and stand in front of the priest. He says: *The blood of Christ,* the communicant answers: *Amen,* and the priest holds out the chalice and purificator. The communicant holds the purificator under his mouth with his left hand, taking care that none of the precious blood is spilled, drinks a little from the chalice, and then returns to his place. The priest wipes the outside of the chalice with the purificator.

d) The priest places the chalice on the altar after all who are receiving under both kinds have drunk from it. If others receive communion under one kind only, he gives it to them and then returns to the altar. The priest drinks whatever remains in the chalice, and it is washed in the usual way.

2 Communion under both kinds by intinction

246.   If there is a deacon or another priest or an acolyte:

a) The celebrant hands him the chalice and purificator and takes the paten or other vessel with the hosts. The priest and the minister of the chalice both go to a convenient place for distributing communion.

b) The communicants approach, make a suitable reverence, and stand in front of the priest. Each holds the plate under his chin. The priest dips a particle into the chalice and, raising it, says: *The body and blood of Christ.* The communicant responds: *Amen,* receives communion from the priest, and returns to his place.

c) The communion of those who do not receive under both kinds and the rest of the rite take place as described above.

247.   If there is no deacon, other priest, or acolyte:

a) After drinking the blood of the Lord, the priest takes the ciborium or paten with the hosts between the index and middle fingers of his left hand and holds the chalice between the thumb and index finger of the same hand. Then he goes to a convenient place for distributing communion.

b) The communicants approach, make a suitable reverence, and stand in front of the priest. Each holds the plate under his chin while the priest takes a particle, dips it into the chalice, and holds it up, saying: *The body and blood of Christ*. The communicant responds: *Amen*, receives communion from the priest and returns to his place.

c) It is also permitted to place a small table covered with a cloth and corporal in an appropriate place. The priest places the chalice or the vessel with the hosts on the table in order to make the distribution of communion easier.

d) The communion of those who do not receive under both kinds and the rest of the rite takes place as described above.

3 Communion under both kinds from a tube

248. In this case the priest also uses a tube when receiving the blood of the Lord.

249. If there is a deacon or another priest or an acolyte:

a) For the communion of the body of the Lord, everything is done as described above, nos. 244b and 244c.

b) The communicant goes to the minister of the chalice and stands in front of him. The minister says: *The blood of Christ*, and the communicant responds: *Amen*. He receives the tube from the minister, places it in the chalice, and drinks a little. He then removes the tube, not spilling any drops, and places it in a container of water which is held by the minister next to the deacon. Then, to cleanse the tube, he drinks a little water from it and places it in a container held by the minister.

250. If there is no deacon, other priest, or acolyte, the celebrant offers the chalice to each communicant in the usual way (no. 245). The minister holds the container of water for cleansing the tube.

4 Communion under both kinds from a spoon

251. If a deacon or another priest or an acolyte assists, he holds the chalice in his left hand. Each communicant holds the plate under his chin while the deacon or priest gives him the blood of the Lord with the spoon, saying: *The blood of Christ*. The communicant should be careful not to touch the spoon with his lips or tongue.

252. If there is no deacon, other priest, or acolyte, the celebrant first gives the host to all who are receiving under both kinds and then gives them the blood of the Lord.

CHAPTER V

ARRANGEMENT AND DECORATION OF CHURCHES FOR THE EUCHARISTIC CELEBRATION

I   General Principles

253. For the celebration of the eucharist, the people of God is normally assembled in a church or, if there is none, in some other place worthy of this great mystery. Churches and such other places should be suitable for celebrating the eucharist and for active participation by the faithful. The buildings and requisites for worship, as signs and symbols of heavenly things, should be truly worthy and beautiful. [67]

254. At all times the Church needs the service of the arts and allows for popular and regional diversity of aesthetic expressions. [68] While preserving the art of former times, [69] the Church also tries to adapt it to new needs and to promote the art of each age. [70]

High artistic standards should be followed when commissioning artists and choosing works of art for the church. These works of art should nourish faith and piety and be in harmony with the meaning and purpose for which they are intended. [71]

255. It is desirable that churches be solemnly consecrated. The faithful should see the cathedral church and their own church as signs of the spiritual Church which their Christian vocation commissions them to build and extend.

256. Everyone involved in planning, constructing, and remodelling churches should consult the diocesan commission for liturgy and art. The local ordinary should use the counsel and help of this commission when giving norms, approving plans for new buildings, and judging important questions. [72]

II   Arrangement of a Church for the Sacred Assembly

257. The people of God assembled at Mass reflects an organic arrangement, expressed by the various ministries and actions for

[67] See SC 122-4; IOe 90; EM 24.   [68] See SC 123.
[69] See EM 24.   [70] See SC 123, 129; IOe 13c.
[71] See SC 123.   [72] See SC 126.

each part of the celebration. The general plan of the building should suggest in some way the image of the congregation. It should also allow the most advantageous arrangement of everything necessary for the celebration and help the carrying out of each function.

The faithful and the choir should have a place which will facilitate their active participation.[73]

The priest and his ministers have their place in the presbyterium or sanctuary. This part of the church shows their hierarchical position as each one presides over prayer, announces the word of God, or ministers at the altar.

While these elements must express a hierarchical arrangement and the difference of offices, they should at the same time form a complete and organic whole which clearly expresses the unity of the people of God. The beauty of the space and appointments should foster prayer and show the holiness of the mysteries which are celebrated.

III Sanctuary

258. The sanctuary should be marked off from the nave either by a higher floor level or by distinctive structure and decor. It should be large enough for all the ministers to carry out their functions conveniently.[74]

IV Altar

259. The altar, where the sacrifice of the cross is made present under sacramental signs, is also the table of the Lord. The people of God is called together to share in this table. Thus the altar is the centre of the thanksgiving accomplished in the eucharist.[75]

260. In a sacred place the eucharist should be celebrated on an altar, either fixed or movable. In other places, especially where the eucharist is not regularly celebrated, a suitable table may be used, but always with a cloth and corporal.

261. An altar is considered fixed if it is attached to the floor so that it cannot be moved. It is a movable altar if it can be transferred from place to place.

[73] See IOe 97-8.   [74] IOe 91.   [75] See EM 24.

262. The main altar should be freestanding so that the ministers can easily walk around it and Mass can be celebrated facing the people. It should be placed in a central position which draws the attention of the whole congregation.[76]

The main altar should ordinarily be a fixed, consecrated altar.

263. According to the traditional practice of the Church and the meaning of an altar, the table of a fixed altar should be of natural stone, but any solid, becoming, and skilfully constructed material may be used with the approval of the conference of bishops.

The support or base of the table may be of any solid, becoming material.

264. A movable altar may be constructed of any solid, becoming material which is suited to liturgical use, according to the traditions and culture of different regions.

265. Fixed altars are consecrated according to the rite as described in the liturgical books; movable altars may be simply blessed. It is not necessary to have a consecrated stone in a movable altar or on the table where the eucharist is celebrated outside a sacred place (see no. 260).

266. It is fitting to maintain the practice of enclosing relics in the altar or of placing them under the altar. These relics need not be those of martyrs, but there must be proof that they are authentic.

267. Minor altars should be few in number. In new churches they should be placed in chapels somewhat separated from the nave.[77]

V Adornment of the Altar

268. Out of respect for the celebration of the Lord's memorial and the banquet in which the body and blood of the Lord are given, there should be at least one cloth on the altar. Its shape, size, and adornment should be in keeping with the structure of the altar.

269. Candles are required during liturgical services to express devotion or the degree of festivity. They should be placed either on the altar or around it, in harmony with the construction of the altar and the sanctuary. The candles should not block the view of what is happening at the altar or what is placed on it.

[76] See IOe 91.   [77] IOe 93.

270. There should also be a cross, easily seen by the congregation, either on the altar or near it.

VI Celebrant's Chair and Other Seats

271. The chair of the celebrating priest should express his office of presiding over the assembly and of directing prayer. Thus the proper place for the chair is in the centre of the sanctuary facing the people, unless the structure or other circumstances are an obstacle, for example, if there is too great a distance between the priest and people. Every appearance of a throne should be avoided. The seats for the ministers should be located in the sanctuary in places convenient for their functions.[78]

VII The Lectern for Proclaiming God's Word

272. The dignity of the word of God requires the church to have a suitable place for announcing his message so that the attention of the people may be easily directed to that place during the liturgy of the word.[79]

Ordinarily the lectern or ambo should be a fixed pulpit and not a simple movable stand. Depending on the structure of the church, it should be so placed that the ministers may be easily seen and heard by the faithful.

The readings, responsorial psalm, and *Exsultet* are proclaimed from the lectern. It may be used also for the homily and general intercessions (prayer of the faithful).

It is less suitable for the commentator, cantor, or choirmaster to use the lectern.

VIII Places for the Faithful

273. The places for the faithful should be arranged so that the people may take full part in the celebration by seeing and by understanding everything. It is usually desirable that there be seats or benches for this purpose, but the custom of reserving seats for

[78] IOe 92.   [79] IOe 96.

132

private persons is reprobated.[80] Seats and benches should be arranged so that the faithful can easily take the positions required during various celebrations and so that they can readily go to communion.

The faithful must be able not only to see the priest and the other ministers but also, with the aid of amplification equipment, to hear them without difficulty.

IX Choir, Organ, and Other Musical Instruments

274. The choir forms part of the assembly of the faithful, but it has a special function and should be so located that its nature may be clearly apparent. The location should facilitate the exercise of the choir's function and the full sacramental participation of its members.[81]

275. The organ and other approved musical instruments should be located in a suitable place so that they may assist both choir and people when they are singing and may be heard properly when played alone.

X Reservation of the Eucharist

276. It is highly recommended that the holy eucharist be reserved in a chapel suitable for private adoration and prayer.[82] If this is impossible because of the structure of the church or local custom, it should be kept on an altar or other place in the church that is prominent and properly decorated.[83]

277. The eucharist is to be kept in a solid, unbreakable tabernacle, and ordinarily there should be only one tabernacle in a church.[84]

---

[80] See SC 32; IOe 98.
[81] See MS 23.
[82] See EM 53; Roman Ritual, *Rite of Holy Communion and Worship of the Eucharist outside Mass*, ed. typ. (1973), 9.
[83] See EM 54; IOe 95.
[84] See EM 52; IOe 95; Congregation for the Sacraments, instruction *Nullo umquam tempore*, 28 May 1938, 4: AAS 30 (1938) 119-200; Roman Ritual, *Rite of Holy Communion and Worship of the Eucharist outside Mass*, ed. typ. (1973), 9.

XI   Images for the Veneration of the Faithful

278.   In accord with ancient traditions, images of Christ, Mary, and the saints are venerated in churches. They should, however, be placed so as not to distract the faithful from the actual celebration.[85] They should not be too numerous, there should not be more than one image of the same saint, and the correct order of saints should be observed. In general, the piety of the entire community should be considered in the decoration and arrangement of the church as regards the images in it.

XII   General Plan of the Church

279.   Church decor should be noble and simple rather than sumptuous. It should reflect truth and authenticity so as to instruct the faithful and enhance the dignity of the sacred place.

280.   The plan of the church and its surroundings should be contemporary. It should meet the needs for the celebration of sacred services and also the usual needs in places where people gather together.

CHAPTER VI

REQUISITES FOR CELEBRATING MASS

I   Bread and Wine

281.   Following the example of Christ, the Church has always used bread and wine with water to celebrate the Lord's Supper.

282.   According to the tradition of the Church, the bread must be made from wheat; according to the tradition of the Latin Church, it must be unleavened.

283.   The nature of the sign demands that the material for the eucharistic celebration appear as actual food. The eucharistic bread,

[85] See SC 125.

even though unleavened and traditional in form, should therefore be made in such a way that the priest can break it and distribute the parts to at least some of the faithful. When the number of communicants is large or other pastoral needs require it, small hosts may be used. The gesture of the breaking of the bread, as the eucharist was called in apostolic times, will more clearly show the eucharist as a sign of unity and charity, since the one bread is being distributed among the members of one family.

284. The wine for the eucharist must be natural and pure, from the fruit of the vine (see Luke 22:18). It should not be mixed with any foreign substance.

285. Care must be taken that the elements be kept in good condition, so that the wine does not sour or the bread spoil or become too hard to be easily broken.

286. If the priest notices after the consecration or when he receives communion that water was poured into the chalice instead of wine, he pours the water into another container, then pours wine with water into the chalice and consecrates it. He says only the part of the narrative for the consecration of the chalice, without consecrating bread again.

II Sacred Furnishings in General

287. As in the case of architecture, the Church admits the artistic style of every region for sacred furnishings and accepts adaptations in keeping with the genius and traditions of each people, if they fit the purpose for which the sacred furnishings are intended.[86]

The noble simplicity which reflects authentic art should be a major factor in selecting furnishings.

288. Besides the traditional materials for sacred furnishings, others may be chosen if they are durable, of good quality according to contemporary taste, and well adapted to sacred use. The conference of bishops will be the judge in this matter.

III Sacred Vessels

289. Sacred vessels are necessary for the celebration of Mass, and

[86] See SC 128; EM 24.

among these the chalice and paten, because of the function they serve, are particularly important.

290. Vessels should be made from solid materials which are considered suitable in each region. The conference of bishops will be the judge in this matter. Materials which do not break or deteriorate easily are to be given preference.

291. Chalices and other vessels which are intended to hold the blood of the Lord should have a cup of non-absorbent material. The base may be of any other solid and worthy material.

292. Vessels which are intended to hold hosts, such as a paten, ciborium, pyx, monstrance, etc., may be made of other materials which are locally considered valuable and appropriate for sacred use, such as ebony or hard woods.

293. It is suitable to use one large paten for the consecration of bread for the priest, ministers, and faithful.

294. Vessels made from metal should ordinarily be gilded on the inside if the metal is one that oxidises; gilding is not necessary, if the metal is precious and does not oxidise.

295. The artist may give a form to the vessels which is in keeping with the culture of the area and their purpose in the liturgy.

296. The rites in the liturgical books should be used to bless or consecrate sacred vessels.

IV Vestments

297. In the Body of Christ not all members have the same function, and this diversity of ministries is shown externally in worship by the diversity of vestments. At the same time, the vestments should contribute to the appearance of the rite itself.

298. The vestment common to all ministers is the alb, tied at the waist with a cincture, unless it is made to fit without a cincture. If the alb does not completely cover the ordinary clothing at the neck, an amice should be worn under it. A surplice may not replace the alb when a chasuble or dalmatic is worn, nor when a stole is used instead of a chasuble or dalmatic.

299. The chasuble, worn over the alb and stole, is the proper

vestment of the priest who celebrates Mass or other services connected with Mass, unless otherwise indicated.

300. The dalmatic, worn over the alb and stole, is the vestment proper to the deacon.

301. Ministers below the order of deacon may wear the alb or other vestment that is lawfully approved in the respective region.

302. The priest wears the stole around his neck and hanging down in front. The deacon wears it over his left shoulder, crossed and fastened at the right side.

303. The priest wears a cope in processions and other services, as indicated in the rubrics of each rite.

304. The conference of bishops may determine adaptations in the form of vestments which correspond to the needs and usages of their regions and propose these to the Apostolic See.[87]

305. In addition to traditional materials, vestments may be made from natural fabrics of the region or artificial fabrics in keeping with the dignity of the sacred action and the person wearing them. The conference of bishops will be the judge in this matter.[88]

306. The beauty of a vestment should derive from its material and form rather than from its ornamentation. Ornamentation should include only symbols, images, or pictures suitable for liturgical use, and anything unbecoming should be avoided.

307. Colours in vestments give an effective expression to the celebration of the mysteries of the faith and, in the course of the year, a sense of progress in the Christian life.

308. The traditional colours should be retained, namely:

a) White is used in the offices and Masses of the Easter and Christmas seasons; on feasts and commemorations of the Lord, other than of his passion; on feasts and memorials of Mary, the angels, saints who were not martyrs, All Saints (1 November), John the Baptist (24 June), John the Evangelist (27 December), the Chair of Peter (22 February), and the Conversion of Paul (25 January).

b) Red is used on Passion Sunday (Palm Sunday) and Good Friday, Pentecost, celebrations of the passion, birthday feasts of the apostles and evangelists, and feasts of martyrs.

[87] See SC 128.   [88] See SC 128.

c) Green is used in the offices and Masses of ordinary time.

d) Violet is used in Lent and Advent. It may also be used in offices and Masses for the dead.

e) Black may be used in Masses for the dead.

f) Rose may be used on *Gaudete* Sunday (Third Sunday of Advent) and *Laetare* Sunday (Fourth Sunday of Lent).

The conference of bishops may determine adaptations suited to the needs and customs of the people and propose these to the Apostolic See.

309. On special occasions more noble vestments may be used, even if not the colour of the day.

310. Ritual Masses are celebrated in the proper colour, or in white, or in a festive colour. Masses for Various Needs are celebrated in the colour of the day or the season, or in purple if the theme is penitential, e.g. nos. 23, 28, 40. Votive Masses are celebrated in the colour suited to the Mass itself or in the colour of the day or season.

V Other Requisites for Church Use

311. Besides vessels and vestments for which some special material is prescribed, any other furnishing which has a liturgical use or is in any other way used in the church should be worthy and suited to its purpose.

312. Even in matters of small importance, every effort should be made to preserve an artistic appearance and to combine cleanliness, simplicity, and quality.

CHAPTER VII

CHOICE OF MASS TEXTS

313. The pastoral effectiveness of a celebration depends in grea⁺ measure on choosing readings, prayers, and songs which correspond to the needs, spiritual preparation, and attitude of the participants. This will be achieved by an intelligent use of the options described below.

In planning the celebration, the priest should consider the spiritual good of the assembly rather than his own desires. The choice of texts is to be made in consultation with the ministers and others who have a function in the celebration, including the faithful, for the parts which belong to them.

Since the variety of options is provided, it is necessary for the deacon, readers, cantors, commentator, and choir to know before-hand the texts for which they are responsible, so that nothing shall mar the celebration. Careful planning and execution will help dispose the people to take their part in the eucharist.

I Choice of Mass

314. On solemnities the priest is bound to follow the calendar of the church where he is celebrating.

315. On Sundays, weekdays of Advent, the Christmas season, Lent, and the Easter season, feasts, and obligatory memorials:

a) if Mass is celebrated with a congregation, the priest should follow the calendar of the church where he is celebrating;

b) if Mass is celebrated without a congregation, the priest may choose the calendar of the church or the calendar he ordinarily follows.

316. On optional memorials:

a) On weekdays of Advent from 17 December to 24 December, during the octave of Christmas, and on the weekdays of Lent, except Ash Wednesday and Holy Week, the priest celebrates the Mass of the day, but he may take the opening prayer from a memorial listed in the general calendar for that day, except on Ash Wednesday and in Holy Week.

b) On the weekdays of Advent before 17 December and the week-days of the Christmas season from 2 January onwards and weekdays of the Easter season, the priest may choose the weekday Mass, the Mass of the saint or of one of the saints whose memorial is observed, or the Mass of a saint listed in the martyrology that day.

c) On the weekdays of ordinary time, the priest may choose the weekday Mass, the Mass of an optional memorial, the Mass of a saint listed in the martyrology for that day, a Mass for various needs and occasions, or a votive Mass.

If he celebrates with a congregation, the priest should first consider the spiritual good of the faithful and avoid imposing his own partic-ular tastes. In particular, he will not omit the readings in the weekday lectionary too frequently or without sufficient reason, since the Church desires that a richer portion of God's word be provided for the people.[89]

For similar reasons the Mass for the dead should be used sparingly. Every Mass is offered for both the living and the dead, and there is a remembrance of the dead in each eucharistic prayer.

Where the optional memorials of Mary or the saints are a part of popular piety, at least one Mass of the memorial should be celebrated.

When there is a choice between a memorial in the general calendar and one in a diocesan or religious calendar, the traditional preference should be given, all things being equal, to the memorial in the particular calendar.

II Choice of Individual Texts

317. In the choice of texts of the several parts of Mass, the following rules are to be observed. They apply to Masses of the season and of the saints.

Readings

318. Sundays and certain feasts have three readings, i.e., from the Old Testament, the writings of the Apostles, and the gospel. These readings teach the Christian people God's plan for salvation.

It is strongly recommended that the three readings be used, but for pastoral reasons and by decree of the conference of bishops the use of two readings is allowed in some places. In such a case, the choice between the first two readings should be based on the norms in the lectionary and the desire to lead the people to a deeper knowledge of scripture and never simply because of the brevity or simplicity of the reading.

319. In the weekday lectionary, readings are provided for each day of the year. Unless a solemnity or feast occurs, these readings are to be used regularly on the days to which they are assigned.

The continuous reading during the week, however, is sometimes interrupted by the occurrence of a feast or particular celebration. In this case the priest should consider in advance the entire week's readings and he may either combine readings so that none will be

[89] See SC 51.

omitted or decide which readings are to be preferred.

In Masses for special groups, the priest may choose readings suitable for the group, provided they are taken from the texts of an approved lectionary.

320. The lectionary has a special selection of readings from scriptures for Masses in which certain sacraments or sacramentals are celebrated and also for particular circumstances.

These selections provide the people with more suitable readings of God's word and lead them to a fuller understanding of the mystery in which they take part. In this way they are formed in a deeper love of his word.

Pastoral considerations and the permission to choose readings should determine which texts are proclaimed to the assembly.

Prayers

321. The various prefaces of the Roman Missal develop the theme of thanksgiving in the eucharistic prayer and bring out more clearly the different aspects of the mystery of salvation.

322. The choice of eucharistic prayer may follow these norms:

a) Eucharistic Prayer I, the Roman canon, may always be used. It is more appropriate on days when there is a special form of *In union with the whole Church* or in Masses which have a special form of *Father, accept this offering.* It is also suitable on the feasts of the apostles and saints mentioned in it and on Sundays, unless for pastoral considerations another eucharistic prayer is preferred.

b) Eucharistic Prayer II has qualities which make it suitable for weekdays and special circumstances.

Although it has its own preface, it may also be used with other prefaces, especially those which present the mystery of salvation succinctly, such as the Sunday preface or the common preface.

When Mass is celebrated for a dead person, the special formula may be inserted in the place indicated.

c) Eucharistic Prayer III may be said with any preface. It is particularly suited for Sundays and feasts.

The special formula for a dead person may be used with this prayer in the place indicated

d) Eucharistic Prayer IV has a fixed preface and provides a fuller synthesis of the history of salvation. It may be used when a Mass has no preface of its own.

Because of its structure no special formula for the dead may be inserted in this prayer.

e) A eucharistic prayer which has its own preface may be used with that preface even when there is a proper seasonal preface.

323.   In any Mass the prayers belonging to that Mass are used unless otherwise noted.

In Masses on a memorial, the opening prayer or collect may be from the Mass itself or from the common; the prayers over the gifts and after communion, unless they are proper, may be taken either from the common or from the weekdays of the current season.

On weekdays of ordinary time, the prayers may be taken from the preceding Sunday, from another Sunday of ordinary time, or from the prayers for various needs and occasions given in the missal. It is always permissible to use only the opening prayer from these Masses.

This makes available a wider selection of texts and affords an opportunity to restate the themes of prayer for the liturgical assembly. It also permits adaptation of the prayer to the needs of the people, the Church, and the world. During the more important seasons of the year, however, this adaptation has already been made in the prayers appointed for weekdays in the missal.

Song

324.   In choosing the chants between the readings, as well as the songs for the entrance, offertory, and communion processions, the guidelines given elsewhere are to be observed.

Special Permissions

325.   In addition to these permissions to choose more suitable texts, the conferences of bishops have the right to make further adaptations of readings for particular circumstances, provided these are taken from an approved lectionary.

CHAPTER VIII

MASS AND PRAYERS FOR VARIOUS OCCASIONS, MASSES FOR THE DEAD

I Masses and Prayers for Various Occasions

326.   For well disposed Christians the liturgy of the sacraments and sacramentals sanctifies almost every event in their lives through God's grace which flows from the paschal mystery.[90] The eucharist is the sacrament of sacraments, and so the missal supplies formularies which may be used in the various circumstances of Christian life, for the needs of the whole world, and for the needs of the Church, both local and universal.

327.   Masses for various occasions should be used with moderation and only when the occasion demands, since the permission to choose readings and prayers allows adequate variety.

328.   In Masses for various occasions, the weekday readings and the chants between them may be used, if these are in harmony with the celebration and no other rule prevails.

329.   There are three kinds of Masses for various occasions:
   a) ritual Masses, which are related to the celebration of certain sacraments or sacramentals;
   b) Masses for various needs, which occur either occasionally or at fixed times;
   c) votive Masses of the mysteries of the Lord or in honour of Mary or of the saints or of all saints, which may be freely chosen in accord with the piety of the faithful.

330.   Ritual Masses are prohibited on the Sundays of Advent, Lent, and the Easter season, on solemnities, weekdays within the Easter octave, on the feast of All Souls, on Ash Wednesday, and in Holy Week. They are also governed by the norms in the ritual books or in the Masses themselves.

331.   The competent authority may choose Masses, from the selection of Masses for various needs, for those times of prayer in the course of the year which are set aside by the conference of bishops.

[90]   See SC 61.

INSTRUCTIONS ON THE REVISED ROMAN RITES

332. When a serious need or pastoral advantage is present, at the direction of the local ordinary or with his permission, an appropriate Mass may be celebrated on any day except solemnities, the Sundays of Advent, Lent and the Easter season, weekdays within the Easter octave, on the feast of All Souls, Ash Wednesday, and Holy Week.

333. On days where there is an obligatory memorial, or the weekdays of Advent up to 16 December, the weekdays of the Christmas season from 2 January onwards, and the weekdays of the Easter season outside the Easter octave, Masses for various needs and Votive Masses are prohibited. However, when some genuine need or pastoral advantage requires it, an appropriate Mass may be used in a celebration with a congregation on obligatory memorials or the weekdays of Advent and the Christmas and Easter seasons when votive Masses are prohibited. The decision is left to the discretion of the rector of the church or the celebrant.

334. On weekdays of ordinary time when there is an optional memorial or the weekday office, any Mass or any prayer for various occasions may be used, except ritual Masses.

II Masses for the Dead

335. The Church offers the paschal sacrifice for the dead so that, through the fellowship of all Christ's members, some obtain spiritual help for others, some obtain the consolation of hope.

336. The funeral Mass has first place among the Masses for the dead and may be celebrated on any day except solemnities which are holydays of obligation, Thursday of Holy Week, the Easter Triduum, and the Sundays of Advent, Lent, and the Easter season.

337. Mass for the dead may also be celebrated on days within the octave of Christmas, days on which there is an obligatory memorial, and weekdays other than Ash Wednesday and Holy Week, in these cases: on learning of a death, on the occasion of final burial, and on the first anniversary.

Other Masses for the dead or daily Masses may be celebrated on optional memorials or on ordinary weekdays of the year, provided the Masses are actually applied for the dead.

338. At the funeral Mass there should ordinarily be a short homily

but never a eulogy. The homily is also encouraged at other Masses for the dead celebrated with a congregation.

339.   All the faithful, and especially the family, should be urged to receive communion at a Mass for a deceased person.

340.   When the funeral Mass is directly connected with the funeral service, the concluding rite (after the prayer after communion) is omitted, and the final commendation or farewell takes place. This rite is celebrated only when the body of the dead person is present.

341.   In planning and selecting the variable parts (e.g., prayers, readings, general intercessions) of the Mass for the dead, especially the funeral Mass, consideration should be given to pastoral circumstances affecting the dead person, his family, and the congregation.

On the occasion of funerals, priests, as ministers of Christ's gospel for all men, should be especially aware of their responsibility to those present, whether Catholic or non-Catholic, who never or almost never take part in the eucharist or who seem to have lost their faith.

HOLY COMMUNION AND THE WORSHIP OF THE EUCHARIST OUTSIDE MASS*: INTRODUCTION

Structure

* Promulgated by Decree dated 21 June 1973.

I The Relationship Between Eucharistic Worship Outside Mass and the Eucharistic Celebration

1. The celebration of the eucharist is the centre of the entire Christian life, both for the Church universal and for the local congregation of the Church. 'The other sacraments, all the ministries of the Church, and the works of the apostolate are united with the eucharist and are directed toward it. For the holy eucharist contains the entire spiritual treasure of the Church, that is, Christ himself, our passover and living bread. Through his flesh, made living and life-giving by the Holy Spirit, he offers life to men, who are thus invited and led to offer themselves, their work, and all creation together with him.'[1]

2. 'The celebration of the eucharist in the sacrifice of the Mass,' moreover, 'is truly the origin and the goal of the worship which is shown to the eucharist outside Mass'.[2] Christ the Lord 'is offered in the sacrifice of the Mass when he becomes present sacramentally as the spiritual food of the faithful under the appearance of bread and wine'. And, 'once the sacrifice is offered and while the eucharist is reserved in churches and oratories, he is truly Emmanuel, "God with us". He is in our midst day and night; full of grace and truth, he dwells among us.'[3]

3. No one therefore may doubt 'that all the faithful show this holy sacrament the veneration and adoration which is due to God himself, as has always been customary in the Catholic Church. Nor is the sacrament to be less the object of adoration because it was instituted by Christ the Lord to be received as food.'[4]

4. In order to direct and to encourage devotion to the sacrament of the eucharist correctly, the eucharistic mystery must be considered in all its fullness, both in the celebration of Mass and in the worship of the sacrament which is reserved after Mass to extend the grace of the sacrifice.[5]

---

[1] PO 5.   [2] EM 3e.
[3] EM 36; Paul VI, encyclical *Mysterium fidei*, near the end: *AAS* 57 (1965) 771.
[4] EM 3f.   [5] EM 3g.

II The Purpose of Eucharistic Reservation

5. The primary and original reason for reservation of the eucharist outside Mass is the administration of viaticum. The secondary reasons are the giving of communion and the adoration of our Lord Jesus Christ who is present in the sacrament. The reservation of the sacrament for the sick led to the praiseworthy practice of adoring this heavenly food in the churches. This cult of adoration rests upon an authentic and solid basis, especially because faith in the real presence of the Lord leads naturally to external, public expression of that faith.[6]

6. In the celebration of Mass the chief ways in which Christ is present in his Church gradually become clear. First he is present in the very assembly of the faithful, gathered together in his name; next he is present in his word, when the Scriptures are read in the Church and explained; then in the person of the minister; finally and above all, in the eucharistic sacrament. In a way that is completely unique the whole and entire Christ, God and man, is substantially and permanently present in the sacrament. This presence of Christ under the appearance of bread and wine 'is called real, not to exclude other kinds of presence as if they were not real, but because it is real *par excellence*'.[7]

Therefore, to express the sign of the eucharist, it is more in harmony with the nature of the celebration that, at the altar where Mass is celebrated, there should if possible be no reservation of the sacrament in the tabernacle from the beginning of Mass. The eucharistic presence of Christ is the fruit of the consecration and should appear to be such.[8]

7. The consecrated hosts are to be frequently renewed and reserved in a ciborium or other vessel, in a number sufficient for the communion of the sick and others outside Mass.[9]

8. Pastors should see that churches and public oratories where, according to law, the holy eucharist is reserved, are open every day at least for some hours, at a convenient time, so that the faithful may easily pray in the presence of the blessed sacrament.[10]

---

[6] EM 49.
[7] Paul VI, encyclical *Mysterium fidei*: *AAS* 57 (1965) 764; see EM 55.
[8] See EM 568-9.
[9] See Roman Missal, General Instruction, nos. 285 and 292.
[10] See EM 51.

III The Place of Eucharistic Reservation

9. The place for the reservation of the eucharist should be truly preeminent. It is highly recommended that the place be suitable also for private adoration and prayer so that the faithful may easily, fruitfully, and constantly honour the Lord, present in the sacrament, through personal worship.

This will be achieved more easily if the chapel is separate from the body of the church, especially in churches where marriages and funerals are celebrated frequently and churches which are much visited by pilgrims or because of their artistic and historical treasures.

10. The holy eucharist is to be reserved in a solid tabernacle. It must be opaque and unbreakable. Ordinarily there should be only one tabernacle in a church; this may be placed on an altar or, at the discretion of the local Ordinary, in some other noble and properly ornamented part of the church other than an altar.[11]

The key to the tabernacle where the eucharist is reserved must be kept carefully by the priest in charge of the church or oratory or by a special minister who has received the faculty to give communion.

11. The presence of the eucharist in the tabernacle is to be shown by a veil or in another suitable way determined by the competent authority.

According to traditional usage, an oil lamp or lamp with a wax candle is to burn constantly near the tabernacle as a sign of the honour which is shown to the Lord.[12]

IV The Competence of Episcopal Conferences

12. It is for episcopal conferences, in the preparation of particular rituals in accord with the Constitution on the Liturgy (no. 63b), to accommodate this title of the Roman Ritual to the needs of individual regions so that, their actions having been confirmed by the Apostolic See, the ritual may be followed in the respective regions.

In this matter it will be for the conferences:

a) to consider carefully and prudently what elements, if any, of popular traditions may be retained or introduced, provided they can be harmonised with the spirit of the liturgy, and then to propose to

[11] See EM 52-3.   [12] See EM 57.

the Apostolic See the adaptations they judge necessary or useful; these may be introduced with the consent of the Apostolic See;

b) to prepare translations of texts which are truly accommodated to the character of various languages and the mentality of various cultures; they may add texts, especially for singing, with appropriate melodies.

Liturgical texts, which are used in respect of a man, may be used with a change of gender for a woman also. And in either case the singular may be changed into the plural.

CHAPTER I
HOLY COMMUNION OUTSIDE MASS

Introduction

I The Relationship Between Communion Outside Mass and the Sacrifice

13. Sacramental communion received during Mass is the more perfect participation in the eucharistic celebration. The eucharistic sign is expressed more clearly when the faithful receive the body of the Lord from the same sacrifice after the communion of the priest.[1] Therefore, recently baked bread, for the communion of the faithful, should ordinarily be consecrated in every eucharistic celebration.

14. The faithful should be encouraged to receive communion during the eucharistic celebration itself.

Priests, however, are not to refuse to give communion to the faithful who ask for it even outside Mass.[2]

In fact it is proper that those who are prevented from being present at the community's celebration should be refreshed with the eucharist. In this way they may realise that they are united not only with the Lord's sacrifice but also with the community itself and are supported by the love of their brothers and sisters.

Pastors should see that an opportunity to receive the eucharist is

---

[1] See SC 55.   [2] See EM 33a.

given to the sick and aged, even though not gravely sick or in imminent danger of death, frequently and, if possible, daily, especially during the Easter season. It is lawful to minister communion under the appearance of wine to those who cannot receive the consecrated bread.[3]

15. The faithful should be instructed carefully that, even when they receive communion outside Mass, they are closely united with the sacrifice which perpetuates the sacrifice of the cross. They are sharers in the sacred banquet in which 'by communion in the body and blood of the Lord the people of God shares in the blessings of the paschal sacrifice, renews the new covenant once made by God with men in the blood of Christ, and by faith and hope prefigures and anticipates the eschatological banquet in the kingdom of the Father, proclaiming the death of the Lord until he comes.'[4]

II The Time of Communion Outside Mass

16. Communion may be given outside Mass on any day and at any hour. It is proper, however, to determine the hours for giving communion, with a view to the convenience of the faithful, so that the celebration may take place in a fuller form and with greater spiritual benefit.

Nevertheless:

a) on Holy Thursday, communion may be given only during Mass; communion may be brought to the sick at any hour of the day;

b) on Good Friday communion may be given only during the celebration of the Passion of the Lord; communion may be brought to the sick who cannot participate in the celebration at any hour of the day;

c) on Holy Saturday communion may be given only as viaticum.[5]

III The Minister of Communion

17. It is, first of all, the office of the priest and the deacon to minister holy communion to the faithful who ask to receive it.[6] It is most fitting, therefore, that they give a suitable part of their time to

---

[3] See EM 40-1.   [4] EM 33a.
[5] See Roman Missal, typical edition 1970; *Missa vespertina in Cena Domini*, 243; *Celebratio Passionis Domini*, 250, no. 3; *Sabbato sancto*, 265.

this ministry of their order, depending on the needs of the faithful. It is the office of an acolyte who has been properly instituted to give communion as a special minister when the priest and deacon are absent or impeded by sickness, old age, or pastoral ministry or when the number of the faithful at the holy table is so great that the Mass or other service may be unreasonably protracted.[7]

The local Ordinary may give other special ministers the faculty to give communion whenever it seems necessary for the pastoral benefit of the faithful and a priest, deacon, or acolyte is not available.[8]

IV The Place of Communion Outside Mass

18. The place where communion outside Mass is ordinarily given is a church or oratory in which the eucharist is regularly celebrated or reserved or a church, oratory, or other place where the local community regularly gathers for the liturgical assembly on Sundays or other days. Communion may be given, however, in other places, including private homes, when it is a question of the sick, prisoners, or others who cannot leave the place without danger or serious difficulty.

V Regulations for Giving Communion

19. When communion is given in a church or oratory, a corporal is to be placed on the altar, which is already covered with a cloth.[9] A communion plate is to be used.

When communion is given in other places, a suitable table is to be prepared and covered with a cloth; candles are also to be provided.

20. The minister of communion, if he is a priest or deacon, is to be vested in an alb, or a surplice over a cassock, and a stole.

Other ministers should wear either the liturgical vesture which may be traditional in their region or the vestment which is appropriate for this ministry and has been approved by the Ordinary.

The eucharist for communion outside a church is to be carried in

---

6 See EM 31.
7 See Paul VI, apostolic letter *Ministeria quaedam*, 15 August 1972, no. VI: *AAS* 64 (1972) 532.
8 See IC 1, 1 and II.
9 See Roman Missal, *General Instruction*, no. 269.

On this account the Church prescribed 'that no one conscious of a pyx or other covered vessel; the vesture of the minister and the manner of carrying the eucharist should be appropriate and in accord with local circumstances.

21. In giving communion the custom of placing the particle of consecrated bread on the tongue of the communicant is to be maintained because it is based on tradition of several centuries.

Episcopal conferences, however, may decree, their actions having been confirmed by the Apostolic See, that communion may also be given in their territories by placing the consecrated bread in the hands of the faithful, provided there is no danger of irreverence or false opinions about the eucharist entering the minds of the faithful.[10]

The faithful should be instructed that Jesus Christ is Lord and Saviour and that, present in the sacrament, he must be given the same worship and adoration which is to be given to God.[11]

In either case, communion must be given by the competent minister, who shows the particle of consecrated bread to the communicant and gives it to him, saying, *The body of Christ*, to which the communicant replies, *Amen*.

In the case of communion under the appearance of wine, the regulations of the instruction *Sacramentali Communione* of 29 June, 1970, are to be followed exactly.[12]

22. Fragments which may remain after communion are to be reverently gathered and placed in a ciborium or in a vessel with water.

Likewise, if communion is given under the appearance of wine, the chalice or other vessel is to be washed with water. The water used for cleansing the vessels may be drunk or poured out in a suitable place.

VI Dispositions for Communion

23. The eucharist continuously makes present among men the paschal mystery of Christ. It is the source of every grace and of the forgiveness of sins. Nevertheless, those who intend to receive the body of the Lord must approach it with a pure conscience and proper dispositions of soul if they are to receive the effects of the paschal sacrament.

[10] See MD.   [11] See IC 4.   [12] See no. 6: *AAS* 62 (1970) 665-6.

mortal sin, even though he seems to be contrite, may go to the holy eucharist without previous sacramental confession.'[13] In urgent necessity and if no confessor is available, he should simply make an act of perfect contrition with the intention of confessing individually, at the proper time, the mortal sins which he cannot confess at present.

It is desirable that those, who receive communion daily or very often, go to the sacrament of penance at regular intervals, depending on their circumstances.

Besides this, the faithful should look upon the eucharist as an antidote which frees them from daily faults and keeps them from mortal sins; they should also understand the proper way to use the penitential parts of the liturgy, especially at Mass.[14]

24. Communicants are not to receive the sacrament unless they have fasted for one hour from solid food and beverages, with the exception of water.

The period of the eucharistic fast, that is, abstinence from food or alcoholic drink, is reduced to about a quarter of an hour for:

1) the sick who are living in hospitals or at home, even if they are not confined to bed;

2) the faithful of advanced age, even if not bedridden, whether they are confined to their homes because of old age or living in a nursing home;

3) sick priests, even if not bedridden, or elderly priests, whether they are to celebrate Mass or to receive communion;

4) persons who care for the sick or aged, and the family of the sick or aged, who wish to receive communion with them, when they cannot conveniently observe the fast of one hour.[15]

25. The union with Christ, to which the sacrament is directed, should be extended to the whole of Christian life. Thus the faithful, constantly reflecting upon the gift they have received, should carry on their daily work with thanksgiving, under the guidance of the Holy Spirit, and should bring forth fruits of rich charity.

So that they may continue more easily in the thanksgiving which is offered to God in an excellent manner through the Mass, it is recommended that each one who has been refreshed by communion should remain in prayer for a period of time.[16]

[13] See Council of Trent, Session XIII, Decree on the Eucharist, 7: Denz-.Schön. 1646-7; ibid., Session XIV Canones de sacramento Paenitentiae, 9: Denz-Schön. 1709; Congregation for the Doctrine of the Faith, Normae pastorales circa absolutionem sacramentalem generali modo impertiendam, 16 June 1972, introduction and no. VI: AAS 64 (1972) 510 and 512.
[14] See EM 35.   [15] See IC 3.   [16] See EM 38.

CHAPTER III

FORMS OF WORSHIP OF THE HOLY EUCHARIST

79. The eucharistic sacrifice is the source and culmination of the whole Christian life. Both private and public devotion towards the eucharist, therefore, including the devotion outside Mass, are strongly encouraged when celebrated according to the regulations of lawful authority.

In the arrangement of devotional services of this kind, the liturgical seasons should be taken into account. Devotions should be in harmony with the sacred liturgy in some sense, take their origin from the liturgy, and lead the people back to the liturgy.[1]

80. When the faithful honour Christ present in the sacrament, they should remember that this presence is derived from the sacrifice and is directed toward sacramental and spiritual communion.

The same piety which moves the faithful to eucharistic adoration attracts them to a deeper participation in the paschal mystery. It makes them respond gratefully to the gifts of Christ who by his humanity continues to pour divine life upon the members of his body. Living with Christ the Lord, they achieve a close familiarity with him and in his presence pour out their hearts for themselves and for those dear to them; they pray for peace and for the salvation of the world. Offering their entire lives with Christ to the Father in the Holy Spirit, they draw from this wondrous exchange an increase of faith, hope and love. Thus they nourish the proper disposition to celebrate the memorial of the Lord as devoutly as possible and to receive frequently the bread given to us by the Father.

The faithful should make every effort to worship Christ the Lord in the sacrament, depending upon the circumstances of their own life. Pastors should encourage them in this by example and word.[2]

81. Prayer before Christ the Lord sacramentally present extends the union with Christ which the faithful have reached in communion. It renews the covenant which in turn moves them to maintain in their lives what they have received by faith and by sacraments. They should try to lead their whole lives with the strength derived from the heavenly food, as they share in the death and resurrection of the

[1] See EM 58.
[2] See EM 50.

Lord. Everyone should be concerned with good deeds and with pleasing God so that he or she may imbue the world with the Christian spirit and be a witness of Christ in the midst of human society.[3]

EXPOSITION OF THE HOLY EUCHARIST

Introduction

I   Relationship Between Exposition and Mass

82.   Exposition of the holy eucharist, either in the ciborium or in the monstrance, is intended to acknowledge Christ's marvellous presence in the sacrament. Exposition invites us to the spiritual union with him that culminates in sacramental communion. Thus it fosters very well the worship which is due to Christ in spirit and in truth.

This kind of exposition must clearly express the cult of the blessed sacrament in its relationship to the Mass. The plan of the exposition should carefully avoid anything which might somehow obscure the principal desire of Christ in instituting the eucharist, namely, to be with us as food, medicine, and comfort.[4]

83.   During the exposition of the blessed sacrament, the celebration of Mass is prohibited in the body of the Church. In addition to the reasons given in no. 6. the celebration of the eucharistic mystery includes in a more perfect way the internal communion to which exposition seeks to lead the faithful.

If exposition of the blessed sacrament is extended for an entire day or over several days, it is to be interrupted during the celebration of Mass. Mass may be celebrated in a chapel distinct from the area of exposition if at least some members of the faithful remain in adoration.[5]

[3]   See EM 13.
[4]   See EM 60.
[5]   See EM 61.

II Regulations for Exposition

84. A single genuflection is made in the presence of the blessed sacrament, whether reserved in the tabernacle or exposed for public adoration.

85. For exposition of the blessed sacrament in the monstrance, four to six candles are lighted, as at Mass, and incense is used. For exposition of the blessed sacrament in the ciborium, at least two candles should be lighted, and incense may be used.

Lengthy Exposition

86. In churches where the eucharist is regularly reserved, it is recommended that solemn exposition of the blessed sacrament for an extended period of time should take place once a year, even though this period is not strictly continuous. In this way the local community may reflect more profoundly upon this mystery and adore Christ in the sacrament.

This kind of exposition, however, may take place, with the consent of the local Ordinary, only if suitable numbers of the faithful are expected to be present.[6]

87. For a grave and general necessity the local Ordinary may direct that a more extended period of supplication before the blessed sacrament exposed take place in churches where the faithful assemble in large numbers.[7]

88. If a period of uninterrupted exposition is not possible, because of too few worshippers, the blessed sacrament may be replaced in the tabernacle during the periods which have been scheduled and announced beforehand. This reposition may not take place more often than twice during the day, for example, about noon and at night.

The following form of simple reposition may be observed: the priest or deacon, vested in an alb, or a surplice over a cassock, and a stole, replaces the blessed sacrament in the tabernacle after a brief period of adoration and a prayer said with those present. The exposition of the blessed sacrament may take place in the same manner (at the scheduled time).[8]

[6] See EM 63.
[7] See EM 64.
[8] See EM 65.

Brief Period of Exposition

89.   Shorter expositions of the eucharist are to be arranged in such a way that the blessing with the eucharist is preceded by a suitable period for readings of the word of God, songs, prayers, and sufficient time for silent prayer.[9]

Exposition which is held exclusively for the giving of benediction is prohibited.

Adoration in Religious Communities

90.   According to the constitutions and regulations of their institute, some religious communities and other groups have the practice of perpetual eucharistic adoration or adoration over extended periods of time. It is strongly recommended that they pattern this holy practice in harmony with the spirit of the liturgy. Thus, when the whole community takes part in adoration before Christ the Lord, readings, songs, and religious silence may foster effectively the spiritual life of a community. This will promote among the members of the religious house the spirit of unity and brotherhood which the eucharist signifies and effects, and the cult of the sacrament may express a noble form of worship.

The form of adoration in which one or two members of the community take turns before the blessed sacrament is also to be maintained and is highly commended. In accordance with the life of the institute, as approved by the Church, the worshippers adore Christ the Lord in the sacrament and pray to him in the name of the whole community and of the Church.

III The Minister of Exposition

91.   The ordinary minister for exposition of the eucharist is a priest or deacon. At the end of the period of adoration, before the reposition, he blesses the people with the sacrament.

In the absence of a priest or deacon or if they are lawfully impeded, the following persons may publicly expose and later repose the holy eucharist for the adoration of the faithful:

a) an acolyte or special minister of communion;

b) a member of a religious community or of a lay association of men or women which is devoted to eucharistic adoration, upon

---

[9]   See EM 66.

appointment by the local Ordinary.

Such ministers may open the tabernacle and also, if suitable, place the ciborium on the altar or place the host in the monstrance. At the end of the period of adoration, they replace the blessed sacrament in the tabernacle. It is not lawful, however, for them to give the blessing with the sacrament.

92. The minister, if he is a priest or deacon, should vest in an alb or a surplice over a cassock, and a stole.

Other ministers should wear either the liturgical vestments which are usual in the region or the vesture which is suitable for this ministry and which has been approved by the Ordinary.

The priest or deacon should wear a white cope and humeral veil to give the blessing at the end of adoration, when the exposition takes place with the monstrance; in the case of exposition in the ciborium, the humeral veil should be worn.

RITE OF PENANCE* : INTRODUCTION

Structure

* Promulgated by Decree dated 2 December 1973.

INSTRUCTIONS ON THE REVISED ROMAN RITES
I The Mystery of Reconciliation in the History of Salvation

1. The Father has shown forth his mercy by reconciling the world to himself in Christ and by making peace for all things on earth and in heaven by the blood of Christ on the cross.[1] The Son of God made man lived among men in order to free them from the slavery of sin[2] and to call them out of darkness into his wonderful light.[3] He therefore began his work on earth by preaching repentance and saying: 'Turn away from sin and believe the good news' (Mark 1:15).

This invitation to repentance, which had often been sounded by the prophets, prepared the hearts of men for the coming of the Kingdom of God through the voice of John the Baptist who came 'preaching a baptism of repentance for the forgiveness of sins' (Mark 1:4).

Jesus, however, not only exhorted men to repentance so that they should abandon their sins and turn wholeheartedly to the Lord,[4] but he also welcomed sinners and reconciled them with the Father.[5] Moreover, by healing the sick he signified his power to forgive sin.[6] Finally, he himself died for our sins and rose again for our justification.[7] Therefore, on the night he was betrayed and began his saving passion,[8] he instituted the sacrifice of the new covenant in his blood for the forgiveness of sins.[9] After his resurrection he sent the Holy Spirit upon the apostles, empowering them to forgive or retain sins[10] and sending them forth to all peoples to preach repentance and the forgiveness of sins in his name.[11]

The Lord said to Peter, 'I will give you the keys of the kingdom of heaven, and whatever you bind on earth will be bound in heaven, and whatever you loose on earth will be loosed also in heaven' (Matthew 16:19). In obedience to this command, on the day of Pentecost Peter preached the forgiveness of sins by baptism: 'Repent and let every one of you be baptised in the name of Jesus Christ for the forgiveness of your sins' (Acts 2:38).[12] Since then the Church has never failed to call men from sin to conversion and by the celebration of penance to show the victory of Christ over sin.

2. This victory is first brought to light in baptism where our fallen nature is crucified with Christ so that the body of sin may be destroyed

---

[1] See 2 Corinthians 5:18ff; Colossians 1:20.
[2] See John 8:34-6.
[3] See 1 Peter 2:9.
[4] See Luke 15.
[5] Luke 5:20, 27-32; 7:48.
[6] See Matthew 9:2-8.
[7] See Romans 4:25.
[8] See *Roman Missal*, Eucharistic Prayer III.
[9] See Matthew 26:28.
[10] See John 20:19-23.
[11] See Luke 24:47.
[12] See Acts 3:19, 26; 17:30.

and we may no longer be slaves to sin, but rise with Christ and live for God.[13] For this reason the Church proclaims its faith in 'the one baptism for the forgiveness of sins'.

In the sacrifice of the Mass the passion of Christ is made present; his body given for us and his blood shed for the forgiveness of sins are offered to God again by the Church for the salvation of the world. In the eucharist Christ is present and is offered as 'the sacrifice which has made our peace'[14] with God and in order that 'we may be brought together in unity'[15] by his Holy Spirit.

Furthermore our Saviour Jesus Christ, when he gave to his apostles and their successors power to forgive sins, instituted in his Church the sacrament of penance. Thus the faithful who fall into sin after baptism may be reconciled with God and renewed in grace.[16] The Church 'possesses both water and tears: the water of baptism, the tears of penance'.[17]

II The Reconciliation of Penitents in the Church's Life

The Church is Holy but always in need of Purification

3.   Christ 'loved the Church and gave himself up for her to make her holy' (Ephesians 5:25-6), and he united the Church to himself as his bride.[18] He filled her with his divine gifts,[19] because she is his body and fullness, and through her he spreads truth and grace to all.

The members of the Church, however, are exposed to temptation and unfortunately often fall into sin. As a result, 'while Christ, "holy, innocent, and unstained" (Hebrews 7:26), did not know sin (2 Corinthians 5:21) but came only to atone for the sins of the people (see Hebrews 2:17), the Church, which includes within itself sinners and is at the same time holy and always in need of purification, constantly pursues repentance and renewal'.[20]

---

[13] See Romans 6:4-10.
[14] *Roman Missal*, Eucharistic Prayer III.
[15] *Roman Missal*, Eucharistic Prayer II.
[16] See Council of Trent, Session XIV, *De sacramento Paenitentiae*, Chapter 1: Denz-Schön. 1668 and 1670; can. 1: Denz-Schön. 1701.
[17] St Ambrose, Letter 41: 12: *PL* 16, 1116.
[18] See Revelation 19:7.
[19] See Ephesians 1:22-23; LG 7.
[20] LG 12.

Penance in the Church's Life and Liturgy

4. The people of God accomplishes and perfects this continual repentance in many different ways. It shares in the sufferings of Christ[21] by enduring its own difficulties, carries out works of mercy and charity,[22] and adopts ever more fully the outlook of the Gospel message. Thus the people of God becomes in the world a sign of conversion to God. All this the Church expresses in its life and celebrates in the liturgy when the faithful confess that they are sinners and ask pardon of God and of their brothers and sisters. This happens in penitential services, in the proclamation of the world of God, in prayer, and in the penitential aspects of the eucharistic celebration.[23]

In the sacrament of penance the faithful 'obtain from the mercy of God pardon for their sins against him; at the same time they are reconciled with the Church which they wounded by their sins and which works for their conversion by charity, example, and prayer'.[24]

Reconciliation with God and with the Church

5. Since every sin is an offence against God which disrupts our friendship with him, 'the ultimate purpose of penance is that we should love God deeply and commit ourselves completely to him'.[25] Therefore, the sinner who by the grace of a merciful God embraces the way of penance comes back to the Father who 'first loved us' (1 John 4:19), to Christ who gave himself up for us,[26] and to the Holy Spirit who has been poured out on us abundantly.[27]

'By the hidden and loving mystery of God's design men are joined together in the bonds of supernatural solidarity, so much so that the sin of one harms the others just as the holiness of one benefits the others.'[28] Penance always entails reconciliation with our brothers and sisters who are always harmed by our sins.

---

[21] See 1 Peter 4:13.
[22] See 1 Peter 4:8.
[23] See Council of Trent, Session XIV, *De sacramento Paenitentiae*: Denz-Schön. 1638, 1740, 1743; EM 35; *Roman Missal, General Instruction*, nos. 29, 30, 56a. b. g.
[24] LG 11.
[25] Paul VI, Apostolic Constitution *Paenitemini*, 17 February 1966: *AAS* 58 (1966) 179; See LG 11.
[26] See Galatians 2:20; Ephesians 5:25.
[27] See Titus 3:6.
[28] Paul VI, Apostolic Constitution *Indulgentiarum doctrina*, 1 January 1967, no. 4: *AAS* 59 (1967) 9; see Pius XII, encyclical *Mystici Corporis*, 29 June 1943: *AAS* 35 (1943) 213.

In fact, men frequently join together to commit injustice. It is thus only fitting that they should help each other in doing penance so that freed from sin by the grace of Christ they may work with all men of good will for justice and peace in the world.

The Sacrament of Penance and Its Parts

6. The follower of Christ who has sinned but who has been moved by the Holy Spirit to come to the sacrament of penance should above all be converted to God with his whole heart. This inner conversion of heart embraces sorrow for sin and the intent to lead a new life. It is expressed through confession made to the Church, due satisfaction, and amendment of life. God grants pardon for sin through the Church, which works by the ministry of priests.[29]

a) Contrition

The most important act of the penitent is contrition, which is 'heartfelt sorrow and aversion for the sin committed along with the intention of sinning no more'.[30] 'We can only approach the Kingdom of Christ by *metanoia*. This is a profound change of the whole person by which one begins to consider, judge, and arrange his life according to the holiness and love of God, made manifest in his Son in the last days and given to us in abundance' (see Hebrews 1:2; Colossians 1:19 and *passim*).[31] The genuineness of penance depends on this heartfelt contrition. For conversion should affect a person from within so that it may progressively enlighten him and render him continually more like Christ.

b) Confession

The sacrament of penance includes the confession of sins, which comes from true knowledge of self before God and from contrition for those sins. However, this inner examination of heart and the exterior accusation should be made in the light of God's mercy. Confession requires in the penitent the will to open his heart to the minister of God, and in the minister a spiritual judgment by which, acting in the person of Christ, he pronounces his decision of forgiveness or retention of sins in accord with the power of the keys.[32]

[29] See Council of Trent, Session XIV, *De sacramento Paenitentae*, Chapter 1: Denz-Schön. 1673-5.

[30] *Ibid.*, Chapter 4: Denz-Schön. 1676.

[31] Paul VI, Apostolic Constitution *Paenitemini*, 17 February 1966: *AAS* 58 (1966) 179.

[32] See Council of Trent, Session XIV, *De sacramento Paenitentiae*, Chapter 5: Denz-Schön. 1679.

165

c) *Act of Penance (Satisfaction)*

True conversion is completed by acts of penance or satisfaction for the sins committed, by amendment of conduct, and also by the reparation of injury.[33] The kind and extent of the satisfaction should be suited to the personal condition of each penitent so that each one may restore the order which he disturbed and through the corresponding remedy be cured of the sickness from which he suffered. Therefore, it is necessary that the act of penance really be a remedy for sin and a help to renewal of life. Thus the penitent, 'forgetting the things which are behind him' (Philippians 3:13), again becomes part of the mystery of salvation and turns himself toward the future.

d) *Absolution*

Through the sign of absolution God grants pardon to the sinner who in sacramental confession manifests his change of heart to the Church's minister, and thus the sacrament of penance is completed. In God's design the humanity and loving kindness of our Saviour have visibly appeared to us,[34] and God uses visible signs to give salvation and to renew the broken covenant.

In the sacrament of penance the Father receives the repentant son who comes back to him, Christ places the lost sheep on his shoulders and brings it back to the sheepfold, and the Holy Spirit sanctifies this temple of God again or lives more fully within it. This is finally expressed in a renewed and more fervent sharing of the Lord's table, and there is great joy at the banquet of God's Church over the son who has returned from afar.[35]

The Necessity and Benefit of the Sacrament

7. Just as the wound of sin is varied and multiple in the life of individuals and of the community, so too the healing which penance provides is varied. Those who by grave sin have withdrawn from the communion of love with God are called back in the sacrament of penance to the life they have lost. And those who through daily weakness fall into venial sins draw strength from a repeated cele-

---

[33] See Council of Trent, Session XIV, *De sacramento Paenitentiae*, Chapter 8: Denz-Schön. 1690-2; Paul VI, Apostolic Constitution *Indulgentiarum doctrina*, 1 January 1967, nos. 2-3: *AAS* 59 (1967) 6-8.

[34] See Titus 3:4-5.

[35] See Luke 15:7, 10, 32.

bration of penance to gain the full freedom of the children of God.

a) To obtain the saving remedy of the sacrament of penance, according to the plan of our merciful God, the faithful must confess to a priest each and every grave sin which they remember upon examination of their conscience.[36]

b) Moreover, frequent and careful celebration of this sacrament is also very useful as a remedy for venial sins. This is not a mere ritual repetition or psychological exercise, but a serious striving to perfect the grace of baptism so that, as we bear in our body the death of Jesus Christ, his life may be seen in us ever more clearly.[37] In confession of this kind, penitents who accuse themselves of venial faults should try to conform more closely to Christ and to follow the voice of the Spirit more attentively.

In order that this sacrament of healing may truly achieve its purpose among Christ's faithful, it must take root in their whole lives and move them to more fervent service of God and neighbour.

The celebration of this sacrament is thus always an act in which the Church proclaims its faith, gives thanks to God for the freedom with which Christ has made us free,[38] and offers its life as a spiritual sacrifice in praise of God's glory, as it hastens to meet the Lord Jesus.

III Offices and Ministries in the Reconciliation of Penitents

The Community in the Celebration of Penance

8. The whole Church, as a priestly people, acts in different ways in the work of reconciliation which has been entrusted to it by the Lord. Not only does the Church call sinners to repentance by preaching the word of God, but it also intercedes for them and helps penitents with maternal care and solicitude to acknowledge and admit their sins and so obtain the mercy of God who alone can forgive sins. Furthermore, the Church becomes the instrument of the conversion and absolution of the penitent through the ministry entrusted by Christ to the apostles and their successors.[39]

---

[36] See Council of Trent, Session XIV, *De sacramento Paenitentiae*, can. 7-8: Denz-Schön. 1707-8.
[37] See 2 Corinthians 4:10.
[38] See Galatians 4:31.
[39] See Matthew 18:18; John 20:23

9. The Minister of the Sacrament of Penance

a) The Church exercises the ministry of the sacrament of penance through bishops and presbyters. By preaching God's word they call the faithful to conversion; in the name of Christ and by the power of the Holy Spirit they declare and grant the forgiveness of sins.

In the exercise of this ministry presbyters act in communion with the bishop and share in his power and office of regulating the penitential discipline.[40]

b) The competent minister of the sacrament of penance is a priest who has the faculty to absolve in accordance with canon law. All priests, however, even though not approved to hear confession, absolve validly and licitly all penitents who are in danger of death.

10. The Pastoral Exercise of this Ministry

a) In order to fulfil his ministry properly and faithfully the confessor should understand the disorders of souls and apply the appropriate remedies to them. He should fulfil his office of judge wisely and should acquire the knowledge and prudence necessary for this task by serious study, guided by the teaching authority of the Church and especially by fervent prayer to God. Discernment of spirits is a deep knowledge of God's action in the hearts of men; it is a gift of the Spirit as well as the fruit of charity.[41]

b) The confessor should always be ready and willing to hear the confessions of the faithful when they make a reasonable request of him.[42]

c) By receiving the repentant sinner and leading him to the light of the truth the confessor fulfils a paternal function: he reveals the heart of the Father and shows the image of Christ the Good Shepherd. He should keep in mind that he has been entrusted with the ministry of Christ, who mercifully accomplished the saving work of man's redemption and who is present by his power in the sacraments.[43]

d) As the minister of God the confessor comes to know the secrets of another's conscience, and he is bound to keep the sacramental seal of confession absolutely inviolate.

---

[40] See LG 26.
[41] See Philippians 1:9-10
[42] See Congregation for the Doctrine of the Faith, *Normae pastorales circa absolutionem sacramentalem generali modo impertiendam*, 16 June 1972, no. XII: *AAS* 64 (1972) 514.
[43] See SC 7.

The Penitent

11.　The acts of the penitent in the celebration of the sacrament are of the greatest importance.

When with proper dispositions he approaches this saving remedy instituted by Christ and confesses his sins, he shares by his actions in the sacrament itself; the sacrament is completed when the words of absolution are spoken by the minister in the name of Christ.

Thus the faithful Christian, as he experiences and proclaims the mercy of God in his life, celebrates with the priest the liturgy by which the Church continually renews itself.

IV The Celebration of the Sacrament of Penance

The Place of Celebration

12.　The sacrament of penance is celebrated in the place and location prescribed by law.

The Time of Celebration

13.　The reconciliation of penitents may be celebrated at any time on any day, but it is desirable that the faithful know the day and time at which the priest is available for this ministry. They should be encouraged to approach the sacrament of penance at times when Mass is not being celebrated and especially during the scheduled periods.[44]

The season of Lent is most appropriate for celebrating the sacrament of penance. Already on Ash Wednesday the people of God has heard the solemn invitation 'Turn away from sin and believe the good news'. It is therefore fitting to have several penitential celebrations during Lent, so that all the faithful may have an opportunity to be reconciled with God and their neighbour and so be able to celebrate the paschal mystery in the Easter triduum with renewed hearts.

Liturgical Vestments

14.　The regulations laid down by the local Ordinaries for the use of liturgical vestments in the celebration of penance are to be observed.

[44] See EM 35.

A. *Rite for the Reconciliation of Individual Penitents*

Preparation of Priest and Penitent

15. Priest and penitent should first prepare themselves by prayer to celebrate the sacrament. The priest should call upon the Holy Spirit so that he may receive enlightenment and charity. The penitent should compare his life with the example and commandments of Christ and then pray to God for the forgiveness of his sins.

Welcoming the Penitent

16. The priest should welcome the penitent with fraternal charity and, if the occasion permits, address him with friendly words. The penitent then makes the sign of the cross, saying: 'In the name of the Father, and of the Son, and of the Holy Spirit. Amen'. The priest may also make the sign of the cross with the penitent. Next the priest briefly urges the penitent to have confidence in God. If the penitent is unknown to the priest, it is proper for him to indicate his state in life, the time of his last confession, his difficulties in leading the Christian life, and anything else which may help the confessor in exercising his ministry.

Reading the Word of God

17. Then the priest, or the penitent himself, may read a text of holy Scripture, or this may be done as part of the preparation for the sacrament. Through the word of God the Christian receives light to recognise his sins and is called to conversion and to confidence in God's mercy.

Confession of Sins and the Act of Penance

18. The penitent then confesses his sins, beginning, where customary, with a form of general confession: *I confess to almighty God.* If necessary, the priest should help the penitent to make a complete confession; he should also encourage him to have sincere sorrow for his sins against God. Finally, the priest should offer suitable counsel to help the penitent begin a new life and, where necessary, instruct him in the duties of the Christian way of life.

If the penitent has been the cause of harm or scandal to others, the priest should lead him to resolve that he will make appropriate restitution.

Then the priest imposes an act of penance or satisfaction on the penitent; this should serve not only to make up for the past but also to help him to begin a new life and provide him with an antidote to weakness. As far as possible, the penance should correspond to the seriousness and nature of the sins. This act of penance may suitably take the form of prayer, self-denial, and especially service of one's neighbour and works of mercy. These will underline the fact that sin and its forgiveness have a social aspect.

The Prayer of the Penitent and the Absolution by the Priest

19. After this the penitent manifests his contrition and resolution to begin a new life by means of a prayer for God's pardon. It is desirable that this prayer should be based on the words of Scripture.

Following this prayer, the priest extends his hands, or at least his right hand, over the head of the penitent and pronounces the formula of absolution, in which the essential words are: 'I absolve you from your sins in the name of the Father and of the Son and of the Holy Spirit'. As he says the final words the priest makes the sign of the cross over the penitent. The form of absolution (see no. 46) indicates that the reconciliation of the penitent comes from the mercy of the Father; it shows the connection between the reconciliation of the sinner and the paschal mystery of Christ; it stresses the role of the Holy Spirit in the forgiveness of sins; finally, it underlines the ecclesial aspect of the sacrament because reconciliation with God is asked for and given through the ministry of the Church.

Proclamation of Praise and Dismissal of the Penitent

20. After receiving pardon for his sins the penitent praises the mercy of God and gives him thanks in a short invocation taken from scripture. Then the priest tells him to go in peace.

The penitent continues his conversion and expresses it by a life renewed according to the Gospel and more and more steeped in the love of God, for 'love covers over a multitude of sins' (1 Peter 4:8).

Short Rite

21. When pastoral need dictates it, the priest may omit or shorten some parts of the rite but must always retain in their entirety the confession of sins and the acceptance of the act of penance, the invitation to contrition (no. 44), and the form of absolution and the dismissal. In imminent danger of death, it is sufficient for the priest to say the essential words of the form of absolution, namely, 'I absolve you from your sins in the name of the Father, and of the Son, and of the Holy Spirit'.

171

B. Rite for Reconciliation of Several Penitents with Individual Confession and Absolution

22. When a number of penitents assemble at the same time to receive sacramental reconciliation, it is fitting that they be prepared for the sacrament by a celebration of the word of God.

Those who will receive the sacrament at another time may also take part in the service.

Communal celebration shows more clearly the ecclesial nature of penance. The faithful listen together to the word of God, which proclaims his mercy and invites them to conversion; at the same time they examine the conformity of their lives with that word of God and help each other through common prayer. After each person has confessed his sins and received absolution, all praise God together for his wonderful deeds on behalf of the people he has gained for himself through the blood of his Son.

If necessary, several priests should be available in suitable places to hear individual confessions and to reconcile the penitents.

Introductory Rites

23. When the faithful are assembled, a suitable hymn may be sung. Then the priest greets them, and, if necessary, he or another minister gives a brief introduction to the celebration and explains the order of service. Next he invites all to pray and after a period of silence completes the (opening) prayer.

The Celebration of the Word of God

24. The sacrament of penance should begin with a hearing of God's word, because through his word God calls men to repentance and leads them to a true conversion of heart.

One or more readings may be chosen. If more than one are read, a psalm, another suitable song, or a period of silence should be inserted between them, so that the word of God may be more deeply understood and heartfelt assent may be given to it. If there is only one reading, it is preferable that it be from the gospel.

Readings should be chosen which illustrate the following:

a) the voice of God calling men back to conversion and ever closer conformity with Christ;

b) the mystery of our reconciliation through the death and resurrection of Christ and through the gift of the Holy Spirit;

c) the judgment of God about good and evil in men's lives as a help in the examination of conscience.

172

25. The homily, taking its theme from the scriptural text, should lead the penitents to examine their consciences and to turn away from sin and towards God. It should remind the faithful that sin works against God, against the community and one's neighbours, and against the sinner himself. Therefore, it would be good to recall:

a) the infinite mercy of God, greater than all our sins, by which again and again he calls us back to himself;

b) the need for interior repentance, by which we are genuinely prepared to make reparation for sin;

c) the social aspect of grace and sin, by which the actions of individuals in some degree affect the whole body of the Church;

d) the duty to make satisfaction for sin, which is effective because of Christ's work of reparation and requires especially, in addition to works of penance, the exercise of true charity toward God and neighbour.

26. After the homily a suitable period of silence should be allowed for examining one's conscience and awakening true contrition for sin. The priest or a deacon or other minister may help the faithful with brief considerations or a litany, adapted to their background, age, etc.

If it is judged suitable, this communal examination of conscience and awakening of contrition may take the place of the homily. But in this case it should be clearly based on the text of scripture that has just been read.

The Rite of Reconciliation

27. At the invitation of the deacon or other minister, all kneel or bow their heads and say a form of general confession (for example, *I confess to almighty God*). Then they stand and join in a litany or suitable song to express confession of sins, heartfelt contrition, prayer for forgiveness, and trust in God's mercy. Finally, they say the Lord's Prayer, which is never omitted.

28. After the Lord's Prayer the priests go to the places assigned for confession. The penitents who desire to confess their sins go to the priest of their choice. After receiving a suitable act of penance, they are absolved by him with the form for the reconciliation of an individual penitent.

29. When the confessions are over, the priests return to the sanctuary. The priest who presides invites all to make an act of thanks-

giving and to praise God for his mercy. This may be done in a psalm or hymn or litany. Finally, the priest concludes the celebration with prayer, praising God for the great love he has shown us.

Dismissal of the People

30. After the prayer of thanksgiving the priest blesses the faithful. Then the deacon or the priest himself dismisses the congregation.

C. Rite for Reconciliation of Penitents with General Confession and Absolution

The Discipline of General Absolution

31. Individual, integral confession and absolution remain the only ordinary way for the faithful to reconcile themselves with God and the Church, unless physical or moral impossibility excuses from this kind of confession.

Particular, occasional circumstances may render it lawful and even necessary to give general absolution to a number of penitents without their previous individual confession.

In addition to cases involving danger of death, it is lawful to give sacramental absolution to several of the faithful at the same time, after they have made only a generic confession but have been suitably called to repentance, if there is grave need, namely when, in view of the number of penitents, sufficient confessors are not available to hear individual confessions properly within a suitable period of time, so that the penitents would, through no fault of their own, have to go without sacramental grace or holy communion for a long time. This may happen especially in mission territories but in other places as well and also in groups of persons when the need is established.

General absolution is not lawful, when confessors are available, for the sole reason of the large number of penitents, as may be on the occasion of some major feast or pilgrimage.[45]

32. The judgment about the presence of the above conditions and the decision concerning the lawfulness of giving general sacramental absolution are reserved to the bishop of the diocese, who is to consult with other members of the episcopal conference.

Over and above the cases determined by the diocesan bishop, if any other serious need arises for giving sacramental absolution to

---

[45] Congregation for the Doctrine of the Faith, *Normae pastorales circa absolutionem sacramentalem generali modo impertiendam*, 16 June 1972, no. III: *AAS* 64 (1972) 511.

several persons together, the priest must have recourse to the local Ordinary beforehand, when this is possible, if he is to give absolution lawfully. Otherwise, he should inform the Ordinary as soon as possible of the need and of the absolution which he gave.[46]

33. In order that the faithful may profit from sacramental absolution given to several persons at the same time, it is absolutely necessary that they be properly disposed. Each one should be sorry for his sins and resolve to avoid committing them again. He should intend to repair any scandal and harm he may have caused and likewise resolve to confess in due time each one of the grave sins which he cannot confess at present. These dispositions and conditions, which are required for the validity of the sacrament, should be carefully recalled to the faithful by priests.[47]

34. Those who receive pardon for grave sins by a common absolution should go to individual confession before they receive this kind of absolution again, unless they are impeded by a just reason. They are strictly bound, unless this is morally impossible, to go to confession within a year. The precept which obliges each of the faithful to confess at least once a year to a priest all the grave sins which he has not individually confessed before also remains in force in this case too.[48]

The Rite of General Absolution

35. For the reconciliation of penitents by general confession and absolution in the cases provided by law, everything takes place as described above for the reconciliation of several penitents with individual confession and absolution, with the following exceptions:

a) After the homily or during it, the faithful who seek general absolution should be instructed to dispose themselves properly, that is, each one should be sorry for his sins and resolve to avoid committing them again. He should intend to repair any scandal and harm he may have caused and likewise resolve to confess in due time each one of the grave sins which cannot be confessed at present.[49] Some act of penance should be proposed for all; individuals may add to this penance if they wish.

[46] *Ibid.*, no. V: *loc. cit.*, 512.
[47] *Ibid.*, nos. VI and XI: *loc. cit.*, 512, 514.
[48] *Ibid.*, nos. VII and VIII: *loc. cit.*, 512-13.
[49] See *Ibid.*, no. VI: *loc. cit.*, 512.

b) The deacon, another minister, or the priest then calls upon the penitents who wish to receive absolution to show their intention by some sign (for example, by bowing their heads, kneeling, or giving some other sign determined by the episcopal conferences). They should also say together a form of general confession (for example, *I confess to almighty God*), which may be followed by a litany or a penitential song. Then the Lord's Prayer is sung or said by all, as indicated in no. 27, above.

c) Then the priest calls upon the grace of the Holy Spirit for the forgiveness of sins, proclaims the victory over sin of Christ's death and resurrection, and gives sacramental absolution to the penitents.

d) Finally, the priest invites the people to give thanks, as described in no. 29, above, and, omitting the concluding prayer, he immediately blesses and dismisses them.

V Penitential Celebrations

Nature and Structure

36. Penitential celebrations are gatherings of the people of God to hear the proclamation of God's word. This invites them to conversion and renewal of life and announces our freedom from sin through the death and resurrection of Christ. The structure of these services is the same as that usually followed in celebrations of the word of God[50] and given in the *Rite for Reconciliation of Several Penitents.*

It is appropriate, therefore, that after the introductory rites (song, greeting, and prayer) one or more biblical readings be chosen with songs, psalms, or periods of silence inserted between them. In the homily these readings should be explained and applied to the congregation. Before or after the readings from scriptures, readings from the Fathers or other writers may be selected which will help the community and each person to a true awareness of sin and heart-felt sorrow, in other words, to bring about conversion of life.

After the homily and reflection on God's word, it is desirable that the congregation, united in voice and spirit, pray together in a litany or in some other way suited to general participation. At the end the Lord's Prayer is said, asking God our Father 'to forgive u our sins as we forgive those who sin against us . . . and deliver u from evil'. The priest or the minister who presides concludes with a prayer and the dismissal of the people.

[50] See IOe 37-9.

Benefit and Importance

37.   Care should be taken that the faithful do not confuse these celebrations with the celebrations of the sacrament of penance.[51] Penitential celebrations are very helpful in promoting conversion of life and purification of heart.[52]

It is desirable to arrange such services especially for these purposes:
—to foster the spirit of penance within the Christian community;
—to help the faithful to prepare for confession which can be made individually later at a convenient time;
—to help children gradually to form their conscience about sin in human life and about freedom from sin through Christ;
—to help catechumens during their conversion.

Penitential celebrations, moreover, are very useful in places where no priest is available to give sacramental absolution. They offer help in reaching that perfect contrition which comes from charity and enables the faithful to attain to God's grace through a desire for the sacrament of penance.[53]

VI Adaptations of the Rite to Various Regions and Circumstances

Adaptations by the Episcopal Conferences

38.   In preparing particular rituals episcopal conferences may adapt the rite of penance to the needs of individual regions so that after confirmation by the Apostolic See the rituals may be used in the respective regions. It is the responsibility of episcopal conferences in this matter:

a) to establish regulations for the discipline of the sacrament of penance, particularly those affecting the ministry of priests and the reservation of sins;

b) to determine more precise regulations about the place proper for the ordinary celebration of the sacrament of penance and about the signs of penance to be shown by the faithful before general absolution (see no. 35, above);

c) to prepare translations of texts adapted to the character and language of each people and also to compose new texts for the prayers

---

[51] See Congregation for the Doctrine of the Faith, *Normae pastorales circa absolutionem sacramentalem generali modo impertiendam*, 16 June 1972, no. X: *AAS* 64 (1972) 513-14.
[52] *Ibid.*
[53] See Council of Trent, Session XIV, *De sacramento Paenitentiae*, Chapter 5: Denz-Schön. 1677.

of the faithful and the minister, keeping intact the sacramental form.

The Competence of the Bishop

39. It is for the diocesan bishop:

a) to regulate the discipline of penance in his diocese,[54] including adaptations of the rite according to the rules proposed by the episcopal conference;

b) to determine, after consultation with the other members of the episcopal conference, when general sacramental absolution may be permitted under the conditions laid down by the Holy See.[55]

Adaptations by the Minister

40. It is for priests, and especially parish priests:

a) in reconciling individuals or the community, to adapt the rite to the concrete circumstances of the penitents. The essential structure and the entire form of absolution must be kept, but if necessary they may omit some parts for pastoral reasons or enlarge upon them, may select the texts of readings or prayers, and may choose a place more suitable for the celebration according to the regulations of the episcopal conference, so that the entire celebration may be rich and fruitful;

b) to propose and prepare occasional penitential celebrations during the year, especially in Lent. In order that the texts chosen and the order of the celebration may be adapted to the conditions and circumstances of the community or group (for example, children, sick persons, etc.), they may be assisted by others, including the laity;

c) to decide to give general sacramental absolution preceded by only a generic confession, when a grave necessity not foreseen by the diocesan bishop arises and when recourse to him is not possible. They are obliged to notify the Ordinary as soon as possible of the need and of the fact that absolution was given.

[54] See LG 26.
[55] See Congregation for the Doctrine of the Faith, *Normae pastorales circa absolutionem sacramentalem generali modo impertiendam*, no. V: *AAS* 64 (1972) 512.

RITE OF ANOINTING AND PASTORAL CARE OF THE SICK APOSTOLIC CONSTITUTION

PAUL, BISHOP
Servant of the Servants of God For Everlasting Memory

The Catholic Church professes and teaches that the anointing of the sick is one of the seven sacraments of the New Testament instituted by Christ and that it is 'alluded to in Mark (6:13) and recommended and promulgated to the faithful by James the Apostle and brother of the Lord. He says: "Is there anyone sick among you? Let him call for the elders of the Church, and let them pray over him and anoint him in the name of the Lord. This prayer, made in faith, will save a sick man. The Lord will restore his health, and if he has committed any sins, they will be forgiven" (James 5:14-15).'[1]

From ancient times testimonies of anointing of the sick have been found in the Church's tradition, particularly in the liturgy, both in the East and in the West. The letter which Innocent I, our predecessor, addressed to Decentius, Bishop of Gubbio,[2] and the venerable prayer used for blessing the oil of the sick: 'Send forth, Lord, your Holy Spirit, the Paraclete', which was inserted in the eucharistic prayer[3] and is still preserved in the Roman Pontifical,[4] are worthy of special note.

In the course of centuries of liturgical tradition, the parts of the sick person's body to be anointed with holy oil were more explicitly defined in different ways. Several formulas were added to accompany the anointings with prayer, and these are contained in the liturgical books of various churches. During the Middle Ages, in the Roman Church the custom prevailed of anointing the sick on the five senses

---

[1] Council of Trent, Session XIV, *Extreme unction*, chapter 1 (cf. *ibid.*, canon 1); CT, VII, 1, 355-6; Denz-Schön. 1695.

[2] Ep. *Si Instituta Ecclesiastica*, chapter 8: PL 20, 559-61; Denz-Schön. 216.

[3] *Liber Sacramentorum Romanae Æclesiae Ordinis Anni Circuli*, ed. L. C. Mohlberg (*Rerum Ecclesiasticorum Documenta, Fontes*, IV), Rome, 1960, p. 61; *Le Sacramentaire Grégorien*, ed. J. Deshusses (*Spicilegium Friburgense*, 16) Fribourg, 1971, p. 172; see *La Tradition Apostolique de Saint Hippolyte*, ed. B. Botte (*Liturgiewissenschaftliche Quellen und Forschungen*, 39), Münster in W., 1963, pp. 18-19; *Le Grand Euchologe du Monastère Blanc*, ed. E. Lanne (*Patrologia Orientalis*, XXVIII, 2), Paris 1958, pp. 392-5.

[4] See *Pontificale Romanum: Ordo benedicendi Oleum Catechumenorum et Infirmorum et conficiendi Chrisma*, Vatican City, 1971, pp. 11-12.

with the formula: '*Per istam sanctam Unctionem, et suam piissimam misericordiam, indulgeat tibi Dominus quidquid deliquisti*', adapted to each sense.[5] In addition, the teaching concerning anointing is expounded in the documents of the ecumenical councils, namely, Florence, Trent especially, and Vatican II.

After the Council of Florence had described the essential elements of the anointing of the sick,[6] the Council of Trent declared its divine institution and explained what is taught in the Letter of James concerning the holy anointing, especially with regard to the reality and effects of the sacrament: 'This reality is in fact the grace of the Holy Spirit, whose anointing takes away sins, if any still remain to be taken away, and the remnants of sin; it also relieves and strengthens the soul of the sick person, arousing in him a great confidence in the divine mercy; thus sustained, he may more easily bear the trials and hardships of his sickness, more easily resist the temptations of the devil "lying in wait" (Genesis 3:15), and sometimes regain bodily health, if this is expedient for the health of the soul.'[7] The same council also declared that these words of the Apostle state with sufficient clarity that 'this anointing is to be administered to the sick, especially those who are in such a condition as to appear to have reached the end of their life, whence it is also called the sacrament of the dying'.[8] Finally, it declared that the priest is the proper minister of the sacrament.[9]

The Second Vatican Council adds the following: '"Extreme Unction", which may also and more fittingly be called "anointing of the sick", is not a sacrament for those only who are at the point of death. Hence, as soon as any one of the faithful begins to be in danger of death from sickness or old age, the appropriate time for him to receive this sacrament has certainly already arrived.'[10] The use of this sacrament is a concern of the whole Church: 'By the sacred anointing of the sick and the prayer of her priests, the whole Church commends the sick to the suffering and glorified Lord, asking

---

[5] See M. Andrieu, *Le Pontifical Romain au Moyen-Age*, t. 1, *Le Pontifical Romain du XIIe siècle* (*Studi e Testi*, 86), Vatican City, 1938, pp. 267-8; t. 2, *Le Pontifical de la Curie Romaine au XIIIe siècle* (*Studi e Testi*, 87) Vatican City, 1940, pp. 491-2.

[6] *Decr. pro Armenis*, G. Hofmann, *Concilium Florentinum*, I-II, p. 130; Denz-Schön. 1324 s.

[7] Council of Trent, Session XIV, *Extreme unction*, chapter 2: *CT*, VII, 1, 356; Denz-Schön. 1696.

[8] *Ibid.*, cap. 3: *CT*, *ibid.*; Denz-Schön. 1698.

[9] *Ibid.*, cap. 3, canon 4: *CT*, *ibid.*; Denz-Schön. 1697-1719.

[10] SC 73.

that he may lighten their suffering and save them (see James 5:14-16). The Church exhorts them, moreover, to contribute to the welfare of the whole people of God by associating themselves freely with the passion and death of Christ (see Romans 8:17; Colossians 1:24; 2 Timothy 2:11-12; 1 Peter 4:13).'[11]

All these considerations had to be weighed in revising the rite of anointing, in order better to adapt to present day conditions those elements which were subject to change.[12]

We thought fit to modify the sacramental formula in such a way that, in view of the words of James, the effects of the sacrament might be more fully expressed. Since olive oil, which had been prescribed until now for the valid administration of the sacrament, is unobtainable or difficult to obtain in some parts of the world, we decreed, at the request of numerous bishops, that from now on, according to the circumstances, other kind of oil could also be used, provided that it be obtained from plants, and thus similar to olive oil.

As regards the number of anointings and the parts of the body to be anointed, it has seemed opportune to simplify the rite.

Therefore, since this revision in certain points touches upon the sacramental rite itself, by our apostolic authority we lay down that the following is to be observed for the future in the Latin Rite:

The sacrament of anointing of the sick is administered to those who are dangerously ill by anointing them on the forehead and hands with blessed olive oil or, according to the circumstances, with another plant oil and saying once only these words: 'Per istam Sanctam Unctionem et suam piissimam misericordiam adiuvet te Dominus gratia Spiritus Sancti, ut a peccatis liberatum te salvet atque propitius allevet.'

In case of necessity, however it is sufficient that a single anointing be given on the forehead or, because of the particular condition of the sick person, on another more suitable part of the body, the whole formula being pronounced.

This sacrament may be repeated if the sick person, recovers after anointing and then falls ill or if, in the course of the same illness, the danger becomes more serious.

Having established and declared all these elements of the essential rite of the sacrament of anointing of the sick, by our apostolic authority we also approve the Rite of Anointing and Pastoral Care of the Sick, which has been revised by the Congregation for Divine

[11] LG 11.   [12] SC 1.

Worship. At the same time, where necessary we derogate from the prescriptions of the Code of Canon Law or other laws hitherto in force or we abrogate them; other prescriptions and laws, which are neither abrogated nor changed by the abovementioned rite, remain valid and in force. The Latin edition of the rite containing the new form will come into force as soon as it is published; the vernacular editions, prepared by the episcopal conferences and confirmed by the Apostolic See, will come into force on the dates to be laid down by the individual conferences. The old rite may be used until 31 December 1973. From 1 January 1974, however, only the new rite is to be used by those concerned.

We intend that everything we have laid down and prescribed should be firm and effective in the Latin Rite, notwithstanding, where relevant, the apostolic constitutions and ordinances issued by our predecessors and other prescriptions, even if worthy of special mention.

Given in Rome at Saint Peter's on 30 November 1972, the tenth year of our pontificate.

PAUL PP. V'

RITE OF ANOINTING AND PASTORAL CARE OF THE SICK * : INTRODUCTION

Structure

---

* Promulgated by Decree dated 7 December 1972.

I Human Sickness and its Meaning in the Mystery of Salvation

1. Sickness and pain have always been a heavy burden for man and an enigma to his understanding. Christians suffer sickness and pain as do all other men; yet their faith helps them to understand better the mystery of suffering and to bear their pain more bravely. From Christ's words they know that sickness has meaning and value for their own salvation and for the world's; they also know that Christ loved the sick and that during his life he often looked upon the sick and healed them.

2. Sickness, while it is closely related to man's sinful condition, cannot be considered a punishment which man suffers for his personal sins (see John 9:3). Christ himself was sinless, yet he fulfilled what was written in Isaiah: he bore all the sufferings of his passion and understood human sorrow (see Isaiah 53:4-5). Christ still suffers and is tormented in his followers whenever we suffer. If we realise that our sufferings are preparing us for eternal life in glory, then they will seem short and even easy to bear (see 2 Corinthians 4:17).

3. It is part of the plan laid down by God's providence that we should struggle against all sickness and carefully seek the blessings of good health, so that we can fulfil our role in human society and in the Church. Yet we should always be prepared to fill up what is lacking in Christ's sufferings for the salvation of the world as we look forward to all creation being set free in the glory of the sons of God (see Colossians 1:24; Romans 8:19-21).

Moreover, the role of the sick in the Church is to remind others not to lose sight of the essential or higher things and so to show that our mortal life is restored through the mystery of Christ's death and resurrection.

4. Not only the sick person should fight against illness; doctors and all who are dedicated to helping the sick should consider it their duty to do whatever they judge will help the sick both physically and spiritually. In doing so they fulfil the command of Christ to visit the sick, for Christ implied that they should be concerned for the whole man and offer both physical relief and spiritual comfort.

II Celebration of the Sacraments of the Sick

A. *Anointing of the Sick*

5. The sacrament of anointing prolongs the concern which the Lord himself showed for the bodily and spiritual welfare of the sick, as the gospels testify, and which he asked his followers to show also. This sacrament has its beginning in Christ and is spoken of in the Letter of James: the Church, by the anointing of the sick and the prayer of the priests, commends those who are ill to the suffering and glorified Lord, that he may raise them up and save them (see James 5:14-16). Moreover, the Church exhorts them to contribute to the welfare of the people of God[1] by associating themselves freely with the passion and death of Christ[2] (see Romans 8:17). The man who is seriously ill needs the special help of God's grace in this time of anxiety, lest he be broken in spirit and subject to temptations and the weakening of faith.

Christ, therefore, strengthens the faithful who are afflicted by illness with the sacrament of anointing, providing them with the strongest means of support.[3]

The celebration of this sacrament consists especially in the laying on of hands by the presbyters of the Church, their offering the prayer of faith, and the anointing of the sick with oil made holy by God's blessing. This rite signifies the grace of the sacrament and confers it.

6. This sacrament provides the sick person with the grace of the Holy Spirit by which the whole man is brought to health, trust in God is encouraged, and strength is given to resist the temptations of the Evil One and anxiety about death. Thus the sick person is able not only to bear his suffering bravely, but also to fight against it. A return to physical health may even follow the reception of this sacrament if it will be beneficial to the sick person's salvation. If necessary, the sacrament also provides the sick person with the forgiveness of sins and the completion of Christian penance.[4]

7. The anointing of the sick, which includes the prayer of faith (see James 5:15), is a sacrament of faith. This faith is important for

---

[1] See Council of Trent, Session XIV, *Extreme unction*, chapter 1: Denz-Schön. 1695; LG 11.
[2] See also Colossians 1:24; 2 Timothy 2:11-12; Peter 4:13.
[3] See Council of Trent, Session XIV, *loc. cit.* Denz-Schön. 1694.
[4] See Council of Trent, Session XIV, foreword and chapter 2: Denz-Schön. 1694 and 1696.

the minister and particularly for the one who receives it. The sick man will be saved by his faith and the faith of the Church which looks back to the death and resurrection of Christ, the source of the sacrament's power (see James 5:15),[5] and looks ahead to the future kingdom which is pledged in the sacraments.

a) Subject of the Anointing of the Sick

8. The Letter of James states that the anointing should be given to the sick to raise them up and save them.[6] There should be special care and concern that those who are dangerously ill due to sickness or old age receive this sacrament.[7]

A prudent or probable judgment about the seriousness of the sickness is sufficient;[8] in such a case there is no reason for scruples, but if necessary a doctor may be consulted.

9. The sacrament may be repeated if the sick person recovers after anointing or if, during the same illness, the danger becomes more serious.

10. A sick person should be anointed before surgery whenever a dangerous illness is the reason for the surgery.

11. Old people may be anointed if they are in weak condition although no dangerous illness is present.

12. Sick children may be anointed if they have sufficient use of reason to be comforted by this sacrament.

13. In public and private catechesis, the faithful should be encouraged to ask for the anointing and, as soon as the time for the anointing comes, to receive it with complete faith and devotion, not misusing this sacrament by putting it off. All who care for the sick should be taught the meaning and purpose of anointing.

14. Anointing may be conferred upon sick people who have lost consciousness or lost the use of reason, if, as Christian believers, they would have asked for it were they in control of their faculties.[9]

15. When a priest has been called to attend a person who is already

---

[5] See St. Thomas, *In IV Sententiarum*, d. 1. q. 1, a. 4. qc. 3.
[6] See Council of Trent, Session XIV, chapter 2: Denz-Schön. 1698.
[7] See SC 73.
[8] See Pius XI, Letter *Explorata res*, 2 February 1923.
[9] See canon 943, C.I.C.

dead, he should pray for the dead person, asking that God forgive his sins and graciously receive him into his kingdom. The priest is not to administer the sacrament of anointing. But if the priest is doubtful whether the sick person is dead, he may administer the sacrament conditionally (no. 135).[10]

b) Minister of Anointing

16. The priest is the only proper minister of the anointing of the sick.[11]

This office is ordinarily exercised by bishops, pastors and their assistants, priests who care for the sick or aged in hospitals, and superiors of clerical religious institutions.[12]

17. These ministers have the pastoral responsibility, with the assistance of religious and laity, first of preparing and helping the sick and others who are present, and then of celebrating the sacrament.

The local Ordinary has the responsibility of supervising celebrations at which sick persons from various parishes or hospitals come together to receive the anointing.

18. Other priests, with the consent of the ministers mentioned in no. 16, may confer the anointing. In case of necessity, a priest may presume this consent, but he should later inform the pastor or the chaplain of the hospital.

19. When two or more priests are present for the anointing of a sick person, one of them says the prayers and performs the anointings, saying the sacramental form. The others take various parts such as the introductory rites, readings, invocations or explanations; they may each lay hands on the sick person.

c) Requirements for Celebrating the Anointing of the Sick

20. The matter proper for the sacrament is olive oil, or according to circumstances, other plant oil.[13]

21. The oil used for anointing the sick must be blessed for this purpose by the bishop or by a priest who has this faculty, either from

[10] See canon 941, C.I.C.
[11] See Council of Trent, Session XIV, *Extreme unction*, chapter 3 and canon 4: Denz-Schön. 1697 and 1719; canon 938, C.I.C.
[12] See canon 938, C.I.C.
[13] See *Ordo benedicendi Oleum catechumenorum et infirmorum et conficienda Chrisma*, Praenotanda, no. 3, Vatican Press, 1970.

the law or by special concession of the Apostolic See.

The law itself permits the following to bless the oil of the sick:

a) those whom the law equates with diocesan bishops;

b) in cases of true necessity, any priest.[14]

The oil of the sick is ordinarily blessed by the bishop on Holy Thursday.[15]

22.   If a priest, according to no. 21b, is to bless the oil during the rite, he may bring the unblessed oil with him, or the family of the sick person may prepare the oil in a suitable vessel. If any of the oil is left after the celebration of the sacrament, it should be absorbed in cotton and burned.

If the priest uses oil that has already been blessed (either by the bishop or by a priest), he brings it with him in the vessel in which it is kept. This vessel, made of a suitable material, should be clean and should contain sufficient oil (soaked in cotton for convenience). In this case, after the anointing the priest returns the vessel to the place where it is reverently kept. He should make sure that the oil remains fit for use and should obtain fresh oil from time to time, either yearly when the bishop blesses the oil on Holy Thursday or more frequently if necessary.

23.   The sacrament is conferred by anointing the sick person on the forehead and on the hands. The formula is divided so that the first part is said while the forehead is anointed, the latter part while the hands are anointed.

In case of necessity, however, a single anointing on the forehead is enough. If the condition of the sick person prevents anointing the forehead, another suitable part of the body is anointed. In either case, the whole formula is said.

24.   Depending on the culture and traditions of different peoples, the number of anointings and the place of anointing may be changed or increased. Provision for this should be made in the preparation of particular rituals.

25.   The following is the formula with which the anointing of the sick is conferred in the Latin Rite:

[14] *Ibid.*, introduction, no. 8.
[15] *Ibid.*, introduction, no. 9.

Through this holy anointing
may the Lord in his love and mercy help you
with the grace of the Holy Spirit.
R. Amen
May the Lord who frees you from sin
save you and raise you up.
R. Amen

B. Viaticum

26.   When the Christian, in his passage from this life, is strengthened by the body and blood of Christ, he has the pledge of the resurrection which the Lord promised: 'He who feeds on my flesh and drinks my blood has life eternal, and I will raise him up on the last day' (John 6:54).

Viaticum should be received during Mass when possible so that the sick person may receive communion under both kinds. Communion received as viaticum should be considered a special sign of participation in the mystery of the death of the Lord and his passage to the Father,[16] the mystery which is celebrated in the eucharist.

27.   All baptised Christians who can receive communion are bound to receive viaticum. Those in danger from any cause are obliged to receive communion. Pastors must see that the administration of this sacrament is not delayed, but that the faithful are nourished by it while still in full possession of their faculties.[17]

28.   It is also desirable that, during the celebration of viaticum, the Christian should renew the faith he professed in baptism, which made him an adopted son of God and a coheir of the promise of eternal life.

29.   The ordinary ministers of viaticum are the pastor and his assistants, the priest who cares for the sick in hospitals, and the superior of clerical religious institutes. In case of necessity, any other priest, with at least the presumed permission of the competent minister, may administer viaticum.

---

[16] See EM 36, 39, 41; Paul VI, apostolic letter *Pastorale munus*, 30 November, 1963, no. 7: *AAS* 56 (1964) 7; canon 882, 4, C.I.C.
[17] See EM 39.

If no priest is available, viaticum may be brought to the sick by a deacon or by another of the faithful, either a man or a woman who by the authority of the Apostolic See has been appointed by the bishop to distribute the eucharist to the faithful. In this case, a deacon follows the rite prescribed in the ritual; other ministers use the rite they ordinarily follow for distributing communion, but with the special formula given in the rite for viaticum (no. 112).

C. Continuous Rite

30. For special cases, when sudden illness or some other cause has unexpectedly placed one of the faithful in danger of death, a continuous rite is provided by which the sick person may be given the sacraments of penance, anointing, and the eucharist as viaticum in one service.

If death is near and there is not enough time to administer the three sacraments in the manner described above, the sick person should be given an opportunity to make a sacramental confession, which of necessity may be a generic confession. Then, he should be given viaticum immediately, since all the faithful are bound by precept to receive this sacrament if they are in danger of death. Afterwards, if there is sufficient time, the sick person is to be anointed.

If because of his illness the sick person cannot receive communion, he should be anointed.

31. If the sick person is to receive the sacrament of confirmation, nos. 117, 124, and 136-137 of this ritual should be consulted.

In danger of death, provided a bishop is not easily available or is lawfully impeded, the law gives the faculty to confirm to the following: pastors and parochial vicars; in their absence, their parochial associates; priests who are in charge of special parishes lawfully established; administrators, substitutes, and assistants; in the absence of all of the preceding, any priest who is not subject to censure or canonical penalty.[18]

III Offices and Ministries for the Sick

32. If one member suffers in the body of Christ, which is the Church, all the members suffer with him (1 Corinthians 12:26).[19] For this

[18] See *Ordo Confirmationis*, Praenotanda, no. 7c. Vatican Press, 1971.
[19] See LG 7.

reason, kindness shown toward the sick and works of charity and mutual help for the relief of every kind of human want should be held in special honour.[20] Every scientific effort to prolong life[21] and every act of heartfelt love for the sick may be considered a preparation for the gospel and a participation in Christ's healing ministry.[22]

33. It is thus fitting that all baptised Christians share in this ministry of mutual charity within the body of Christ: by fighting against disease, by love shown to the sick, and by celebrating the sacraments of the sick. Like the other sacraments, these too have a communal aspect, which should be brought out as much as possible when they are celebrated.

34. The family and friends of the sick and those who take care of them have a special share in this ministry of comfort. It is their task to strengthen the sick with words of faith and by praying with them, to commend them to the Lord who suffered and is glorified, and to urge the sick to unite themselves willingly with the passion and death of Christ for the good of God's people.[23] If the sickness grows worse, the family and friends of the sick and those who take care of them have the responsibility to inform the pastor and by their kind words prudently to dispose the sick person for the reception of the sacraments at the proper time.

35. Priests, particularly pastors and those mentioned in no. 16, should remember that they are to care for the sick, visiting them and helping them by works of charity.[24] Especially when they administer the sacraments, priests should stir up the hope of those present and strengthen their faith in Christ who suffered and was glorified. By expressing the Church's love and the consolation of faith, they should comfort believers and raise the minds of others to God.

36. The faithful should clearly understand the meaning of the anointing of the sick so that these sacraments may nourish, strengthen, and express faith. It is most important for the faithful in general, and above all for the sick, to be aided by participating in it, especially if it is to be carried out communally. The prayer of faith which accompanies the celebration of the sacrament is supported by the profession of this faith.

[20] See AA 8.   [21] See GS 18.   [22] See LG 28.
[23] See LG 21.   [24] See canon 468, 1, C.I.C.

37. When the priest prepares for the celebration of the sacraments, he should ask about the condition of the sick person. He should take this information into account when he arranges the rite, in choosing readings and prayers, in deciding whether he will celebrate Mass for viaticum, and the like. As far as possible he should plan all this with the sick person or his family beforehand, while he explains the meaning of the sacraments.

IV Adaptations by the Conferences of Bishops

38. According to the Constitution on the Liturgy (no. 63b), it is for the conferences of bishops to prepare a title in particular rituals corresponding to this title of the Roman Ritual. It should be accommodated to the needs of the region so that, after the decisions have been reviewed by the Apostolic See, the ritual can be used in the region for which it was prepared.

The following pertains to the episcopal conferences:

a) to specify adaptations, as mentioned in no. 39 of the Constitution on the Liturgy;

b) carefully and prudently to consider what can properly be accepted from the genius and the traditions of each nation; to propose to the Apostolic See further adaptations which seem useful or necessary and to introduce them with its consent;

c) to retain elements in the rites of the sick which now exist in particular rituals, so long as they are compatible with the Constitution on the Liturgy and with contemporary needs; or to adapt any of these elements;

d) to prepare translations of the texts so that they are truly accommodated to the genius of different languages and cultures, with the addition of melodies for singing when this is appropriate;

e) to adapt and enlarge, if necessary, the introduction given in the Roman Ritual so as to encourage the conscious and active participation of the faithful;

f) to arrange the material in the editions of liturgical books prepared under the direction of the episcopal conferences so that they will be suitable for pastoral use.

39. Wherever the Roman Ritual gives several optional formulas, particular rituals may add other texts of the same kind.

V Adaptations by the Minister

40. The minister should be aware of particular circumstances and other needs, as well as the wishes of the sick and of other members of the faithful, and should freely use the different options provided in the rite.

a) He should be especially aware that the sick tire easily and that their physical condition can change from day to day and even from hour to hour. For this reason he may shorten the rite if necessary.

b) When the faithful are not present, the priest should remember that the Church is already present in his own person and in the person of the one who is ill. For this reason he should try to offer the sick person the love and help of the Christian community both before and after the celebration of the sacrament, or he may ask another Christian from the local community to do this if the sick person will accept this help.

c) If the sick person regains his health after being anointed, he should be encouraged to give thanks for the favours he has received, for example, by participating in a Mass of thanksgiving or in some other suitable manner.

41. The priest should follow the structure of the rite in the celebration, while accommodating it to the place and the people involved. The penitential rite may be part of the introductory rite or take place after the reading from scripture. In place of the thanksgiving over the oil, the priest may give an instruction. This is particularly appropriate when the sick person is in a hospital and the other sick people in the room do not take part in the celebration of the sacrament.

RITE OF FUNERALS*:
INTRODUCTION

Structure

Introduction 1-15

Offices and Ministries towards the Dead 16-20

Adaptations by the Conferences of Bishops 21-2

The Function of the Priest in Preparing and Planning the Celebration 23-5

* Promulgated by Decree dated 15 August 1969.

Introduction

1. In the funeral rites the Church celebrates the paschal mystery of Christ. Those who in baptism have become one with the dead and risen Christ will pass with him from death to life, to be purified in soul and welcomed into the fellowship of the saints in heaven. They look forward in blessed hope to his second coming and the bodily resurrection of the dead.

The Church therefore celebrates the eucharistic sacrifice of Christ's passover for the dead, and offers prayers and petitions for them. In the communion of all Christ's members, the prayers which bring spiritual help to some may bring to others a consoling hope.

2. In celebrating the funeral rites of their brothers and sisters, Christians should certainly affirm their hope in eternal life, but in such a way that they do not seem to neglect or ignore the feeling and practice of their own time and place. Family traditions, local customs, groups established to take care of funerals, anything that is good may be used freely, but anything alien to the Gospel should be changed so that funeral rites for Christians may proclaim the paschal faith and the spirit of the Gospel.

3. The bodies of the faithful, which were temples of the Holy Spirit, should be shown honour and respect, but any kind of pomp or display should be avoided. Between the time of death and burial there should be sufficient opportunities for the people to pray for the dead and profess their own faith in eternal life.

Depending on local custom, the significant times during this period would seem to be the following: the vigil in the home of the deceased; the time when the body is laid out; the assembly of the relatives and, if possible, the whole community, to receive hope and consolation in the liturgy of the word, to offer the eucharistic sacrifice, and to bid farewell to the deceased in the final commendation, followed by the carrying of the body to the grave or tomb.

4. The rite of funerals for adults has been arranged in three plans to take into account conditions in all parts of the world:

a) the first plan provides for three stations: in the home of the deceased, in the church, and at the cemetery;

b) the second plan has two stations; in the cemetery chapel and at the grave;

c) the third plan has one station: at the home of the deceased.

5. The first plan is the one found until now in the Roman Ritual. Ordinarily it includes three stations, at least when celebrated in rural areas. These stations are in the home of the deceased, in the church, and at the cemetery, with two intervening processions. Such processions, however, are uncommon or inconvenient for various reasons, especially in large cities. On the other hand, priests are frequently unable to lead the services in the home and at the cemetery because of the limited number of clergy or the distance from the church to the cemetery. The faithful themselves should therefore be urged to recite the appointed prayers and psalms in the absence of a priest or deacon; if this is impossible, the stations in the home and at the cemetery may be omitted.

6. According to this first plan, the station in the church usually includes the celebration of the funeral Mass. The latter is prohibited only during the triduum of Holy Week, on solemnities, and on the Sundays of Advent, Lent, and the Easter season. For pastoral reasons the funeral rites may be celebrated in church on such days but without Mass (which should be celebrated on another day if possible). In such cases the celebration of the liturgy of the word is prescribed. Thus the station in the church will always include the liturgy of the word, with or without the eucharistic sacrifice, and will be completed by the rite formerly called the 'absolution' of the deceased and now called the 'final commendation and farewell'.

7. The second plan has only two stations, in the cemetery chapel and at the grave. The eucharistic celebration is not provided for, but it will take place, in the absence of the body, either before or after the funeral.

8. The funeral rite, according to the third plan, is to be celebrated in the home of the deceased. In some places this plan is not at all useful, but in some regions it is actually necessary. In view of the variety of circumstances, specific points have not been considered, but it seemed desirable to mention this rite so that it may include elements common to the others, for example, in the liturgy of the word and in the rite of final commendation and farewell. For the rest the conferences of bishops may make their own arrangements.

9. When particular rituals are prepared in harmony with the new Roman Ritual, the conference of bishops may retain the three plans for funeral rites, change the order, or omit one or other of them. It may be that in a country a single plan, for example, the first one with

three stations, is the only one in use and therefore should be retained to the exclusion of the others; in another country all three plans may be necessary. The conference of bishops, after considering pastoral needs, will make suitable arrangements.

10.   After the funeral Mass the rite of final commendation and farewell is celebrated.

This rite is not to be understood as a purification of the dead—which is effected rather by the eucharistic sacrifice—but as the last farewell with which the Christian community honours one of its members before the body is buried. Although in death there is a certain separation, Christians, who are members of Christ and are one in him, can never be really separated by death.[1]

The priest introduces this rite with an invitation to pray: then follows a period of silence, the sprinkling with holy water, the incensation, and the song of farewell. The text and melody of the latter should be such that it may be sung by all present and be experienced as the climax of this entire rite.

The sprinkling with holy water, which recalls the person's entrance into eternal life through baptism, and the incensation, which honours the body of the deceased as a temple of the Holy Spirit, may also be considered signs of farewell.

The rite in final commendation and farewell is to be held only in the funeral celebration itself, that is, with the body present.

[In the United States, however, although the rite of final commendation at the catafalque or pall is excluded, it is permitted to celebrate the funeral service, including the commendation, in those cases where it is physically or morally impossible for the body of the deceased person to be present.]

11.   In celebrations for the dead, whether the funeral service or any other, emphasis should be given to the biblical readings. These proclaim the paschal mystery, support the hope of reunion in the kingdom of God, teach respect for the dead, and encourage the witness of Christian living.

12.   The Church employs the prayer of the psalms in the offices for the dead to express grief and to strengthen genuine hope. Pastors must therefore try by appropriate catechesis to lead their communities to understand and appreciate at least the chief psalms of the funeral liturgy. When pastoral considerations indicate the use of other

[1] Cf. Simeon of Thessalonica, *De ordine sepulturae*: P.G. 155, 685 B.

sacred songs, these should reflect a 'warm and living love for sacred scripture'[2] and a liturgical spirit.

13.   In the prayers, too, the Christian community expresses its faith and intercedes for adults who have died so that they may enjoy eternal happiness with God. This is the happiness which deceased children, made sons of adoption through baptism, are believed to enjoy already. Prayers are offered for the parents of these infants, as for the relatives of all the dead, so that in their sorrow they may experience the consolation of faith.

14.   In places where, by particular law, endowment, or custom, the Office of the Dead is usually said not only at the funeral rites but also apart from them, this office may continue to be celebrated with devotion. In view of the demands of modern life and pastoral considerations, a vigil or celebration of God's word (nos. 27-9) may take the place of the office.

15.   Christian funeral rites are permitted for those who choose to have their bodies cremated unless it is shown that they have acted for reasons contrary to Christian principles. See the norms in the Instruction of the Sacred Congregation of the Holy Office, *de cadaverum crematione*, 8 May 1963, nos. 2-3.[3]

These funeral rites should be celebrated according to the plan in use for the region but in a way that does not hide the Church's preference for the custom of burying the dead in a grave or tomb, as the Lord himself willed to be buried. In the case of cremation any danger of scandal or confusion should be removed.

The rites ordinarily performed at the cemetery chapel or at the grave or tomb may be used in the crematorium building. If there is no other suitable place for the rites, they may be celebrated in the crematorium hall itself, provided that the danger of scandal and religious indifferentism is avoided.

Offices and Ministries toward the Dead

16.   In funeral celebrations all who belong to the people of God should keep in mind their office and ministry: the parents or relatives, those who take care of funerals, the Christian community as a whole, and finally the priest. As teacher of the faith and minister of consola-

[2] SC 24.   [3] Cf. *AAS* 56 (1964) 822-3.

tion, the priest presides over the liturgical service and celebrates the eucharist.

17. Priests and all others should remember that, when they commend the dead to God in the funeral liturgy, it is their duty to strengthen the hope of those present and to foster their faith in the paschal mystery and the resurrection of the dead. In this way the compassionate kindness of Mother Church and the consolation of the faith may lighten the burden of believers without offending those who mourn.

18. In preparing and arranging funeral celebrations priests should consider the deceased and the circumstances of his life and death and be concerned also for the sorrow of the relatives and their Christian needs. Priests should be especially aware of persons, Catholic or non-Catholic, who seldom or never participate in the eucharist or who seem to have lost their faith, but who assist at liturgical celebrations and hear the Gospel on the occasion of funerals. Priests must remember that they are ministers of Christ's Gospel to all men.

19. The funeral rites, except the Mass, may be celebrated by a deacon. If pastoral necessity demands, the conference of bishops may, with the permission of the Holy See, permit a lay person to celebrate the service.

In the absence of a priest or deacon, it is urged that in the funeral rites according to the first plan the stations in the home of the deceased and at the cemetery be conducted by lay persons; the same holds for vigil services for the dead.

20. Apart from distinctions based on liturgical function and sacred orders and the honours due to civil authorities according to liturgical law, no special honours are to be paid to any private persons or classes of persons, whether in the ceremonies or by external display.[4]

Adaptations by the Conferences of Bishops

21. In accordance with article 63b of the Constitution on the Sacred Liturgy, the conference of bishops have the right to prepare a section of their particular rituals, which will correspond to this section of the Roman Ritual but is adapted to the needs of each

[4] See SC 32.

region. After review by the Apostolic See it may be used in the regions for which it has been prepared.

In making this adaptation, it is for the conferences of bishops:

1) To define the adaptations, within the limits stated in this section of the Roman Ritual.

2) To consider carefully and prudently which elements from the traditions and cultures of individual countries may be appropriately admitted and to submit such other adaptations, which they feel to be useful or necessary, to the Apostolic See, by whose consent they may be introduced.

3) To retain or adapt special elements of existing particular rituals, if any, provided that they can be brought into harmony with the Constitution on the Liturgy and contemporary needs.

4) To prepare translations of texts which are truly suited to the genius of the various languages and cultures, adding, when appropriate, melodies for singing.

5) To adapt and supplement the introductory material of the Roman Ritual so that the ministers will fully understand the significance of the rites and celebrate them effectively.

6) To arrange the material in the liturgical books prepared under the direction of the conferences of bishops so that the order is best suited to pastoral purposes. None of the material contained in this typical edition is to be omitted.

If it seems advisable to add rubrics and texts, they should be distinguished typographically from the rubrics and texts of the Roman Ritual.

22. In preparing particular rituals for funerals, it is for the conferences of bishops:

1) To arrange the rite according to one or more plans, as indicated above in no. 9.

2) To substitute, if preferred, texts from Chapter VI for those which appear in the basic rite.

3) To add, according to the rule in no. 21, 6, other formulas of the same kind whenever the Roman Ritual provides a choice of texts.

4) To judge whether lay persons are to be deputed to celebrate the funeral rites (see above, no. 19).

5) To decree, if there are pastoral reasons, that the sprinkling with holy water and the incensation may be omitted or another rite substituted.

6) To determine the liturgical colour for funerals in accordance

with the popular feeling. The colour should not be offensive to human sorrow but should express Christian hope enlightened by the paschal mystery.

The Function of the Priest in Preparing and Planning the Celebration

23. The priest should consider the various circumstances, and in particular the wishes of the family and the community. He should make free use of the choices afforded in the rite.

24. The rite for each plan is so described that it may be celebrated very simply. On the other hand, a generous selection of texts is given for use according to circumstances.

For example:

1) In general, all the texts are interchangeable and may be chosen, with the help of the community or family, to reflect the individual situation.

2) Some elements of the rite are not obligatory but may be freely added, for example, the prayer for the mourners at the home of the deceased.

3) In keeping with liturgical tradition, greater freedom of choice is given in the case of texts for processions.

4) Whenever a psalm, indicated or preferred for liturgical reasons, may offer some pastoral difficulty, another psalm is provided for optional use. In addition, one or other psalm verse which seems pastorally unsuitable may be omitted.

5) Since the text of the prayers is always given in the singular, masculine form, the gender and number must be adapted.

6) In the prayers, the lines within parentheses may be omitted.
[If an individual prayer or other text is clearly not appropriate to the circumstances of the deceased person, it is the responsibility of the priest to make the necessary adaptation.]

25. The celebration of the funeral liturgy with meaning and dignity and the priest's ministry to the dead presuppose an integral understanding of the Christian mystery and the pastoral office.

Among other things, the priest should:

1) Visit the sick and the dying, as indicated in the relevant section of the Roman Ritual.

2) Teach the significance of Christian death.

3) Show loving concern for the family of the deceased person, support them in the time of sorrow, and as much as possible involve them in planning the funeral celebration and the choice of the options made available in the rite.

4) Integrate the liturgy for the dead with the whole parish liturgical life and the pastoral ministry.

RITE OF MARRIAGE*:
INTRODUCTION

Structure

* Promulgated by Decree dated 19 March 1969.

Importance and Dignity of the Sacrament of Matrimony

1. Married Christians, in virtue of the sacrament of matrimony, signify and share in the mystery of that unity and fruitful love which exists between Christ and his Church;[1] they help each other to attain to holiness in their married life and in the rearing and education of their children; and they have their own special gift among the people of God.[2]

2. Marriage arises in the covenant of marriage, or irrevocable consent, which each partner freely bestows on and accepts from the other. This intimate union and the good of the children impose total fidelity on each of them and argue for an unbreakable oneness between them. Christ the Lord raised this union to the dignity of a sacrament so that it might more clearly recall and more easily reflect his own unbreakable union with his Church.[3]

3. Christian couples, therefore, nourish and develop their marriage by undivided affection, which wells up from the fountain of divine love, while, in a merging of human and divine love, they remain faithful in body and in mind, in good times as in bad.[4]

4. By their very nature, the institution of matrimony and wedded love are ordained for the procreation and education of children and find in them their ultimate crown. Therefore, married Christians, while not considering the other purposes of marriage of less account, should be steadfast and ready to cooperate with the love of the Creator and Saviour, who through them will constantly enrich and enlarge his own family.[5]

5. A priest should bear in mind these principles of faith, both in his instructions to those about to be married and when giving the homily during the marriage ceremony. He should relate his instructions to the texts of the sacred readings.[6]

   The bridal couple should be given a review of the fundamentals of Christian doctrine. This may include instruction on the teachings about marriage and the family, on the rites used in the celebration of the sacrament itself, and on the prayers and readings. In this way the bridegroom and the bride will receive far greater benefit from the celebration.

[1] Ephesians 5:32.   [2] LG 11.   [3] GS 48.
[4] GS 48, 49.   [5] GS 48, 50.   [6] SC 52; IOe 54.

6. In the celebration of marriage (which normally should be within the Mass), certain elements should be stressed, especially the liturgy of the word, which shows the importance of Christian marriage in the history of salvation and the duties and responsibility of the couple in caring for the holiness of their children. Also of supreme importance are the consent of the contracting parties, which the priest asks and receives; the special nuptial blessing for the bride and for the marriage covenant; and finally, the reception of holy communion by the groom and the bride, and by all present, by which their love is nourished and all are lifted up into communion with our Lord and with one another.[7]

7. Priests should first of all strengthen and nourish the faith of those about to be married, for the sacrament of matrimony presupposes and demands faith.[8]

Choice of Rite

8. In a marriage between a Catholic and a baptised person who is not Catholic, the regulations which appear below in the rite of marriage outside Mass (nos. 39-54) shall be observed. If suitable, and if the Ordinary of the place gives permission, the rite for celebrating marriage within Mass (nos. 19-38) may be used, except that, according to the general law, communion is not given to the non-Catholic.

In a marriage between a Catholic and one who is not baptised, the rite which appears in nos. 55-6 is to be followed.

9. Furthermore, priests should show special consideration to those who take part in liturgical celebrations or hear the gospel only on the occasion of a wedding, either because they are not Catholics, or because they are Catholics who rarely, if ever, take part in the eucharist or seem to have abandoned the practice of their faith. Priests are ministers of Christ's gospel to everyone.

10. In the celebration of matrimony, apart from the liturgical laws providing for due honours to civil authorities, no special honours are to be paid to any private persons or classes of person, whether in the ceremonies or by external display.[9]

[7] AA 3; LG 12. [8] SC 59. [9] SC 32.

11. Whenever marriage is celebrated during Mass, white vestments are worn and the wedding Mass is used. If the marriage is celebrated on a Sunday or solemnity, the Mass of the day is used with the nuptial blessing and, where appropriate, the special final blessing.

The liturgy of the word is extremely helpful in emphasising the meaning of the sacrament and the obligations of marriage. When the wedding Mass may not be used, one of the readings in nos. 67-105 should be chosen, except from Holy Thursday to Easter and on the feasts of Christmas, Epiphany, Ascension, Pentecost, Corpus Christi, and other holydays of obligation. On the Sundays of the Christmas season and throughout the year, in Masses which are not parish Masses, the wedding Mass may be used without change.

When a marriage is celebrated during Advent or Lent or other days of penance, the parish priest should advise the couple to take into consideration the special nature of these times.

Preparation of Local Rituals

12. In addition to the faculty spoken of below in no. 17 for regions where the Roman Ritual for matrimony is used, particular rituals shall be prepared, suitable for the customs and needs of individual areas, according to the principle of art. 63b and 77 of the Constitution on the Sacred Liturgy. These are to be reviewed by the Apostolic See. In making adaptations, the following points must be remembered:

13. The formulas of the Roman Ritual may be adapted or, as the case may be, filled out (including the questions before the consent and the actual words of the consent).

When the Roman Ritual has several optional formulas, local rituals may add other formulas of the same type.

14. Within the rite of the sacrament of matrimony, the arrangement of its parts may be varied. If it seems more suitable, even the questions before the consent may be omitted as long as the priest asks and receives the consent of the contracting parties.

15. After the exchange of rings, the crowning or veiling of the bride may take place according to local custom.

In any region where the joining of hands or the blessing or exchange of rings does not fit in with the practice of the people, the conference of bishops may allow these rites to be omitted or other rites substituted.

16. As for the marriage customs of nations that are now receiving the gospel for the first time, whatever is good and is not indissolubly bound up with superstition and error should be sympathetically considered and, if possible, preserved intact. Sometimes the Church admits such things into the liturgy itself, as long as they harmonise with its true and authentic spirit.[10]

Right to Prepare a Completely New Rite

17. Each conference of bishops may draw up its own marriage rite suited to the usages of the place and people and approved by the Apostolic See. The rite must always conform to the law that the priest assisting at such marriages must ask for and receive the consent of the contracting parties,[11] and the nuptial blessing should always be given.[12]

18. Among peoples where the marriage ceremonies customarily take place in the home, sometimes over a period of several days, these customs should be adapted to the Christian spirit and to the liturgy. In such cases the conference of bishops, according to the pastoral needs of the people, may allow the sacramental rite to be celebrated in the home.

[10] SC 37.
[11] SC 77.
[12] SC 78.

RITE OF ORDINATION OF DEACONS, PRESBYTERS AND BISHOPS*
APOSTOLIC LETTER

Issued Motu Proprio
Laying down certain norms
regarding The Holy Order of Deacons

POPE PAUL VI

For the nurturing and constant growth of the people of God, Christ the Lord instituted in the Church a variety of ministries which work for the good of the whole body.[1]

From the apostolic age the diaconate has had a clearly outstanding position among these ministries, and it has always been held in great honour by the Church. Explicit testimony of this is given by the apostle Saint Paul both in his letter to the Philippians, in which he sends his greetings not only to the bishops but also to the deacons,[2] and in a letter to Timothy, in which he highlights the qualities and virtues that deacons must have in order to be proved worthy of their ministry.[3]

Later, when the early writers of the Church acclaim the dignity of deacons, they do not fail to extol also the spiritual qualities and virtues that are required for the performance of that ministry, namely, fidelity to Christ, moral integrity, and obedience to the bishop.

Saint Ignatius of Antioch declares that the office of the deacon is nothing other than 'the ministry of Jesus Christ, who was with the Father before all ages and has been manifested in the final time'.[4] He also made the following observation: 'The deacons too, who are ministers of the mysteries of Jesus Christ, should please all in every way, for they are not servants of food and drink, but ministers of the

---

* Promulgated by Decree dated 15 August 1968.
[1] See LG 18.
[2] See Philippians 1:1.
[3] See 1 Timothy 3:8-13.
[4] *Ad Magnesios*, VI, 1: *Patres Apostolici*, ed. F. X. Funk, I (Tübingen, 1901), p. 235.

Church of God'.[5]

Saint Polycarp of Smyrna exhorts deacons to 'be moderate in all things, merciful, diligent, living according to the truth of the Lord, who became the servant of all'.[6] The author of the *Didascalia Apostolorum*, recalling the words of Christ: 'Anyone who wants to be great among you must be your servant',[7] addresses the following fraternal exhortation to deacons: 'Accordingly you deacons also should behave in such a way that, if your ministry obliges you to lay down your lives for a brother or a sister, you should do so . . . If the Lord of heaven and earth served us and suffered and sustained everything on our behalf, should not this be done for our brothers and sisters all the more by us, since we are imitators of him and have been given the place of Christ?'[8]

Furthermore, when the writers of the first centuries insist on the importance of the deacons' ministry, they give many examples of the manifold important tasks entrusted to them and clearly show how much authority they held in the Christian communities and how great was their contribution to the apostolate. The deacon is described as 'the bishop's ear, mouth, heart, and soul'.[9] The deacon is at the disposal of the bishop in order that he may serve the whole people of God and take care of the sick and the poor;[10] he is correctly and rightly called 'one who shows love for orphans, for the devout and for the widowed, one who is fervent in spirit, one who shows love for what is good'.[11] Furthermore, he is entrusted with the mission of taking the holy eucharist to the sick confined to their homes,[12] of conferring baptism,[13] and of attending to preaching the word of God in accordance with the express will of the bishop.

Accordingly, the diaconate flourished in a wonderful way in the

---

[5] *Ad Trallianos*, II, 3: *Patres Apostolici*, ed. F. X. Funk, I (Tübingen, 1901), p. 245.

[6] Epistola *Ad Philippenses*, V, 2: *Patres Apostolici*, ed. F. X. Funk, I (Tübingen, 1901), pp. 301-3.

[7] Matthew 20:26-7.

[8] *Didascalia Apostolorum*, III, 13, 2-4: *Didascalia et Constitutiones Apostolorum*, ed. F. X. Funk, I, (Paderborn, 1906), p. 214.

[9] *Didascalia Apostolorum*, II, 44, 4; ed. F. X. Funk, I, p. 138.

[10] See *Traditio Apostolica*, 39 and 34; *La Tradition Apostolique de Saint Hippolyte. Essai de reconstitution* by B. Botte (Münster, 1963), pp. 87 and 81.

[11] *Testamentum D. N. Iesu Christi*, I, 38; ed. and trans. into Latin by I. E. Rahmani (Mainz, 1899), p. 93.

[12] See Saint Justin, *Apologia* I, 65, 5 and 67, 5: Saint Justin, *Apologiae duae*; ed. G. Rauschen (Bonn, 1911), pp. 107 and 111.

[13] See Tertullian, *De Baptismo*, XVII, 1: *Corpus Christianorum*, I, *Tertulliani Opera*, pars I (Turnholt, 1954), p. 291.

Church and at the same time gave an outstanding witness of love for Christ and the brethren through the performance of works of charity,[14] the celebration of sacred rites,[15] and the fulfilment of pastoral duties.[16]

The exercise of the office of deacon enables those who were to become presbyters to give proof of themselves, to display the merit of their work, and to acquire preparation—all of which were requirements for receiving the dignity of the priesthood and the office of pastor.

As time went on, the discipline concerning this holy order was changed. The prohibition against conferring ordination without observing the established sequence of orders was strengthened, and there was a gradual decrease in the number of those who preferred to remain deacons all their lives instead of advancing to a higher order. As a consequence, the permanent diaconate almost entirely disappeared in the Latin Church. It is hardly necessary to mention what was decided by the Council of Trent when it proposed to restore the holy orders in accordance with their own nature as ancient functions within the Church;[17] it was only much later that the idea matured of restoring this important order also as a truly permanent rank. Our predecessor Pius XII briefly alluded to this matter.[18]

Finally, the Second Vatican Council supported the wishes and requests that, where such would lead to the good of souls, the permanent diaconate should be restored as an intermediate order between the higher ranks of the Church's hierarchy and the rest of the people of God, as an expression of the needs and desires of the Christian communities, as a driving force for the Church's service or *diaconia* towards the local Christian communities, and as a sign or sacrament of the Lord Christ himself, who 'came not to be served but to serve'.[19]

For this reason, at the third session of the Council, in October 1964, the Fathers ratified the principle of the renewal of the diaconate and in the following November the dogmatic constitution *Lumen*

[14] See *Didascalia Apostolorum*, II, 31, 2: ed. F. X. Funk, I, p. 112; see *Testamentum D. N. Iesu Christi*, I, 31: ed. and trans. into Latin by I. E. Rahmani (Mainz, 1899), p. 75.
[15] See *Didascalia Apostolorum*, II, 57, 6; 58, 1; ed. F. X. Funk, I. pp. 162 and 166.
[16] See Saint Cyprian, Epistolae XV and XVI: ed. G. Hartel (Vienna, 1971), pp. 513-520; see Saint Augustine, *De catechizandis rudibus*, I, cap. I, 1: PL 40, 309-10.
[17] Session XXIII, capp. I-IV: *Mansi*, XXXIII, 138-40.
[18] Address to the Participants in the Second International Congress of the Lay
[19] Apostolate, 5 October 1957: *AAS* 49 (1957) 925.
Matthew 20:28.

gentium was promulgated. In article 29 of this document a description is given of the principal characteristics proper to that state: 'At a lower level of the hierarchy are deacons, upon whom hands are imposed "not for priesthood, but for ministry". For, strengthened by sacramental grace, in communion with the bishop and his presbyterium, they serve the people of God in the *diaconia* of the liturgy, of the word, and of charity'.[20]

The same constitution made the following declaration about permanency in the rank of deacon: 'These duties (of deacons), so very necessary for the life of the Church, can in many areas be fulfilled only with difficulty according to the prevailing discipline of the Latin Church. For this reason, the diaconate can in the future be restored as a proper and permanent rank of the hierarchy'.[21]

However, this restoration of the permanent diaconate required that the instructions of the Council be more profoundly examined and that there be mature deliberation concerning the juridical status of both the celibate and married deacon. Similarly, it was necessary that matters connected with the diaconate of those who are to become priests should be adapted to contemporary conditions, so that the time of diaconate would furnish that proof of way of life, of maturity, and of aptitude for the priestly ministry which ancient discipline demanded from candidates for the presbyterate.

Thus on 18 June 1967, we issued *motu proprio* the apostolic letter *Sacrum Diaconatus Ordinem*, by which suitable canonical norms for the permanent diaconate were established.[22] On 17 June of the following year, through the apostolic constitution *Pontificalis Romani Recognitio*,[23] we authorised the new rite for the conferring of the sacred orders of deacons, presbyters, and bishops, and at the same time defined the matter and the form of the ordination itself.

Now that we are proceeding further and are today promulgating the apostolic letter *Ministeria Quaedam*, we consider it fitting to issue certain norms concerning the diaconate. We also desire that candidates for the diaconate should know what ministries they are to exercise before sacred ordination and when and how they are to take upon themselves the responsibilities of celibacy and liturgical prayer.

Since entrance into the clerical state is deferred until diaconate, there no longer exists the rite of first tonsure, by which a layman used

---

[20] *AAS* 57 (1965) 36.
[21] *Ibid.*
[22] *AAS* 59 (1967) 697-704.
[23] *AAS* 60 (1968) 369-73.

to become a cleric. But a new rite is introduced, by which one who aspires to ordination as deacon or presbyter publicly manifests his will to offer himself to God and the Church, so that he may exercise a sacred order. The Church, accepting this offering, selects and calls him to prepare himself to receive a sacred order, and in this way he is properly numbered among candidates for the diaconate or presbyterate.

It is especially fitting that the ministries of readers and acolyte should be entrusted to those who, as candidates for sacred orders, desire to devote themselves to God and to the Church in a special way. For the Church, which 'does not cease to receive the bread of life from the table of the word of God and the body of Christ and offer it to the faithful',[24] considers it to be very opportune that, both by study and by gradual exercise of the ministry of the word and of the altar, candidates for sacred orders should through intimate contact understand and reflect upon the double aspect of the priestly office. Thus it comes about that the authenticity of the ministry shines out with the greatest effectiveness. In this way the candidates are to approach holy orders fully aware of their vocation, fervent in spirit, serving the Lord, constant in prayer, and aware of the needs of the faithful.[25] Having weighed every aspect of the question well, having sought the opinion of experts, having consulted with the conferences of bishops and taken their views into account, and having taken counsel with our venerable brothers who are members of the Sacred Congregations competent in this matter, by our apostolic authority we enact the following norms, derogating—if and insofar as necessary—from provisions of the Code of Canon Law now in force, and we promulgate them with this letter.

1. a) A rite of admission for candidates for ordination as deacons and presbyters is now introduced. In order that this admission be properly made, the free petition of the aspirant, made out and signed in his own hand, is required, as well as the written acceptance of the competent ecclesiastical superior, through which the selection by the Church is brought about.

Professed members of clerical congregations who seek the presbyterate are not bound to this rite.

b) The competent superior for this acceptance is the Ordinary (the bishop, or in clerical institutes, the major superior). Those can be accepted who give signs of an authentic vocation and, endowed with good moral qualities and free from mental and physical defects, wish

[24] See DV 21.   [25] See Romans 12:11-13.

to dedicate their lives to the service of the Church for the glory of God and the good of souls. It is necessary that those who aspire to the diaconate leading to the presbyterate will have completed at least their twentieth year and have begun their course of theological studies.

c) In virtue of the acceptance the candidate must care for his vocation in a special way and foster it. He also acquires the right to the necessary spiritual assistance by which he can develop his vocation and submit unconditionally to the will of God.

2. Candidates for the permanent diaconate and for the diaconate leading to the presbyterate, as well as candidates for the presbyterate itself, are to receive the ministries of reader and acolyte, unless they have already done so, and are to exercise them for a fitting time, in order to be better disposed for the future service of the word and of the altar.

Dispensation from receiving these ministries on the part of such candidates is reserved to the Holy See.

3. The liturgical rites by which admission of candidates for ordination as deacons and presbyters takes place and by which the above-mentioned ministries are conferred should be performed by the Ordinary of the aspirant (the bishop or, in clerical institutes, the major superior).

4. The intervals established by the Holy See or by the conferences of bishops between the conferring—during the course of theological studies—of the ministry of readers and that of acolytes, and between the ministry of acolytes and the order of deacons, must be observed.

5. Before ordination candidates for the diaconate shall give to the Ordinary (the bishop or, in clerical institutes, the major superior) a declaration made out and signed in their own hand, by which they testify that they are about to receive the order freely and of their own accord.

6. The special consecration of celibacy observed for the sake of the kingdom of heaven and its obligation for candidates to the priesthood and for unmarried candidates to the diaconate are linked with the diaconate. The public commitment to celibacy before God and the Church is to be celebrated in a particular rite, even by religious, and it is to precede ordination to the diaconate. Celibacy taken on in this way is a diriment impediment to entering marriage.

In accordance with the traditional discipline of the Church, a married deacon who has lost his wife cannot enter a new marriage.[26]

7. a) Deacons called to the presbyterate are not to be ordained until they have completed the course of studies prescribed by the norms of the Apostolic See.

b) In regard to the course of theological studies to precede the ordination of permanent deacons, the conferences of bishops, with attention to the local situation, will issue the proper norms and submit them for the approval of the Sacred Congregation for Catholic Education.

8. In accordance with norms 29-30 of the General Instruction for the Liturgy of the Hours:

a) Deacons called to the presbyterate are obliged by their sacred ordination to celebrate the liturgy of the hours.

b) It is most fitting that permanent deacons should recite daily at least a part of the liturgy of the hours, to be determined by the conference of bishops.

9. Entrance into the clerical state and incardination into a diocese are brought about by ordination to the diaconate.

10. The rite of admission for candidates for ordination as deacons and presbyters and of the special consecration of celibacy is to be published soon by the competent department of the Roman Curia.

Transitional Norms: Candidates for the sacrament of orders who have already received first tonsure before the promulgation of this letter retain all the duties, rights, and privileges of clerics. Those who have been promoted to the order of subdiaconate are held to the obligations taken on in regard to both celibacy and the liturgy of the hours. But they must celebrate once again their public commitment to elibacy before God and the Church by the new special rite preceding ordination to the diaconate.

All that has been decreed by us in this letter, issued *motu proprio*, we order to be confirmed and ratified, anything to the contrary notwithstanding. We also determine that it shall come into force on 1 January 1973.

Given at Rome, at Saint Peter's, 15 August 1972, the Solemnity of the Assumption, the tenth year of our pontificate.

PAUL PP. VI

[26] See Paul VI, apostolic letter *Sacrum Diaconatus Ordinem*, no. 16: *AAS* 59 (1967) 701.

APOSTOLIC CONSTITUTION

PAUL, BISHOP
Servant of the Servants of God For an Everlasting Memorial

The revision of the Roman Pontifical is prescribed in a general way by the Second Vatican Ecumenical Council[1] and is also governed by special norms in which the holy Synod ordered that the rites of ordination be changed 'in ceremonies and in texts'.[2]

Among the rites of ordination the first to be considered are those which constitute the hierarchy through the sacrament of orders, conferred in several grades: 'Thus the divinely instituted ministry of the Church is exercised in various orders by those who already in antiquity are called bishops, presbyters, and deacons'.[3]

In the revision of the rites of sacred ordination, besides the general principles which must direct the entire restoration of the liturgy according to the decrees of the Second Vatican Council, the greatest attention should be paid to the Council's important teaching, in the Constitution on the Church, on the nature and effects of the sacrament of orders. It is evident that the liturgy itself should express this doctrine in its own way, for 'the texts and rites should be drawn up so that they express more clearly the holy things they signify; the Christian people, so far as possible, should be able to understand them with ease and to take part in them fully, actively, and as befits a community'.[4]

The holy Synod teaches that 'by episcopal consecration the fullness of the sacrament of orders is conferred, that fullness which is truly called—in the Church's liturgical usage and in the language of the Fathers—the high priesthood, the apex of the sacred ministry. But together with the office of sanctifying, episcopal consecration also confers the offices of teaching and governing. These, however, of their very nature can be exercised only in hierarchical communion with the head and members of the college (of bishops). From

---

[1] SC 25.   [2] SC 76.
[3] LG 28.   [4] SC 21.

tradition which is expressed especially through liturgical rites and through the practice of the Church in both East and West, it is clear that by the laying on of hands and the words of consecration the grace of the Holy Spirit is so conferred and the sacred character so impressed that bishops undertake Christ's own role as Teacher, Shepherd, and Bishop in an eminent and visible way and that they act in his person.'[5]

To these words should be added a number of important doctrinal statements (of the Council) concerning the apostolic succession of bishops and their duties and functions. Even if these matters are now found in the rite of episcopal consecration, still it seems that they should be better and more precisely expressed. To achieve this, it appeared appropriate to take from ancient sources the consecratory prayer which is found in the document called the *Apostolic Tradition of Hippolytus of Rome*, written at the beginning of the third century. This consecratory prayer is still used, in large part, in the ordination rites of the Coptic and West Syrian liturgies. Thus the very act of ordination is witness to the harmony of tradition in East and West concerning the apostolic office of bishops.

With regard to presbyters, the following should be recalled from the acts of the Second Vatican Council: 'Although presbyters do not possess the highest degree of the pontificate and although they are dependent upon the bishops in the exercise of their power, they are nevertheless united with the bishops in priestly dignity; and in virtue of the sacrament of orders they are consecrated in the image of Christ the eternal high priest (see Hebrews 5:1-10; 7:24, 9:11-28) as true priests of the New Testament to preach the Gospel, shepherd the faithful, and celebrate the worship of God.'[6] In another place the Council says: 'By sacred ordination and by the mission they receive from the bishops, presbyters are promoted to the service of Christ the Teacher, the Priest, and the King. They share in his ministry of unceasingly building up the Church on earth into the People of God, the Body of Christ, and the Temple of the Holy Spirit.'[7] In the ordination of presbyters, as found in the Roman Pontifical, the mission and grace of the presbyter as a helper of the episcopal order have been very clearly described. Yet it seemed necessary to restore the entire rite, which had been divided into several parts, to greater unity and to express in sharper light the central part of the ordination, that is, the laying on of hands and

[5] LG 21. [6] LG 28. [7] PO 1.

the consecratory prayer.

Finally, with regard to deacons, in addition to the content of our apostolic letter *Sacrum Diaconatus Ordinem* issued *motu proprio* on 18 June 1967, the following should be especially recalled: 'In the lower grade of the hierarchy are deacons, on whom hands are laid "not for the priesthood, but for the ministry" (Constitutions of the Church of Egypt, III, 2). Strengthened by sacramental grace, they serve the People of God in the *diaconia* of liturgy, word, and charity, in communion with the bishop and his *presbyterium*.'[8] In the ordination of deacons a few changes had to be made to satisfy the recent prescriptions about the diaconate as a distinct and permanent grade of the hierarchy in the Latin Church or to achieve a greater simplicity and clarity in the rites.

Among the other documents of the supreme magisterium pertaining to sacred orders, we consider one worthy of particular mention, namely, the apostolic constitution *Sacramentum Ordinis* published by our predecessor, Pius XII, on 30 November 1947. In this constitution he declared that 'the sole matter of the sacred orders of diaconate and presbyterate is the laying on of hands; likewise the sole form is the words determining the application of this matter, which univocally signify the sacramental effects—namely, the power of orders and the grace of the Holy Spirit—and are accepted and used as such by the Church'.[9] After this, the document determines which laying on of hands and which words constitute the matter and form in the conferring of each order.

It was necessary in the revision of the rite to add, delete, or change certain things, either to restore texts to their earlier integrity, to clarify the meaning, or to bring out more clearly the sacramental effects. We therefore think it necessary, in order to remove all controversy and to avoid anxiety of conscience, to declare what is to be considered as belonging to the very nature of the rite in each case. By our supreme apostolic authority we decree and establish the following with regard to the matter and form in the conferring of each order.

In the ordination of deacons, the matter is the laying of the bishop's hands upon the individual candidates, which is done in silence before the consecratory prayer; the form consists of the words of the consecratory prayer, of which the following belong to the nature of the rite and are consequently required for validity:

[8] LG 29.   [9] *AAS* 40 (1948)6.

> Lord,
> send forth upon them the Holy Spirit,
> that they may be strengthened
> by the gift of your sevenfold grace
> to carry out faithfully the work of the ministry.

In the ordination of presbyters, the matter is likewise the laying of the bishop's hands upon the individual candidates, which is done in silence before the consecratory prayer; the form consists of the words of the consecratory prayer, of which the following belong to the nature of the rite and are consequently required for validity:

> Almighty Father,
> grant to these servants of yours
> the dignity of the priesthood.
> Renew within them the Spirit of holiness.
> As co-workers with the order of bishops
> may they be faithful to the ministry
> that they receive from you, Lord God,
> and be to others a model of right conduct.

Finally, in the ordination of a bishop, the matter is the laying of hands on the head of the bishop-elect by the consecrating bishops, or at least by the principal consecrator, which is done in silence before the consecratory prayer; the form consists of the words of the consecratory prayer, of which the following belong to the nature of the rite and are consequently required for validity:

> So now pour out upon this chosen one
> that power which is from you,
> the governing Spirit
> whom you gave to your beloved Son, Jesus Christ,
> the Spirit given by him to the holy apostles,
> who founded the Church in every place
> to be your temple
> for the unceasing glory and praise of your name.

This rite for the conferring of the sacred orders of diaconate, presbyterate, and episcopate has been revised by the Consilium for the Implementation of the Constitution on the Sacred Liturgy 'with the assistance of experts, and with the consultation of bishops, from various parts of the world'.[10] By our apostolic authority we approve

[10] SC 25.

this rite so that it may be used in the future for the conferral of these orders in place of the rite now found in the Roman Pontifical.

It is our will that these our decrees and prescriptions be firm and effective now and in the future, notwithstanding, to the extent necessary, the apostolic constitutions and ordinances issued by our predecessors and other prescriptions, even those requiring particular mention and derogation.

Given at Rome, at Saint Peter's, 18 June 1968, the fifth year of our pontificate.

PAUL PP. VI

219

ORDINATION OF DEACONS:
INTRODUCTION

1. The ordination of deacons should take place on a Sunday or holyday, when a large number of the faithful can attend, unless pastoral reasons suggest another day.

The public commitment to celibacy by candidates for ordination as priests and by unmarried candidates for the diaconate, including religious, must be made before the rite of ordination of deacons (see no. 14 below).

2. The ordination should take place ordinarily at the *cathedra* or bishop's chair; or, to enable the faithful to participate more fully, a chair for the bishop may be placed before the altar or elsewhere. Seats for those to be ordained should be placed so that the faithful may have a complete view of the liturgical rites.

3. Those to be ordained wear an alb (with amice and cincture unless other provisions are made).

4. In addition to what is needed for the celebration of Mass, there should be ready: (a) the Roman Pontifical; (b) stoles and dalmatics for the individual candidates.

The chalice should be sufficiently large for the communion of those ordained.

5. When everything is ready, the procession moves through the church to the altar in the usual way. A deacon carries the Book of the Gospels; he is followed by the candidates and finally by the bishop between two deacons.

ORDINATION OF PRIESTS:
INTRODUCTION

1. The ordination of priests should take place on a Sunday or holyday, when a large number of the faithful can attend, unless pastoral reasons suggest another day.

2. The ordination should take place ordinarily at the *cathedra* or bishop's chair; or, to enable the faithful to participate more fully, a chair for the bishop may be placed before the altar or elsewhere. Seats for those to be ordained should be placed so that the faithful may have a complete view of the liturgical rites.

3. All the priests concelebrate with the bishop in their ordination Mass. It is most appropriate for the bishop to admit other priests to the concelebration; in this case and on this day the newly ordained priests take the first place ahead of the others who concelebrate.

4. Those to be ordained wear an alb (with an amice and cincture unless other provisions are made) and deacon's stole. In addition to what is needed for the concelebration of Mass, there should be ready: (a) the Roman Pontifical; (b) stoles for the priests who lay hands upon the candidates; (c) chasubles for the individual candidates; (d) a linen gremial; (e) holy chrism; (f) whatever is needed for the washing of hands.

5. When everything is ready, the procession moves through the church to the altar in the usual way. A deacon carries the Book of the Gospels; he is followed by the candidates, then the concelebrating priests, and finally the bishop between two deacons.

ORDINATION OF A BISHOP: INTRODUCTION

1. The ordination of a bishop should take place on a Sunday or holyday when a large number of the faithful can attend, unless pastoral reasons suggest another day, such as the feast of an apostle.

2. The principal consecrator must be assisted by at least two other consecrating bishops, but it is fitting for all the bishops present together with the principal consecrator to ordain the bishop-elect.

3. Two priests assist the bishop-elect.

4. It is most appropriate for all the consecrating bishops and the priests assisting the bishop-elect to concelebrate the Mass with the principal consecrator and with the bishop-elect. If the ordination takes place in the bishop-elect's own church, some priests of his diocese should also concelebrate.

5. If the ordination takes place in the bishop-elect's own church, the principal consecrator may ask the newly ordained bishop to preside over the concelebration of the eucharistic liturgy. If the ordination does not take place in the bishop-elect's own church, the principal consecrator presides at the concelebration; in this case the new bishop takes the first place among the other concelebrants.

6. The principal consecrator and the concelebrating bishops and priests wear the vestments required for Mass. The bishop-elect wears all the priestly vestments, the pectoral cross, and the dalmatic. If the consecrating bishops do not concelebrate, they wear the rochet or alb, pectoral cross, stole, cope, and mitre. If the priests assisting the bishop-elect do not concelebrate, they wear the cope over an alb or surplice.

7. The blessing of the ring, pastoral staff, and mitre ordinarily takes place at a convenient time prior to the ordination service.

8. In addition to what is needed for the concelebration of a pontifical Mass, there should be ready: (a) the Roman Pontifical; (b)

222

copies of the consecratory prayer for the consecrating bishops; (c) a linen gremial; (d) holy chrism; (e) a ring, staff, and mitre for the bishop-elect.

9. Seats for the principal consecrator, consecrating bishops, the bishop-elect, and concelebrating priests are arranged as follows:

a) For the liturgy of the word, the principal consecrator should sit at the *cathedra* or bishop's chair, with the consecrating bishops near the chair. The bishop-elect sits between the assisting priests in an appropriate place within the sanctuary.

b) The ordination should usually take place at the bishop's chair; or, to enable the faithful to participate more fully, seats for the principal consecrator and consecrating bishops may be placed before the altar or elsewhere. Seats for the bishop-elect and his assisting priests should be placed so that the faithful may have a complete view of the liturgical rites.

When everything is ready, the procession moves through the church to the altar in the usual way. A deacon carries the Book of the Gospels; he is followed by the priests who will concelebrate, the bishop-elect between the priests assisting him, the consecrating bishops, and, finally, the principal consecrator between two deacons.

INSTITUTION OF READERS AND ACOLYTES*
APOSTOLIC LETTER

Issued Motu Proprio
by which the discipline of First Tonsure, Minor Orders,
and Subdiaconate in the Latin Church is reformed

POPE PAUL VI

Even in the most ancient times certain ministries were established by the Church for the purpose of suitably giving worship to God and for offering service to the people of God according to their needs. By these ministries, duties of a liturgical and charitable nature, deemed suitable to varying circumstances, were entrusted to the performance of the faithful. The conferring of these functions often took place by a special rite, in which, after God's blessing had been implored, a Christian was established in a special class or rank for the fulfilment of some ecclesiastical function.

Some of these functions, which were more closely connected with the liturgical celebration, slowly came to be considered as preparatory instructions for the reception of sacred orders, so that the offices of porter, reader, exorcist, and acolyte were called minor orders in the Latin Church in relation to the subdiaconate, diaconate, and presbyterate, which were called major orders. Generally, though not everywhere, these minor orders were reserved to those who received them on their way to the priesthood.

Nevertheless, since the minor orders have not always been the same and many tasks connected with them, as at present, have also been exercised by the laity, it seems fitting to reexamine this practice and to adapt it to contemporary needs, so that what is obsolete in these offices may be removed, what is useful retained, what is necessary defined, and at the same time what is required of candidates for holy orders may be determined.

While the Second Vatican Council was in preparation, many

* Promulgated by Decree dated 3 December 1972.

pastors of the Church requested that the minor orders and sub-diaconate should be reexamined. Although the Council did not decree anything concerning this for the Latin Church, it enunciated certain principles for solving the question. There is no doubt that the norms laid down by the Council regarding the general and orderly renewal of the liturgy[1] also included those areas which concern ministries in the liturgical assembly, so that from the very arrangement of the celebration the Church clearly appears structured in different orders and ministries.[2] Thus the Second Vatican Council decreed that 'in liturgical celebrations each person, minister or layman, who has an office to perform, should do all, and only, those parts which pertain to his office by the nature of the rite and the principles of liturgy'.[3]

With this assertion is closely connected what was written a little before in the same constitution: 'Mother Church earnestly desires that all the faithful be led to that full, conscious, and active participation in liturgical celebrations which is demanded by the nature of the liturgy. Such participation by the Christian people as "a chosen race, a royal priesthood, a holy nation, a purchased people" (1 Peter 2:9; see 2:4-5) is their right and duty by reason of their baptism. In the restoration and promotion of the sacred liturgy, this full and active participation by all the people is the aim to be considered before all else; for it is the primary and indispensable source from which the faithful are to derive the true Christian spirit. Therefore, through the needed programme of instruction, pastors of souls must zealously strive to achieve it in all their pastoral work.'[4]

Among the particular offices to be preserved and adapted to contemporary needs are those which are in a special way more closely connected with the ministries of the word and of the altar and in the Latin Church are called the offices of reader and acolyte and the subdiaconate. It is fitting to preserve and adapt these in such a way, that from this time on there will be two offices: that of reader and that of acolyte, which will include the functions of the subdiaconate.

Besides the offices common to the Latin Church, there is nothing to prevent episcopal conferences from requesting others of the Apostolic See, if they judge the establishment of such offices in their region to be necessary or very useful because of special reasons. To these belong, for example, the offices of porter, exorcist, and

---

[1] See SC 62.
[2] See General Instruction on the Roman Missal 58.
[3] SC 28.
[4] SC 14.

catechist,[5] as well as other offices to be conferred upon those who are dedicated to works of charity, where this service has not been given to deacons.

It is in accordance with the reality itself and with the contemporary outlook that the above-mentioned ministries should no longer be called minor orders; their conferring will not be called 'ordination', but 'institution'. Only those, however, who have received the diaconate will be properly known as clerics. Thus there will better appear the distinction between clergy and laity, between what is proper and reserved to the clergy and what can be entrusted to the laity; thus there will appear more clearly their mutual relationship, insofar as 'the common priesthood of the faithful and the ministerial or hierarchical priesthood, while they differ in essence and not only in degree, are nevertheless interrelated. Each of them shares in its own special way in the one priesthood of Christ.'[6]

Having weighed every aspect of the question well, having sought the opinion of experts, having consulted with the episcopal conferences and taken their views into account, and having taken counsel with our venerable brothers who are members of the Sacred Congregations competent in this matter, by our apostolic authority we enact the following norms, derogating—if and insofar as necessary—from provisions of the Code of Canon Law now in force, and we promulgate them with this letter.

1. First tonsure is no longer conferred; entrance into the clerical state is joined to the diaconate.

2. What up to now were called minor orders are henceforth called 'ministries'.

3. Ministries may be committed to lay Christians; hence they are no longer to be considered as reserved to candidates for the sacrament of orders.

4. Two ministries, adapted to present-day needs, are to be preserved in the whole of the Latin Church, namely those of reader and acolyte. The functions heretofore committed to the subdeacon are entrusted to the reader and the acolyte; consequently, the major order of subdiaconate no longer exists in the Latin Church. There is nothing, however, to prevent the acolyte being also called a subdeacon in some places, if the episcopal conference judges it opportune.

[5] See AG 15.   [6] LG 10.

5. The reader is appointed for a function proper to him, that of reading the word of God in the liturgical assembly. Accordingly, he is to read the lessons from sacred Scripture, except for the gospel, in the Mass and other sacred celebrations; he is to recite the psalm between the readings when there is no psalmist; he is to present the intentions for the general intercessions in the absence of a deacon or cantor; he is to direct the singing and the participation by the faithful; he is to instruct the faithful for the worthy reception of the sacraments. He may also, insofar as necessary, take care of preparing other faithful who by a temporary appointment are to read the Scriptures in liturgical celebrations. That he may more fittingly and perfectly fulfil these functions, let him meditate assiduously on sacred Scripture.

Let the reader be aware of the office he has undertaken and make every effort and employ suitable means to acquire that increasingly warm and living love[7] and knowledge of Scripture that will make him a more perfect disciple of the Lord.

6. The acolyte is appointed in order to aid the deacon and to minister to the priest. It is therefore his duty to attend to the service of the altar and to assist the deacon and the priest in liturgical celebrations, especially in the celebration of Mass; he is also to distribute holy communion as an auxiliary minister when the ministers spoken of in canon 845 of the Code of Canon Law are not available or are prevented by ill health, age, or another pastoral ministry from performing this function, or when the number of those approaching the sacred table is so great that the celebration of Mass would be unduly prolonged.

In the same extraordinary circumstances he may be entrusted with publicly exposing the Blessed Sacrament for adoration by the faithful and afterward replacing it, but not with blessing the people. He may also, to the extent needed, take care of instructing other faithful who by temporary appointment assist the priest or deacon in liturgical celebrations by carrying the missal, cross, candles, etc., or by performing other such duties. He will perform these functions more worthily if he participates in the holy eucharist with increasingly fervent piety, receives nourishment from it and deepens his knowledge of it.

Destined as he is in a special way for the service of the altar, the acolyte should learn all matters concerning public divine worship and strive to grasp their inner spiritual meaning: in that way he will

[7] See SC 24; DV 25.

be able each day to offer himself entirely to God, be an example to all by his seriousness and reverence in the sacred building, and have a sincere love for the Mystical Body of Christ, the people of God, especially the weak and the sick.

7. In accordance with the venerable tradition of the Church, institution in the ministries of reader and acolyte is reserved to men.

8. The following are requirements for admission to the ministries:

a) the presentation of a petition freely made out and signed by the aspirant to the ordinary (the bishop and, in clerical institutes, the major superior) who has the right to accept the petition;

b) a suitable age and special qualities to be determined by the episcopal conference;

c) a firm will to give faithful service to God and the Christian people.

9. The ministries are conferred by the ordinary (the bishop and, in clerical institutes, the major superior) according to the liturgical rite *De institutione lectoris* and *De institutione acolythi* revised by the Apostolic See.

10. Intervals, determined by the Holy See or the episcopal conferences, shall be observed between the conferring of the ministries of reader and acolyte whenever more than one ministry is conferred on the same person.

11. Candidates for ordination as deacons and priests are to receive the ministries of reader and acolyte, unless they have already done so, and are to exercise them for a suitable time, in order to be better disposed for the future service of the word and of the altar. Dispensation from receiving these ministries on the part of such candidates is reserved to the Holy See.

12. The conferring of ministries does not confer the right to sustenance or remuneration from the Church.

13. The rite of institution of readers and acolytes is to be published by the competent department of the Roman Curia.

All that has been decreed by us in this letter, issued *motu proprio*, we order to be confirmed and ratified, anything to the contrary notwithstanding. We also determine that it shall come into force on 1 January 1973.

Given in Rome, at Saint Peter's, on 15 August, the Solemnity of the Assumption, in the year 1972, the tenth of our pontificate.

PAUL PP. VI

RITE OF THE BLESSING OF OILS
AND CONSECRATION OF CHRISM*
INTRODUCTION

Structure

* Promulgated by Decree dated 3 December 1970.

1. The bishop is to be considered as the high priest of his flock. The life in Christ of his faithful is in some way derived and dependent upon the bishop.[1]

The chrism Mass is one of the principal expressions of the fullness of the bishop's priesthood and signifies the close unity of the priests with him. During the Mass, which he concelebrates with priests from various sections of the diocese, the bishop consecrates the chrism and blesses the other oils. The newly baptised are anointed and confirmed with the chrism consecrated by the bishop. Catechumens are prepared and disposed for baptism with the second oil. And the sick are anointed in their illness with the third oil.

2. The Christian liturgy has assimilated this Old Testament usage of anointing kings, priests, and prophets with consecratory oil because the name of Christ, whom they prefigured, means 'the anointed of the Lord'.

Chrism is a sign: by baptism Christians are plunged into the paschal mystery of Christ; they die with him, are buried with him, and rise with him;[2] they are sharers in his royal and prophetic priesthood. By confirmation Christians receive the spiritual anointing of the Spirit who is given to them.

By the oil of catechumens the effect of the baptismal exorcisms is extended. Before they go to the font of life to be reborn the candidates for baptism are strengthened to renounce sin and the devil.

By the use of the oil of the sick, to which Saint James is a witness,[3] the sick receive a remedy for the illness of mind and body, so that they may have strength to bear suffering and resist evil and obtain the forgiveness of sins.

I The Oils

3. The matter proper for the sacraments is olive oil or, according to circumstances, other plant oil.

4. Chrism is made of oil and perfumes or other sweet smelling matter.

5. The preparation of the chrism may take place privately before the rite of consecration or may be done by the bishop during the liturgical service.

[1] See SC 42.   [2] SC 6.   [3] James 5:14.

II The Minister

6. The consecration of the chrism belongs to the bishop alone.

7. If the use of the oil of catechumens is retained by the conferences of bishops, it is blessed by the bishop with the other oils during the chrism Mass.

In the case of the baptism of adults, however, priests have the faculty to bless the oil of catechumens before the anointing in the designated stage of the catechumenate.

8. The oil used for anointing the sick must be blessed for this purpose by the bishop or by a priest who has this faculty, either from the law or by special concession of the Apostolic See.

The law itself permits the following to bless the oil of the sick:
   a) those whom the law equates with diocesan bishops;
   b) in case of true necessity, any priest.

III Time of Blessing

9. The blessing of the oil and the consecration of the chrism are ordinarily celebrated by the bishop at the chrism Mass celebrated on Holy Thursday morning.

10. If it is difficult for the clergy and people to assemble with the bishop on Holy Thursday morning, the blessing may be held on an earlier day, near Easter, with the celebration of the proper chrism Mass.

IV Place of the Blessing in the Mass

11. According to the tradition of the Latin liturgy, the blessing of the oil of the sick takes place before the end of the eucharistic prayer; the blessing of the oil of catechumens and the consecration of the chrism, after communion.

12. For pastoral reasons, however, the entire rite of blessing may be celebrated after the liturgy of the word, according to the order described below.

LECTIONARY FOR MASS*
INTRODUCTION

Structure

* Promulgated by Decree dated 25 May 1969.

LECTIONARY FOR MASS: INTRODUCTION

CHAPTER I

GENERAL ARRANGEMENT OF THE LECTIONARY FOR MASS

I   General Principles

1. The Church loves sacred scripture and is anxious to deepen its understanding of the truth and to nourish its own life by studying these sacred writings. The Second Vatican Council likened the bible to a fountain of renewal within the community of God's people and directed that in the revision of liturgical celebrations there should be 'more abundant, varied, and appropriate reading from sacred scripture'.[1] The council further directed that at Mass 'the treasures of the bible should be opened up more lavishly so that richer fare might be provided for the faithful at the table of God's word. In this way a more representative portion of sacred scripture will be read to the people over a set cycle of years'.[2]

It is clear why the council expressed such principles. By means of sacred scripture, read during the liturgy of the word and explained during the homily, 'God speaks to his people, revealing the mystery of their redemption and salvation and offering them spiritual nourishment. Through his word, Christ himself is present in the assembly of his people.'[3] Thus the Church at Mass 'receives the bread of life from the table of Christ's body and God's word and unceasingly offers it to the faithful'.[4]

2. In response to the directives of the council, the Consilium for the Implementation of the Constitution on the Sacred Liturgy has prepared this order of readings, which lists texts for Sundays and feasts, for weekdays throughout the year, for Masses of the saints and for other special occasions.

In arranging these texts the purpose was to assign those of greatest importance to Sundays and feasts when the Christian people are bound to celebrate the eucharist together. In this way the faithful will be able to hear the principal portions of God's revealed word over a suitable period of time. Other biblical readings which to some degree complement these texts are arranged in a separate

[1] SC 35.
[2] SC 51.
[3] General Instruction on the Roman Missal 33.
[4] DV 21.

234

series for weekdays. Neither part of the lectionary is dependent on the other: the readings for Sundays and feasts proceed independently of the weekday readings and vice versa.

The selection of texts for Masses of the saints, ritual Masses, votive Masses, and other special Masses has been determined by their own rules.

II   Lectionary for Sundays and Feasts

3. The following norms apply to the readings for Sundays and feasts:

a) Three readings are provided for each Mass: the first from the Old Testament, the second from the writings of the apostles (from an epistle or from the Book of Revelation, depending on the time of the year), and the third from the gospel. This arrangement best illustrates the basic unity of both Testaments and of the history of salvation: a unity which has Christ in the memorial of his paschal mystery as its centre; a unity which should be one of the main subjects of instruction. Furthermore this arrangement is traditional and has long been followed in the Eastern Churches.

b) This lectionary provides a more varied reading of sacred scripture on Sundays and feasts by arranging the texts in a three-year cycle. Thus the same text is read only once every fourth year.

Each year is designated A, B, or C. Year C is a year whose number is equally divisible by three, as if the cycle began with the first year of the Christian era. Thus 1968 is year C, 1969 is year A, 1970 is year B, 1971 is year C, etc.

c) Readings for Sundays and feasts have been arranged according to two principles which are called 'semi-continuous' or 'thematic'. The different seasons of the year and the themes of each liturgical season determine which principle applies in specific cases.

The Old and New Testament readings best harmonise when their relationship is self-evident, that is, when the events and teachings of the New Testament are more or less explicitly related to those of the Old. The Old Testament readings in this lectionary have been chosen primarily because of their relationship to the New Testament selections, especially the gospel reading.

Common themes provide another kind of harmonisation among the readings for each Mass. Seasons which best illustrate this principle are Advent, Lent, and Easter, each of which has its own spirit and message.

The Sundays of the year, on the other hand, have no particular theme. The epistle and gospel readings for these days are arranged semi-continuously, while the Old Testament readings have been chosen because of their relationship to the gospel passages.

III Weekday Lectionary

4.   The following norms apply to the weekday readings:

a) The Lenten cycle is based on the principal themes of this season, baptism and penance.

b) The gospel readings for other weekdays are arranged in a single series. During the thirty-four weeks of the year the first reading is arranged in a two-year cycle with separate readings for alternate years. Series I is for the odd years (1969, 1971, etc.), and series II is for the even years (1970, 1972, etc.).

c) The readings in the weekday lectionary, as in the Sunday lectionary, are arranged either semi-continuously or thematically depending on the presence of a theme for a particular season.

IV Lectionary for the Celebrations of the Saints

5.   Two series of readings are provided for Masses of the saints:

a) The Proper of the Saints provides the first series of readings for solemnities, feasts, and memorials, especially if a reading is especially appropriate for an individual feast. Sometimes, however, a more appropriate text is indicated as preferable and will be found in the Common of the Saints.

b) The Common of the Saints provides a more complete series of readings especially appropriate for various kinds of celebrations of saints (martyrs, pastors, virgins), as well as an extensive selection of texts speaking of holiness in general, for optional use whenever one is referred to the Common to choose a reading.

Texts in this Common are arranged in the order in which they are read at Mass: Old Testament selections, texts from the writings of the apostles, psalms and verses between the readings, and finally gospel selections. Unless expressly stated otherwise, the celebrant may choose the readings at will, considering the pastoral needs of the participating group.

V   Lectionary for Ritual Masses, Masses for Various Occasions, and Votive Masses

6. Texts for use at ritual Masses, votive Masses, and other special Masses are arranged in the same way. An extensive list of optional texts is provided, as in the Common of the Saints, to enable the celebrant to consider the particular occasion and the pastoral needs of the participating group when he chooses from a variety of readings.

VI   Criteria for the Choice and Arrangement of Readings

7. In addition to the principles governing the arrangement of readings in specific parts of the lectionary, these general norms also apply:

a) *Liturgical Seasons*. The importance of scriptural reading at Mass, as well as liturgical tradition, demands that in this new lectionary certain scriptural books should be reserved for specific liturgical seasons. The tradition of reading the Acts of the Apostles during the Easter season is preserved, as common to East and West (in the Ambrosian and Spanish rites). These readings beautifully illustrate how the total life of the Church springs from the paschal mystery. The Eastern and Western traditions of reading John's Gospel during the last weeks of Lent and throughout the Easter season is likewise preserved, since it is the 'spiritual' gospel which brings out the mystery of Christ more deeply.

The reading of Isaiah, especially the first part of the book, is traditionally assigned to Advent. Parts of this prophet's writings are also read during the Christmas season, along with the First Letter of John.

b) *Length of texts*. The new lectionary has tried to establish a balance in determining the length of texts. A distinction has been made between narratives which demand a longer reading but are likely to hold the listeners' attention and other texts which should not be too lengthy because of their doctrinal depth.

Certain lengthy passages have been carefully abbreviated and appear in both long and short forms. The celebrant may decide which to use. Optional verses should be indicated by appropriate typographical signs.

c) *Difficult texts*. Biblical texts which contain serious literary, critical, or exegetical problems or which the faithful may find difficult to understand have been omitted from the readings for Sundays and solemnities. It would be wrong, of course, to keep from the faithful the wealth of spiritual meaning contained in these texts on the premise that they are too difficult to understand, if this difficulty can be overcome, since every faithful member of the Church should have a basic Christian education and every pastor should have a basic biblical formation. Frequently a passage will become easier to grasp when associated with another reading from the same Mass.

d) *Omission of verses.* Many liturgies, including the Roman liturgy, traditionally omit certain verses from biblical readings. One should not be too quick to do this because the style, purpose, or meaning, of the scriptural text may easily be damaged. But, for pastoral reasons it seemed best to continue this tradition, taking care that the essential meaning of the text remain unchanged. Otherwise some texts would be too lengthy or readings of greater spiritual value to the people would have to be entirely omitted because of the one or two verses of little pastoral worth or involving truly difficult questions.

VII Celebrant's Choice of Texts

8. This lectionary sometimes provides the celebrant with a choice of two texts or a choice among several optional texts for one reading. This seldom occurs on Sundays, solemnities, and feasts because such a choice might easily obscure the spirit of the liturgical season or unduly interrupt the semi-continuous reading of the book of the bible. However, such a choice is frequently possible in Masses of the saints, ritual Masses, votive Masses, and other special Masses.

To keep a sound order in the choice of readings, these guidelines should be noted:

a) When three readings are assigned for a Mass, it is most desirable that all three be read. If however, for pastoral reasons, the conference of bishops decides to permit only two readings, one of the first two should be chosen which is of greater value in presenting the mystery of salvation to the faithful. Unless expressly stated otherwise in another part of the lectionary, it is preferable to choose the reading which is more closely related to the day's gospel, more helpful in presenting an organised and unified instruction over a period of time, or which permits a semi-continuous reading of a book of the bible.

For instance, the Old Testament readings throughout Lent present the development of salvation history. Semi-continuous selections from the writings of the apostles are provided for Sundays of the year. The priest should choose the readings systematically for a number of Sundays so that his teaching will be logically and coherently presented. It would hardly be consistent to choose a reading from the Old Testament one week and from the writings of the apostles the next week, with no order or harmony at all.

b) Pastoral reasons should also determine the choice between the long and the short forms of the same text. These reasons are the capacity of the hearers to listen to a longer or shorter reading with profit, their ability to understand difficult texts correctly, and their appreciation of a more complete text which is to be explained in the homily.

Whenever this choice is given it should be indicated by the way the text is printed.

c) When a choice between appointed texts is permitted, the needs of the people should be considered by choosing a text which is easier or more suited to the congregation, by repeating or postponing a text appointed for a particular celebration and using it optionally on another occasion when it is helpful pastorally.

These provisions are especially useful in circumstances where a text may present difficulties for a certain group, or when the same text might be repeated within a few days, on Sunday and again during the week.

d) When the weekday lectionary is used, it is important to determine in advance whether any feasts will occur in a given week to interrupt the course of weekday readings. Then the priest, considering the entire week's readings, may omit less important selections from the weekday lectionary or combine them with other readings when this will give a unified presentation of a specific theme.

e) For Masses of the saints *special readings* are sometimes provided which are appropriate to the saint's life or the mystery remembered at the Mass (feast of the conversion of Paul, memorial of Mary Magdalen). Even in the case of a memorial, these readings should replace those prescribed by the weekday lectionary for that day.

Sometimes *appropriate readings* are provided to focus on a certain aspect of the spiritual life or the saint's accomplishments. It is not necessary to use these readings every time they are provided, unless pastoral reasons so demand. Generally it would be preferable to use the semi-continuous readings from the book assigned in the weekday lectionary to that liturgical season.

In addition, the Common of the Saints provides *general readings* which are appropriate for various kinds of saints (martyrs, pastors, virgins) or for the saints in general. When several texts are given for the same reading, the celebrant may choose the one most suitable for the congregation. However:

1. On solemnities, when three readings are assigned the first choice should be from the Old Testament, the second from the writings of the apostles, and the third from the gospel, unless the conference of bishops decides to permit only two readings.

2. On feasts and memorials, when only two readings are assigned the first choice is from the Old Testament or from the writings of the apostles, and the second from the gospel. During Easter time, however, it is customary to use the writings of the apostles for the first reading and John's Gospel for the second.

f) The guidelines above, governing the choice of readings from the Common of the Saints, also apply to ritual Masses, votive Masses, and other special Masses when several texts are provided for the same reading.

VIII Chants between the Readings

9. According to the norms of the General Instruction of the Roman Missal (nos. 36-40), there is to be a song after each reading.

The more important song is the psalm following the first reading. Ordinarily the psalm should be the one assigned to the reading, except for readings from the Common of the Saints, ritual Masses, votive Masses, and other special Masses for which the celebrant may choose the psalm most pastorally useful.

To make it easier for the people to join in the psalm, some selected texts and responses have been chosen for different times of the year and for different kinds of saints, and these may be used in place of the assigned response if the psalm is sung.

The other song, between the second reading and the gospel, is either specified for the Mass and related to the day's gospel, or it may be chosen from the series of texts given for the particular season or in the Common.

During Lent the following acclamations (or similar ones) may be used before and after the verse which precedes the gospel:

Praise to you, Lord Jesus Christ, king of endless glory!
Praise and honour to you, Lord Jesus Christ!
Glory and praise to you, Lord Jesus Christ!
Glory to you, Word of God, Lord Jesus Christ!

IX Purpose of the Lectionary

10. The purpose of this lectionary is primarily a pastoral one, in the spirit of the Second Vatican Council. The general principles governing it and the wealth of texts within it are all pastorally oriented. It is the result of cooperation and effort among a large number of people from all parts of the world: experts in scripture, pastoral work, catechetics, and liturgy.

This extended reading and explanation of sacred scripture to Christians during the celebration of the eucharist will, it is hoped, help to reach the goal which the Second Vatican Council so often spoke of and which Pope Paul VI expressed in these words: 'The revision of the lectionary was indeed a wise directive, aimed at developing among the faithful an ever-increasing hunger for God's word, the word which leads the people of the new covenant to the perfect unity of the Church under the guidance of the Holy Spirit. We are fully confident that priests and faithful alike will prepare their hearts together more earnestly for the Lord's Supper, meditating more thoughtfully on sacred scripture, nourishing themselves daily with the words of the Lord. The fulfilment of the wishes of the Second Vatican Council will be the inevitable consequence of this experience of God's word: sacred scripture will become a perpetual source of spiritual life, an important instrument for transmitting Christian teachings, and the centre of all theological formation.'[5]

---

[5] Apostolic Constitution on the Roman Missal.

CHAPTER II
DESCRIPTION OF THE ORDER OF READINGS

This arrangement of the order of readings according to the different seasons of the year is to help clarify the structure of the entire lectionary and its relationship to the liturgical year.

I Season of Advent

11. 1. *Sundays*. Each gospel reading has a specific theme: the Lord's coming in glory at the end of time (first Sunday), John the Baptist (second and third Sundays), and the events which immediately prepared for the Lord's birth (fourth Sunday).

The Old Testament readings are prophecies about the Messiah and messianic times, especially those taken from the Book of Isaiah.

The selections from the writings of the apostles present exhortations and instructions on different themes of this season.

2. *Weekdays*. Two series of readings are given: one from the beginning of Advent to 16 December, the other from 17 December to 24 December.

The first part of Advent is devoted to a semi-continuous reading of the Book of Isaiah, including those important passages which are also read on Sundays. Gospel passages for these days have been chosen because of their relationship to the first reading.

Beginning on Thursday of the second week the gospel passages are about John the Baptist, while the first readings either continue the book of Isaiah or come from a text related to the day's gospel.

The gospels of the last week before Christmas are from Matthew (Chapter 1) and Luke (Chapter 1), the events which immediately prepared for the Lord's birth. Selections for the first reading are from different books of the Old Testament which have important messianic prophecies and a relationship to the gospel texts.

II Christmas Season

12. 1. *Solemnities, Feasts, and Sundays*. For the vigil and the three Masses of Christmas, the first reading is from Isaiah.

These passages are traditional in the Roman liturgy and have been retained in various local rites. With two exceptions, the other readings follow the Roman Missal.

The gospel of the Sunday within the octave of Christmas, (the feast of the Holy Family), tells of Jesus' childhood. The other readings concern family life.

The readings for the octave of Christmas and solemnity of Mary the Mother of God are about the virgin-mother of God (the gospel and second reading) and about the naming of the child Jesus (the gospel and first reading) since this feast is no longer in the calendar.

The readings for the second Sunday after Christmas refer to the mystery of the incarnation.

On Epiphany the second reading speaks of the call of all people to salvation.

The readings for the Sunday after Epiphany (the feast of the Baptism of the Lord) speak of that mystery.

2. *Weekdays.* The reading of the First Letter of John begins on his feast, 27 December. It is continued on the feast of the Holy Innocents (28 December) and the following days.

The gospels present the Lord's manifestations: the events of Jesus' childhood from Luke's Gospel (29-30 December), the first chapter of John's Gospel (31 December-5 January), and the significant manifestations recorded in the three synoptic gospels (7-12 January).

III Lenten Season

13. 1. *Sundays.* The gospel selections for the first two Sundays recount the Lord's temptations and transfiguration as recorded in the synoptic gospels.

For year A the gospel accounts: concerning the Samaritan woman, the man born blind, and Lazarus are assigned to the following three Sundays. Since these passages are very important in relation to Christian initiation they may also be used for years B and C, especially when candidates for baptism are present. However, for pastoral reasons, many wished another choice of texts for years B and C and alternative selections have been provided: year B, John's text about Christ's future glorification through his cross and resurrection; year C, Luke's texts on conversion.

The Old Testament readings are about the history of salvation, one of the main topics of Lenten instruction. A series of texts has been prepared for each year to present the principal elements of this history from the beginning to the promise of the new covenant; especially readings about Abraham (second Sunday) and about the deliverance of God's people from slavery (third Sunday).

The selections from the writings of the apostles have been chosen because of their relationship to the Gospel and Old Testament readings, and as far as possible should harmonise with them.

2. *Weekdays.* The gospel and Old Testament readings were chosen for their mutual relationship and for their treatment of various themes for Lenten instruction. Whenever possible, most of the readings from the Roman Missal were preserved. It seemed best, however, to arrange the readings from John's Gospel in a better sequence since most of it used to be read without any special order. Therefore a semi-continuous reading of John's Gospel, with a better relation to Lenten themes, begins on Monday of the fourth week.

Since the readings about the Samaritan woman, the man born blind, and Lazarus are assigned for Sundays only in year A (and are optional in years B and C), additional Masses with these texts have been inserted at the beginning of the third, fourth, and fifth weeks. During years B and C they may be used on any day of these weeks in place of the assigned weekday readings.

IV Easter Season

14. 1. *Sundays.* Until the third Sunday of Easter the gospel selections recount the appearances of the risen Christ. To avoid interrupting the narrative, the reading about the Good Shepherd, previously assigned to the second Sunday after Easter, are now assigned to the fourth Sunday of Easter (that is, the third Sunday after Easter). The gospels of the fifth, sixth, and seventh Sundays of Easter are excerpts from the teaching and prayer of Christ after the last supper.

The first reading is from the Acts of the Apostles, arranged in a three-year cycle of parallel and progressive selections. Thus the life, growth, and witness of the early Church are presented every year.

The selections from the writings of the apostles are year A, First Letter of Peter; year B, First Letter of John; year C, the Book of

Revelation. These texts seem most appropriate to the spirit of the Easter season, a spirit of joyful faith and confident hope.

2. *Weekdays.* As on Sunday, the first reading is from the Acts of the Apostles, arranged semi-continuously.

The gospel readings during Easter week tell of the Lord's appearances with the conclusions of the synoptic gospels reserved for the Ascension. A semi-continuous reading of John's Gospel follows, appropriate for the Easter theme and complementary to the Lenten readings. These readings are largely devoted to the teaching and prayer of the Lord after the last supper.

V Season 'Of the Year'

I. Arrangement and Choice of Texts

15. The remainder of the liturgical year consists of thirty-three or thirty-four weeks of the year. It begins on Monday after the Sunday following 6 January and goes to the Tuesday before Ash Wednesday inclusive, and from Monday after Pentecost Sunday until first Vespers of the first Sunday of Advent.

This lectionary provides readings for all thirty-four weeks. Sometimes, however, there are only thirty-three weeks since certain seasonal feasts, e.g., the Lord's baptism and Pentecost as well as other solemnities, e.g., Holy Trinity, Christ the King, replace some of these Sundays.

The following guidelines should be followed for the correct use of the readings during the weeks of the year.

1. The Sunday celebrated as the feast of the Lord's Baptism takes the place of the first Sunday of the year. Therefore the readings for the first week begin on Monday after the first Sunday following 6 January.

2. The Sunday following the feast of the Lord's baptism is the second Sunday of the year, and the following Sundays are numbered consecutively until the beginning of Lent. The readings for the week in which Lent begins continue until Tuesday inclusive. On Ash Wednesday the Lenten readings begin.

3. The weeks of the year begin again after Pentecost Sunday in the following order:

a) When there are thirty-four Sundays of the year, the readings are resumed at the week immediately following the last one used before

Lent. For instance, if Lent begins during the sixth week of the year, then the Monday after Pentecost Sunday begins the seventh week of the year. The Solemnity of the Trinity takes the place of a Sunday of the year.

b) When there are only thirty-three Sundays of the year, the week of the year which would ordinarily follow Pentecost is omitted. Thus the eschatological readings with which the liturgical year concludes will still be read during the last two weeks of the year. For instance, if Lent begins during the fifth week of the year, the sixth week is omitted and the seventh week begins on Monday after Pentecost.

II. Sunday Readings

16. 1. *Gospel readings.* The gospel for the second Sunday of the year refers to the manifestation of the Lord, already celebrated on Epiphany, with the traditional passage about the wedding at Cana and two other passages from John's Gospel.

The third Sunday of the year begins the semi-continuous reading of the three synoptic gospels. This arrangement provides a presentation of each gospel's distinctive doctrine as well as a development of the Lord's life and preaching.

The above arrangement and distribution of texts also allows a certain harmony between the meaning of each gospel and the development of the liturgical year. The readings after Epiphany are concerned with the beginning of the Lord's preaching and are related to his baptism and first manifestation, which are celebrated on Epiphany and the following Sundays. At the end of the liturgical year the eschatological themes of these last Sundays occur in sequence because the chapters of the synoptic gospels which precede the passion narratives treat these themes more or less extensively.

In year B after the sixteenth Sunday of the year, there are five readings from the sixth chapter of John's Gospel (the teaching on the bread of life). This insertion is only natural since the multiplication of the bread in John's Gospel parallels the same narrative in Mark. In year C the first text in the semi-continuous reading of Luke, (third Sunday of the year), is the preface to his gospel in which he outlines his purpose for writing the gospel; there did not seem to be another appropriate place for this reading.

2. *Old Testament readings* were chosen for their relationship to each gospel passage. This serves a twofold purpose: any great contrast between the readings in the same Mass is avoided, and at

the same time the unity of Old and New Testaments is clearly shown. This relationship between the readings for each Mass is indicated by the careful selection of titles for the readings.

As far as possible the selection of readings has been made so that the texts are short and easy to grasp, but another purpose is to read the most important parts of the Old Testament on Sundays. Although these readings are ordinarily related to the gospel passage and thus lack their own set order, nevertheless the treasures of the word of God are opened up so that all who participate in Sunday Mass will hear most of the Old Testament principal sections.

3. *Writings of the Apostles.* A semi-continuous reading of the letters of Paul and James is presented. (The letters of Peter and John are read during the Easter and Christmas seasons.)

Paul's First Letter to the Corinthians, since it is lengthy and discusses so many different questions, is arranged in a three-year cycle at the beginning of this season of the year. It seemed best to divide the Letter to the Hebrews into one part for year B and another for year C.

All selections are short and should be quite easy for the faithful to understand.

Table II (below, page 254) indicates the distribution of passages from the epistles in the three-year cycle of the Sundays of the year.

4. The theme of the readings chosen for the thirty-fourth and last Sunday of the liturgical year is Christ the King, prefigured by David and proclaimed in the humiliations he suffered by dying for us on the cross, who governs and guides his Church until his return at the end of time.

III. Weekday Readings

17. 1. *The gospel selections* are arranged so that Mark is read first (weeks 1-9), then Matthew (weeks 10-21), and finally Luke (weeks 22-34). The first twelve chapters of Mark are read in their entirety, omitting only those two passages from the sixth chapter which are read on weekdays at other times of the year. Everything omitted in Mark is read from Matthew and Luke. Thus all the elements which give the different gospels their distinctive style and which are necessary for an intelligent understanding of each gospel are read two or three times. The complete eschatological teaching of Luke's Gospel completes the readings of the liturgical year.

2. *The first reading* consists of selections from either testament, depending on the length of books to be read.

a) Extensive selections from the books of the New Testament are read so that the listener is given something of each letter's substance. However, passages having little pastoral relevance today have been omitted, such as those concerning the gift of tongues or the discipline of the early Church.

b) The limited readings from the Old Testament are an attempt to give something of the individual character of each book. The historical texts have been chosen for their presentation of an overall view of the history of salvation before the incarnation. Lengthy narratives could not be included: sometimes a few verses have been selected to make up a short reading. In addition the religious significance of some historical events is brought out by selections from the wisdom books which serve as introductions or conclusions to a series of historical events.

Almost all the Old Testament books will be found in the weekday lectionary in the proper of the season. The only books omitted are the very short prophetic books (Obadiah, Zephaniah) and a poetic book not suited to reading (Song of Songs). Some texts written for edification require a lengthy reading to be understood. Of these the books of Tobit and Ruth are read and the rest omitted (Esther and Judith). Texts from these are also assigned to Sundays and weekdays at other times of the year.

Table III (below, page 255) indicates the distribution of the books of each testament in a two-year cycle among the weekdays of the year.

c) The books of Daniel and Revelation are assigned to the end of the liturgical year since they have appropriate eschatological themes.

CHAPTER III

FORMAT OF THE READINGS

For each reading the Lectionary gives text references, title, and introductory phrase. The notes below concern these features:

18. A. *Text references* (chapters and verses) are given according to the Vulgate translation, with additional references to the original texts (Hebrew, Aramaic, Greek) whenever these differ.* It is the responsibility of the competent authorities for each language group to decide which numerical system to follow in the vernacular translations. Chapters and verses should always be listed so that these may easily be referred to in the margin or in the text itself.

The liturgical books should also provide a phrase, not included in this book, to announce the readings during the celebration of God's word. The following guidelines should be followed, although these may be changed by the competent authorities to fit the usage and language of each country:

1. The announcement of the reading should always be: 'A *reading* from the Book (or Letter, Gospel) . . .' Phrases such as 'the beginning of . . .' (except where this is actually the case) and 'The continuation of . . .' should be avoided.

2. The names of the biblical books should follow the present practice of the Roman Missal, with these changes:

a) When two books have the same name, the reader should clearly indicate from which one he is reading: 'A reading from the first (or second) Book of Maccabees.' 'A reading from the first (or second) Letter . . .'

b) Contemporary titles should be used for the following books:

I and II Books of Samuel (for I and II Kings);
I and II Books of Kings (for III and IV Kings);
I and II Chronicles (for I and II Paralipomenon);
Books of Ezra and Nehemiah (for I and II Ezra).

c) The wisdom books were formerly designated by a single name, 'the Book of Wisdom'. They now should be distinguished as follows: Book of Job, Proverbs, Ecclesiastes (Qohelet, in some translations), Song of Songs, Wisdom, Ecclesiasticus (Sirach, in some translations).

---

* This, of course, refers to the original *Ordo Lectionum Missae.*

d) All books listed in the Vulgate among the prophets should be announced as such, even though some do not consider them truly prophetic books: 'A reading from the Book of the Prophet N.'

e) Since there is general agreement today that Lamentations and the Letter to the Hebrews were not actually written by Jeremiah and Paul respectively, these authors should not be mentioned in the announcement of the reading: 'A reading from the Book of Lamentations.' 'A reading from the Letter to the Hebrews.'

19. B. The *title* of each text has been carefully chosen (usually from the text itself) to summarise the theme of the passage and, if necessary, to indicate the relationship between the readings assigned to a given Mass.

Vernacular translations should not appear without such titles, although the competent authorities may decide whether to translate the titles or to prepare new titles suited to various cultures. In addition to the title, an explanation of the text's general meaning of a passage may also be given if desired.

20. C. The *introductory phrase* is given wit theh usual words. 'At that time . . .', 'In those days . . .', 'Brothers . . .', 'Dear friends . . .', or 'The Lord says . . .'. These may be omitted when the passage itself gives sufficient indication of the time and persons involved, or when such an introduction is not in harmony with the nature of the text. These introductions may be changed or omitted by the competent authorities when preparing the vernacular translations.

The *opening line* of each reading is given, adding or omitting words whenever necessary for a better understanding of a selection taken out of context. Suitable indications are also given whenever verses have been omitted, if other changes will be necessitated by such omissions.

21. D. At the end of the reading the reader adds, 'This is the word of the Lord' or 'This is the gospel of the Lord,' to facilitate the acclamation made by the people. Other customary phrases may also be used.

CHAPTER IV

PREPARATION OF TRANSLATIONS OF THE LECTIONARY

22. In addition to the notes above, especially nos. 18-20, the following guidelines should be observed in preparing translations of this lectionary:

All editions should have a section explaining the *structure and purpose* of the lectionary, i.e., at least Chapter I of this introduction.

23. Because of the scope of this lectionary, vernacular editions will necessarily consist of *several volumes*, but no specific division is prescribed.

One possibility is the traditional division: the Book of Gospels and the Book of Epistles (containing Old Testament selections as well).

An even better arrangement is to have a Sunday lectionary with excerpts from the Masses of Saints as well as from the weekday lectionary. This Sunday lectionary may be compiled in three sections corresponding to the three yearly cycles, thus presenting a continuous arrangement of readings for each individual year.

Any other suitable arrangements may be used as well.

24. Texts of the *intervenient songs* should always be provided with the readings, especially for use at recited Masses. Separate books may also be published containing only these songs. It is suggested that these texts be arranged in verses.

Whenever the reading consists of different sections, this *structure of the text* should be made clear typographically. It is also suggested that these texts, even prose selections, be arranged in sense-lines for easy reading, especially as an aid to inexperienced readers.

When *long and short forms* are provided, these should be separated for easy reading. Where such a separation is impossible, the optional verses should be clearly marked to avoid errors in the public reading of the text.

All editions should contain a biblical index similar to the one in the *editio typica*.

25. The principles governing the preparation of vernacular translations of the biblical readings and intervenient songs are found in the Instruction on the Translation of Liturgical Texts (25 January

1969) sent to the presidents of the conferences of bishops and the national liturgical commissions by the Consilium for the Implementation of the Constitution on the Sacred Liturgy. Further instructions are given in the declaration Translations of Liturgical Texts for Interim Use (Notitiae 5 1969, p. 69), which states the obligation of submitting for confirmation by the Sacred Congregation of Divine Worship even those translations which have been given interim approval for liturgical use.

TABLE I

TABLE OF MOVABLE FEASTS AND SUNDAYS

Year	Sunday Cycle	Week-day Cycle	Ash Wednes-day	Easter	Ascension	Pentecost	Corpus Christi	Ordinary Weeks of the Year				First Sunday of Advent	Year
								Before Lent		After Pentecost			
								Until	Week	From	Week		
1979	B	I	28 Feb.	15 Apr.	24 May	3 June	14 June	27 Feb.	8	4 June	9	2 Dec.	1979
1980	C	II	20 Feb.	6 Apr.	15 May	25 May	5 June	19 Feb.	6	26 May	8	30 Nov.	1980
1981	A	I	4 Mar.	19 Apr.	28 May	7 June	18 June	3 Mar.	8	8 June	10	29 Nov.	1981
1982	B	II	24 Feb.	11 Apr.	20 May	30 May	10 June	23 Feb.	7	31 May	9	28 Nov.	1982
1983	C	I	16 Feb.	3 Apr.	12 May	22 May	2 June	15 Feb.	6	23 May	8	27 Nov.	1983
1984	A	II	7 Mar.	22 Apr.	31 May	10 June	21 June	6 Mar.	9	11 June	10	2 Dec.	1984
1985	B	I	20 Feb.	7 Apr.	16 May	26 May	6 June	19 Feb.	6	27 May	8	1 Dec.	1985
1986	C	II	12 Feb.	30 Mar.	8 May	18 May	29 May	11 Feb.	5	19 May	7	30 Nov.	1986
1987	A	I	4 Mar.	19 Apr.	28 May	7 June	18 June	3 Mar.	8	8 June	10	29 Nov.	1987
1988	B	II	17 Feb.	3 Apr.	12 May	22 May	2 June	16 Feb.	6	23 May	8	27 Nov.	1988
1989	C	I	8 Feb.	26 Mar.	4 May	14 May	25 May	7 Feb.	5	15 May	6	3 Dec.	1989
1990	A	II	28 Feb.	15 Apr.	24 May	3 June	14 June	27 Feb.	8	4 June	9	2 Dec.	1990
1991	B	I	13 Feb.	31 Mar.	9 May	19 May	30 May	12 Feb.	5	20 May	7	1 Dec.	1991
1992	C	II	4 Mar.	19 Apr.	28 May	7 June	18 June	3 Mar.	8	8 June	10	29 Nov.	1992
1993	A	I	24 Feb.	11 Apr.	20 May	30 May	10 June	23 Feb.	7	31 May	9	28 Nov.	1993
1994	B	II	16 Feb.	3 Apr.	12 May	22 May	2 June	15 Feb.	6	23 May	8	27 Nov.	1994
1995	C	I	1 Mar.	16 Apr.	25 May	4 June	15 June	28 Feb.	8	5 June	9	3 Dec.	1995
1976	A	II	21 Feb.	7 Apr.	16 May	26 May	6 June	20 Feb.	7	27 May	8	1 Dec.	1996
1977	B	I	12 Feb.	30 Mar.	8 May	18 May	29 May	11 Feb.	5	19 May	7	30 Nov.	1997
1998	C	II	25 Feb.	12 Apr.	21 May	31 May	11 June	24 Feb.	7	1 June	9	29 Nov.	1998
1999	A	I	17 Feb.	4 Apr.	13 May	23 May	3 June	16 Feb.	6	24 May	8	28 Nov.	1999

TABLE II

ORDER FOR THE SECOND READING FOR SUNDAYS
OF THE SEASON OF THE YEAR

Sunday	Year A	Year B	Year C
2	1 Corinthians, 1-4	1 Corinthians, 6-11	1 Corinthians, 12-15
3	,,	,,	,,
4	,,	,,	,,
5	,,	,,	,,
6	,,	,,	,,
7	,,	2 Corinthians	,,
8	,,	,,	,,
9	Romans	,,	Galatians
10	,,	,,	,,
11	,,	,,	,,
12	,,	,,	,,
13	,,	,,	,,
14	,,	,,	,,
15	,,	Ephesians	Colossians
16	,,	,,	,,
17	,,	,,	,,
18	,,	,,	,,
19	,,	,,	Hebrews, 11-12
20	,,	,,	,,
21	,,	,,	,,
22	,,	James	,,
23	,,	,,	Philemon
24	,,	,,	1 Timothy
25	Philippians	,,	,,
26	,,	,,	,,
27	,,	Hebrews, 2-10	2 Timothy
28	,,	,,	,,
29	1 Thessalonians	,,	,,
30	,,	,,	,,
31	,,	,,	2 Thessalonians
32	,,	,,	,,
33	,,	,,	,,

TABLE III

ORDER OF THE FIRST READING FOR WEEKDAYS FOR THE SEASON OF THE YEAR

Week	Year I	Year II
1	Hebrews	1 Samuel
2	"	"
3	"	2 Samuel
4	"	2 Samuel, 1 Kings, 1-16
5	Genesis, 1-11	1 Kings, 1-16
6	"	James
7	Sirach (Ecclesiasticus)	"
8	"	1 Peter; Jude
9	Tobit	2 Peter, 2 Timothy
10	2 Corinthians	1 Kings, 17-22
11	"	1 Kings, 17-22; 2 Kings
12	Genesis, 12-50	2 Kings; Lamentations
13	"	Amos
14	"	Hosea; Isaiah
15	Exodus	Isaiah; Micah
16	"	Micah; Jeremiah
17	Exodus; Leviticus	Jeremiah
18	Numbers; Deuteronomy	Jeremiah; Nahum; Habakkuk
19	Deuteronomy; Joshua	Ezekiel
20	Judges; Ruth	"
21	1 Thessalonians	2 Thessalonians; 1 Corinthians
22	1 Thessalonians; Colossians	1 Corinthians
23	Colossians; 1 Timothy	"
24	1 Timothy	"
25	Ezra; Haggai; Zachariah	Proverbs; Qoheleth (Ecclesiastes)
26	Zachariah; Nehemiah; Baruch	Job
27	Jonah; Malachiah; Joel	Galatians
28	Romans	Galatians; Ephesians
29	"	Ephesians
30	"	"
31	"	Ephesians; Philippians
32	Wisdom	Titus; Philemon; 2 and 3 John
33	1 and 2, Maccabees	Revelation
34	Daniel	"

INDEX

Abraham, 243

absolution: in danger of death, 9, 168, 171, 174; formula of, 171, 178; general, 174–8; in penitential rite at Mass, 89; in sacrament of Penance, 166, 167, 169, 173

acolyte: assistance to deacon and priest, 227–8; functions at Mass, 100, 111; ministry for candidates for orders, 212, 213; office of, 224; office to include functions of subdiaconite, 225, 226

actions and postures, sign of unity, 87, 99; uniformity of, 87

Acts of the Apostles, readings at Easter, 70, 237, 244

adaptations: allowed, 12; of Baptismal rite, 22–3, 49–52; at celebration of eucharist, 83; at Christian initiation, 37, 41–2; of Confirmation rite, 66; of funeral rites, 199–201; of Marriage rite, 206–7; of Mass texts, 142; of penitential celebrations, 178; of postures and actions, 87; of prayers, 81–2, 142; of rite of Penance, 177–8

Advent, Season of, readings, 235, 237, 242

Agnus Dei, invocation, 86, 96–7, 107, 118

alb, wearing of: common to all ministers, 136–7; at communion outside Mass, 152; at Exposition, 159; at Mass, 103, 114; at ordinations, 220, 221

Alleluia, singing of, 86, 92, 104

altar: adornment, 131; fixed, 130–1; incensation, 88, 114; minor, 131; movable, 130, 131; preparation for eucharistic liturgy, 94, 102; veneration, 88, 122

Ambrose, St, 79

amice, wearing of: at ordinations, 220, 221; with alb, 103, 136

anaphoras, 69

anointing: assimilation of Old Testament usage, 239; with chrism at Baptism, 17, 33, 48, 49, 50; with chrism at Confirmation, 54–8, 63–4; with chrism at ordination of priest, 221; with oil of catechumens, 32, 39, 41

Anointing of the Sick: ancient tradition, 179; appropriate time, 180, 186–7; blessing of oil, 188, 231; effect of oil, 230; formulas accompanying anointing, 179, 188–9; minister of, 187; number of anointings, 179, 181, 188; oil to be used, 181, 187

Apostles, writings of the: readings from, 235, 236, 239, 240; readings for Advent, 242; readings for Easter, 244–5; readings for Lent, 244; readings during Sundays 'of the Year', 247

apostolic succession, 216

Apostolic Tradition of Hippolytus of Rome, 216

Ash Wednesday, 245

Augustine, St, 71, 86

Baptism, rite of: adaptations, 22–3; anointing with chrism, 17, 33, 48, 49, 50; for children, 44, 46–7, 50; in danger of death, 46, 47, 49; during Mass, 51; Easter candle, 21; *Ephphetha*, 32, 39, 48, 50; and forgiveness of sins, 162–3; full celebrations, 47–8; godparents, 17, 18–19, 45, 48, 49; by immersion or infusion, 21, 33, 48; laying on of hands, 48; lighted candle: symbolism, 33, 48; ministers of, 19–20; ministry and role of parents, 44–5, 48; never repeated once validly celebrated, 17, 28; participation of community, 45, 46;